D1809745

ARISTOTLE ON PERCEIVING OBJECTS

ARISTOTLE ON
PERCEIVING OBJECTS

Anna Marmodoro

OXFORD
UNIVERSITY PRESS

OXFORD

UNIVERSITY PRESS

Oxford University Press is a department of the University of Oxford.
It furthers the University's objective of excellence in research, scholarship,
and education by publishing worldwide.

Oxford   New York
Auckland   Cape Town   Dar es Salaam   Hong Kong   Karachi
Kuala Lumpur   Madrid   Melbourne   Mexico City   Nairobi
New Delhi   Shanghai   Taipei   Toronto

With offices in
Argentina   Austria   Brazil   Chile   Czech Republic   France   Greece
Guatemala   Hungary   Italy   Japan   Poland   Portugal   Singapore
South Korea   Switzerland   Thailand   Turkey   Ukraine   Vietnam

Oxford is a registered trademark of Oxford University Press
in the UK and certain other countries.

Published in the United States of America by
Oxford University Press
198 Madison Avenue, New York, NY 10016

© Oxford University Press 2014

Library of Congress Cataloging-in-Publication Data

Cataloging in Publication data on file with the Library of Congress

ISBN 978-0-19-932600-6

1 3 5 7 9 8 6 4 2
Printed in the United States of America
on acid-free paper

CONTENTS

ACKNOWLEDGMENTS

I started working on this book project in 2008 as a British Academy postdoctoral fellow and a junior research fellow of Corpus Christi College at the University of Oxford. The project took a new direction in 2011 when I came to a fresh understanding of Aristotle's metaphysics within my research program *Power Structuralism in Ancient Ontologies,* supported by a starting investigator award (number 263484) from the European Research Council. Throughout the years, the two Oxford institutions to which I belong, namely the Faculty of Philosophy and Corpus Christi College, have offered me the most supportive environment for this research. I am thankful to my colleagues, as well as to the many who engaged with my research on different occasions, from different institutions. During the preparation of this book I benefitted further from visiting research fellowships at the University of Harvard (Center for Hellenic Studies) and the Australian National University, as well as a research period at the Rockefeller Foundation Bellagio Center. I was fortunate to be invited to give talks on a variety of topics related to this book in a number of places in Europe, the United States, Australia, and Brazil, and on all occasions I profited from the audience's feedback. Thanks are also due to the OUP anonymous readers for their insightful comments. The book is dedicated to my loved ones, without whose support it would not have been written.

Introduction

How can one explain the structure of experience? What is it that we perceive? How is it that we perceive objects and not disjoint arrays of properties? By which sense or senses do we perceive objects? Does this type of perception require a further sense over and above the five senses?

Perception for Aristotle is an instance of causal interaction between the properties of objects in the world and the perceiver's sense organs. It is the mutual activation of the respective causal powers in the object and the perceiver that comprises this causal interaction, which grounds the perceiver's experience on the one hand, and the object's sounding, coloring, etc., on the other. For Aristotle, the perceiver is the means for the fullest activation of the perceptible properties of objects in the world—which are activated as properties of objects rather than as experiences of perceivers. This is Aristotle's subtle realist view of perception. It shows that (and in what way) the perceptual input we gather about a colorful, noisy, etc. world is veridical.

Our only means for perceiving the world are the five senses, each individuated by the type of perceptible qualities it is sensitive to: colors for sight, sounds for hearing, etc. Is our perceptual grasp of the world limited to only one perceptible quality per perceptual content at a time, or even to several such contents from the disparate senses? If this were the case, we would not perceive objects, or discriminate their qualities; but we do perceive objects and discriminate their qualities. So how is it that we can become aware of perceptual content comprising more than isolated perceptible qualities at a time? How is complex perceptual content realized?

Aristotle was the first to investigate these questions to a depth that makes his account fruitful even for contemporary philosophy, but also challenging. He addressed them by means of the metaphysical modeling of the unity of the perceptual faculty and of experiential content. In this book I reconstruct the six metaphysical models offered by Aristotle to address these and related questions, focusing on their metaphysical underpinning in his theory of causal powers. By doing so, I bring out what is especially valuable and even surprising about the topic: Aristotle's metaphysics of perception is fundamentally different from his metaphysics of substance—which has received so much attention in the last forty years, generating a neo-Aristotelian movement in metaphysics.

For generations scholars attempted to fit Aristotle's metaphysics of perception to his metaphysics of substance. Yet, for precisely this reason, his models of complex perceptual content are unexplored territory. This book charts the new territory: it offers an understanding of Aristotle's metaphysics of the content of perceptual experience and of the faculty of perception; it aims at systematizing them—explicating and exploring them—and at bringing out the metaphysical breakthroughs Aristotle achieved. The book also makes a scholarly contribution to the field in that it brings textual evidence to bear on the most recent work on this topic.

Chapter 1

The Metaphysical
Foundations of Perception

INTRODUCTION

One of the cornerstones of Aristotle's theory of perception is that the world is truly as colorful as it looks to us, as noisy as it sounds to us, etc. By generalization, Aristotle holds that we perceive the world through the senses *as it is*; in other words, the contents of our perceptions are just like the real properties of the external objects we perceive.[1] While there is scholarly consensus on Aristotle's realism with respect to perceptible qualities, a variety of ways of interpreting it have been put forward in the literature. This book makes an original contribution to the debate by motivating the view that Aristotle's theory of perception is aligned with one of his most fundamental positions in metaphysics, namely that all properties are causal powers (δυνάμεις, potentialities), and that causation is to be accounted for in terms of powers and their activation (ἐν ἐνεργείᾳ or ἐνεργείᾳ, actuality).[2] Thus, in the case of perception the perceptible qualities of objects are real powers of the object to interact causally with the perceivers, and perception itself is the activation of the relevant powers in the perceiver by the objects of perception. The activation of the object's perceptible qualities and the activity of the corresponding perceptual experience in the agent are mutually dependent in a variety of ways, which are unique to Aristotle's perceptual realism.

Before exploring this view in more detail, it will be helpful to briefly introduce the key terms that will be relevant for the following discussion. The Aristotelian scholar might indeed already be surprised by my use of the terms 'power' for 'potentiality' on the one hand, and 'activation' for 'actuality' on the other. These are interpretative choices, and in some ways departures from the received tradition; I will explain them presently. The Greek term δύναμις, as Aristotle uses it, refers to a property whose nature is defined in terms of the change it can bring about, or which it can allow its bearer to suffer. The most common English translation of δύναμις thus understood is 'potentiality'. This translation, albeit well established, is unhelpful when we embark on an investigation of Aristotle's views, for three main reasons. Firstly, it blurs the conceptual distinction between the property itself, that is, the causal power, and the state it is in, because they both end up being referred to as 'potentiality'. Secondly, it obscures the relevance of Aristotle's view to contemporary metaphysics: the term 'potentiality' does not figure in the contemporary discourse, although what it refers to in Aristotle is very much at the center of current discussion in metaphysics.[3] Thirdly, it generates unnecessary difficulties for our understanding of what an activated power is. I thus propose to use the term 'power' as a translation of δύναμις when it refers to causal powers, and to use the term 'potentiality' when referring to the state that causal powers are in when not activated.

Some powers, for Aristotle, exist in nature ἐν δυνάμει or δυνάμει and others ἐν ἐνεργείᾳ or ἐνεργείᾳ. For these expressions I use the current translation 'in potentiality' or 'potentially', and 'in actuality' or 'actually', respectively. While keeping to the standard translation, I offer however an original interpretation of what it is for a power to be in actuality. I argue that the actuality of a power is to be interpreted as its *state of activation*; its *exercising* powerfulness. For Aristotle, a power does not cease to be powerful while activated, nor is its powerfulness reducible to mere potentiality, as we will see in more detail later. The powerfulness of a power is either the potentiality to bring about change, or the actuality of bringing about change. That the powerfulness and the potentiality of a power are not reducible one to the other can be derived from the following stance Aristotle takes. He differentiates three states a subject *s* may be in in relation to a power: *s* may have a power in potentiality (as in the case of a child having the power to learn to play soccer); *s* may have a power in first actuality (when the child has learned to play soccer); and *s* may have a power in second actuality (when the child is playing soccer).[4] For Aristotle some powers retain their potentiality only up to the state of first actuality, but not in second actuality. For example, when water is freezing and becoming an ice cube, in the first stages of this process the ice cube in the making is not actually fragile but can acquire the capacity to break if it cooled down more. When it is cooled down more the ice cube becomes harder and brittle, and can potentially break (e.g. by being crushed). Crushing it activates its brittleness, namely its power to break. When the ice cube is actively breaking it loses the potentiality to break. By contrast, other powers retain their potentiality when in second actuality; for instance, the child's potentiality to play soccer is preserved while playing soccer, namely while the power is activated. Aristotle explains:

> Even the term 'being acted upon' is not used in a single sense, but sometimes it means a kind of destruction of something by its contrary, and sometimes rather a preservation of that which is potential by something actual which is like it, as potency is related to actuality. For when the one merely possessing knowledge comes to exercise it, he is not altered (for the development

is into his real self or actuality), or else this is a different kind of alteration (DA 417b2–7)

οὐκ ἔστι δ' ἁπλοῦν οὐδὲ τὸ πάσχειν, ἀλλὰ τὸ μὲν φθορά τισ
ὑπὸ τοῦ ἐναντίου, τὸ δὲ σωτηρία μᾶλλον τοῦ δυνάμει ὄντος
ὑπὸ τοῦ ἐντελεχείᾳ ὄντος, καὶ ὁμοίου οὕτως ὡς δύναμις ἔχει
πρὸς ἐντελέχειαν· θεωροῦν γὰρ γίνεται τὸ ἔχον τὴν ἐπιστήμην,
ὅπερ ἢ οὐκ ἔστιν ἀλλοιοῦσθαι (εἰς αὑτὸ γὰρ ἡ ἐπίδοσις καὶ εἰς
ἐντελέχειαν) ἢ ἕτερον γένος ἀλλοιώσεως.

A power is powerful because of its relation to change—it can lead to change, or it engages in change that preserves it.[5]

1.1 ARISTOTLE'S POWER ONTOLOGY

Aristotle's power ontology, as briefly sketched thus far, bears on his theory of perception. For him, the perceptible qualities that characterize the world around us are *real causal powers* objects have, as we will see in the next chapters. Why are powers so central to Aristotle's metaphysics, and consequently to all domains of his investigation, including perception? How did he reach this view? Aristotle aims at a rational explanation of the world all the way down to the bedrock of reality. In the *De Generatione et Corruptione* he states that at this fundamental level of reality there are properties and bodies, and there is a rationale to the number of bodies and the way the properties are distributed among them. He writes,

> The [fundamental] differences [i.e., properties] are *reasonably* distributed among the primary bodies, and the number of the latter is *consonant with theory*. (GC 330b6–7, my emphasis)
> εὐλόγως διανέμεσθαι τὰς διαφορὰς τοῖς πρώτοις σώμασι, καὶ τὸ πλῆθος αὐτῶν εἶναι κατὰ λόγον.

In thinking about the properties that characterize the primary bodies, Aristotle narrows down the candidates for this role of fundamental property to the *tangible contrarieties* (GC 329b6–9), which for him are:

> [Properties]…capable of acting [and] being affected…said of things in virtue of their acting upon something else or being acted upon by something else. (GC 329b21–22)
>
> … ποιητικά…παθητικά…τῷ ποιεῖν τι ἕτερον ἢ πάσχειν ὑφ' ἑτέρου λέγονται.

Clearly then for Aristotle these properties are *powers*: they are properties whose nature is to bring about or allow their bearer to suffer change. Aristotle goes through an analysis of the list of tangible contrarieties, and concludes that they are all reducible to four primary or fundamental ones. These primary powers are heat, cold, wetness, and dryness:

> It is clear…that all the other differences reduce to the first four, but that these admit of no further reduction…Hence these must be four. (GC 330a24–29)
>
> Δῆλον…ὅτι πᾶσαι αἱ ἄλλαι διαφοραὶ ἀνάγονται εἰς τὰς πρώτας τέτταρας. Αὗται δὲ οὐκέτι εἰς ἐλάττους…ὥστ' ἀνάγκη τέτταρας εἶναι ταύτας.

These primary powers do not exist separately each on its own; they pair up and constitute the *four simple elements*: namely fire, air, water, and earth:

> Fire is hot and dry, whereas Air is hot and moist…and Water is cold and wet, while Earth is cold and dry. (GC 330b3–5)
>
> τὸ μὲν γὰρ πῦρ θερμὸν καὶ ξηρόν, ὁ δ' ἀὴρ θερμὸν καὶ ὑγρόν…τὸ δ' ὕδωρ ψυχρὸν καὶ ὑγρόν, ἡ δὲ γῆ ψυχρὸν καὶ ξηρόν.

Aristotle holds that there are no other primary properties that any of the simple elements possesses in addition to the two contrary powers each simple element is qualified by. The simple elements can reciprocally transform into one another by gaining or losing their powers.[6] For example the simple elements water and fire have two contrarieties each, and when they come in contact the interaction between them results in the heat of fire overpowering the coldness of the water while the wetness of water overpowers the dryness of fire, giving rise to what is hot and wet, namely air. And when air loses its primary power of heat, which is replaced by the power of cold, it transforms into water again. Aristotle writes:

> For these bodies [Fire, Water and the like] change into one another (they are not immutable as Empedocles and other thinkers assert, since alteration would then have been impossible), whereas the *contrarieties do not change*. (GC 329a35–b3, my emphasis)
>
> ταῦτα μὲν γὰρ μεταβάλλει εἰς ἄλληλα, καὶ οὐχ ὡς Ἐμπεδοκλῆς καὶ ἕτεροι λέγουσιν (οὐδὲ γὰρ ἂν ἦν ἀλλοίωσις), αἱ δ' ἐναντιώσεις οὐ μεταβάλλουσιν.
>
> There will be Air, when the cold of the Water and the dry of the Fire have passed away (since the hot of the latter and the moist of the former are left); whereas, when the hot of the Fire and the moist of the Water have passed-away, there will be Earth, owing to the survival of the dry of the Fire and the cold of the Water. So, too, in the same way Fire and Water will result from Air and Earth. For there will be Water, when the hot of the Air and the dry of the Earth have passed-away (since the moist of the former and the cold of the latter are left); whereas, when the moist of the Air and the cold of the Earth have passed-away, there will be Fire, owing to the survival of the hot of the Air

and the dry of the Earth—qualities constitutive of Fire. (GC 331b14–24)

Ὅταν μὲν γὰρ τοῦ ὕδατος φθαρῇ τὸ ψυχρὸν τοῦ δὲ πυρὸς τὸ ξηρόν, ἀὴρ ἔσται (λείπεται γὰρ τοῦ μὲν τὸ θερμὸν τοῦ δὲ τὸ ὑγρόν), ὅταν δὲ τοῦ μὲν πυρὸς τὸ θερμὸν τοῦ δ' ὕδατος τὸ ὑγρόν, γῆ, διὰ τὸ λείπεσθαι τοῦ μὲν τὸ ξηρὸν τοῦ δὲ τὸ ψυχρόν. ὡσαύτως δὲ καὶ ἐξ ἀέρος καὶ γῆς πῦρ καὶ ὕδωρ· ὅταν μὲν γὰρ τοῦ ἀέρος φθαρῇ τὸ θερμὸν τῆς δὲ γῆς τὸ ξηρόν, ὕδωρ ἔσται (λείπεται γὰρ τοῦ μὲν τὸ ὑγρὸν τῆς δὲ τὸ ψυχρόν), ὅταν δὲ τοῦ μὲν ἀέρος τὸ ὑγρὸν τῆς δὲ γῆς τὸ ψυχρόν, πῦρ, διὰ τὸ λείπεσθαι τοῦ μὲν τὸ θερμὸν τῆς δὲ τὸ ξηρόν, ἅπερ ἦν πυρός.

The simple elements can combine between them in different proportions to make up more complex kinds of stuff. Thus the (instantiated) primary powers are the primitive (or basic) and fundamental building blocks of reality. The primary powers are primitive because they are not constituted of any further items as their building blocks. There are no items constituting the primary properties, and therefore there are no further items constituting the simple elements—air, water, earth, and fire—apart from their primary powers. On the other hand, they are fundamental because the primary properties, to which the other properties are reducible,[7] interact with each other in the cyclical transformations of the primary elements they constitute,[8] thereby making up a structure of interacting powers that is the foundation of all there is in nature. In view of the fact that for Aristotle everything in physical nature is built out of the four simple elements and their mixtures, and the simple elements are built out of the primary properties, it follows that all there is in nature is built out of *powers*. All physical changes in nature derive from changes in the combinations of the primary powers. Since, on Aristotle's view, powers require other powers to activate them, this gives rise to a net of interdependent powers, which, ultimately, constitute everything in nature. It is a structure of dependences, not of relations between powers. Nor is it a structure of relations that constitute powers; dependence does not introduce relations or make powers relational entities in their constitution. Furthermore, as we shall see, for Aristotle the manifestation of each power is intrinsic to the power itself. Being activated is simply exercising the powerfulness that defines what the power is.[9]

1.2 THE NATURE OF CAUSAL POWERS

In general terms, for Aristotle, a power is first and foremost the capacity to *bring about change*:

> All potentialities that conform to the same type are *starting points* of some kind, and are called *potentialities* in reference to one primary kind, which is a starting point of *change* in another thing or in the thing itself *qua* other. (*Met.* 1046a9–11, my emphasis)[10]
>
> ὅσαι δὲ πρὸς τὸ αὐτὸ εἶδος, πᾶσαι ἀρχαί τινές εἰσι, καὶ πρὸς πρώτην μίαν λέγονται, ἥ ἐστιν ἀρχὴ μεταβολῆς ἐν ἄλλῳ ἢ ᾗ ἄλλο.

It is important to note from the start that Aristotle's very explanation of powers as being sources of change, and nothing other than that, commits him, albeit implicitly, to the view that all there is to a power is what it can do, or is doing. Nothing inert or impotent is needed in the power's nature to anchor the power to reality.[11] This commitment (which is shared by a number of contemporary power metaphysicians)[12] is not uncontroversial;[13] however, it is crucial to free Aristotle's power ontology from any of the regresses that ensue for other power ontologies, as we will see later.

In addition to the primary type of powers just mentioned, that is the *active* ones which can initiate change, for Aristotle there exist *passive* powers that are capacities to suffer change:

> For one kind is a potentiality for being acted on (i.e., the principle in the very thing acted on) which makes it capable of being changed and acted on by another thing or by itself regarded as other. (*Met.* 1046a11–13)
>
> ἡ μὲν γὰρ τοῦ παθεῖν ἐστι δύναμις, ἡ ἐν αὐτῷ τῷ πάσχοντι ἀρχὴ μεταβολῆς παθητικῆς ὑπ' ἄλλου ἢ ᾗ ἄλλο.

Examples of such capacities or powers are, for example, fragility, or malleability, or flexibility, etc. For Aristotle being able to change is as much a capacity or power as being able to effect change, as he states:

> In a sense the potentiality of acting and of being acted on is one (for a thing may be capable either because it can be acted on or because something else can be acted on by it), but in a sense the potentialities are different. For the one is in the thing acted on; it is because it contains a certain motive principle, and because even the matter is a motive principle, that the thing acted on is acted on...for that which is oily is inflammable; and that which yields in a particular way can be crushed; and similarly in all other cases. But the other potency is in the agent (e.g. heat and the art of building are present, one in that which can produce heat and the other in the man who can build). (*Met.* 1046a19–28)
>
> φανερὸν οὖν ὅτι ἔστι μὲν ὡς μία δύναμις τοῦ ποιεῖν καὶ πάσχειν (δυνατὸν γάρ ἐστι καὶ τῷ ἔχειν αὐτὸ δύναμιν τοῦ παθεῖν καὶ τῷ ἄλλο ὑπ' αὐτοῦ), ἔστι δὲ ὡς ἄλλη. ἡ μὲν γὰρ ἐν τῷ πάσχοντι (διὰ γὰρ τὸ ἔχειν τινὰ ἀρχήν, καὶ εἶναι καὶ τὴν ὕλην ἀρχήν τινα,

πάσχει τὸ πάσχον... τὸ λιπαρὸν μὲν γὰρ καυστὸν τὸ δ᾽ ὑπεῖκον ὡδὶ θλαστόν, ὁμοίως δὲ καὶ ἐπὶ τῶν ἄλλων), ἡ δ᾽ ἐν τῷ ποιοῦντι, οἷον τὸ θερμὸν καὶ ἡ οἰκοδομική, ἡ μὲν ἐν τῷ θερμαντικῷ ἡ δ᾽ ἐν τῷ οἰκοδομικῷ·

A notion that is distinctive to Aristotle's account is conceiving of passive powers as *originative sources of change* (see *Met.* 1046a11–13; a23). It is natural for us to think that an originative source of change is a power to *bring about* change; but it is not as natural to think that an originative source of change is a capacity to *suffer* change. Yet Aristotle sees both active and passive powers as originative sources of change, the one as a source that changes something, and the other as a source of suffering change. In fact, Aristotle gives several examples of originative sources of suffering change to make his point clear, such as, for example, oil or brittle matter.[14] Both active and passive powers are mentioned in Aristotle's definition of power in *Met.* V 12:

Things which are called capable (δυνατόν) in one sense will be those which originate change or alteration... in other things or *qua* other; in another sense, if something else possesses such capacity over them. (*Met.* 1019a33–b1)

καὶ τὸ δυνατὸν ἕνα μὲν τρόπον λεχθήσεται τὸ ἔχον κινήσεως ἀρχὴν ἢ μεταβολῆς...ἐν ἑτέρῳ ἢ ᾗ ἕτερον, ἕνα δ᾽ ἐὰν ἔχῃ τι αὐτοῦ ἄλλο δύναμιν τοιαύτην.

The former is the primary case for Aristotle; 'the others are called capable either from something else's possessing a capability of that kind over them, or from its not possessing it, or from its possessing it in a particular way' (*Met.* 1020a2–4).

As I will argue below, it is a fundamental tenet for Aristotle that powers are *dependent on other powers* in order to be activated. For example the solubility of salt requires salt to be placed in an appro-priate liquid in order for it to dissolve. The position was first put forward by Heraclitus, endorsed by Plato,[15] and then developed by Aristotle; interestingly it is gaining consensus among contempo-rary metaphysicians too.[16] But it is a distinctive Aristotelian view (and far from being a point of consensus among contemporary power metaphysicians) that *active* powers depend on *passive* pow-ers for their activation (and vice versa). Aristotle defines an active power as one that exercises its powerfulness on a corresponding passive one.[17] As I will argue below, the distinction between active and passive powers is pivotal for a sound account of causation, for it gives metaphysical underpinning to its asymmetry.[18]

1.3 CAUSAL POWERS IN ACTUALITY

Powers are capacities for change; the change is the end (τέλος) they are directed toward.[19] For a power, reaching its end is exercising its powerfulness, and thereby becoming actual. Most importantly, for Aristotle the actuality of a power is its *activation*, namely a transi-tion to a different *status* of the power itself.[20] This new stage reached by the activated power is the causal *activity* the power is engaged in. For example, the power to heat when activated is heat*ing* something else. Aristotle in fact distinguishes between powers whose activa-tion is an *activity* in the strict sense (ἐνέργεια, πρᾶξις), and others whose activation is a *process* (κίνησις). The powers whose ends are activities are realized instantaneously, such as in the case of the power to see; at any one moment one sees and has seen. The powers whose ends are processes are realized in stages, such as in the case of the power to build a house; while one is building a house, one has not built a house. Processes have a natural completion point: when the end of the process is reached, such as the completion of the house; activities do not have a natural completion point (e.g., in the case of seeing). Strictly speaking Aristotle associates *change* with *processes* only, because in the case of processes the resulting state is qualitatively different from the initial state—as for instance in the case of heating (process), but not of seeing (activity).[21] To make Aristotle's point even clearer we might say that processes only have an output, while both processes and activities have an effect. Aristotle's distinctions are mainly presented in the following text from the *Metaphysics*:

> Since of the actions which have a limit none is an end but all are relative to the end (e.g., the process of making thin is of this sort) and the things themselves when one is making them thin are in movement in this way (i.e., without being already that at which the movement aims), this is not an action or at least not a complete one (for it is not an end); but that in which the end is present is an action. For example, at the same time we are seeing and have seen, are understanding and have understood, are thinking and have thought: but it is not true that at the same time we are learning and have learned, or are being cured and have been cured. At the same time we are living well and have lived well, and are happy and have been happy. If not, the process would have had sometime to cease, as the process of making thin ceases: but, as it is, it does not cease: we are living and have lived. Of these processes, then, we must call the one set movements (κινήσεις), and the other actualities (ἐνεργείας). For every movement is incomplete—making thin, learning, walking, building—these are movements, and incomplete movements. For it is not true that at the same time we are walking [to a destination] and have walked [to the destination], or are building and have built, or are coming to be and have come to be—it is a different thing that is being moved

and that has been moved, and that is moving [to a location] and that has moved; but it is the same thing that at the same time has seen and is seeing, or is thinking and has thought. The latter sort of process, then, I call an actuality (ἐνέργεια), and the former a movement (κίνησις). What, and what kind of thing, the actual is, may be taken as explained by these and similar considerations. (*Met.* 1048b18–36)

Ἐπεὶ δὲ τῶν πράξεων ὧν ἔστι πέρας οὐδεμία τέλος ἀλλὰ τῶν περὶ τὸ τέλος, οἷον τὸ ἰσχναίνειν [ἡ ἰσχνασία] [αὐτό], αὐτὰ δὲ ὅταν ἰσχναίνῃ οὕτως ἐστὶν ἐν κινήσει, μὴ ὑπάρχοντα ὧν ἕνεκα ἡ κίνησις, οὐκ ἔστι ταῦτα πρᾶξις ἢ οὐ τελεία γε· οὐ γὰρ τέλος· ἀλλ' ἐκείνη <ἧ> ἐνυπάρχει τὸ τέλος καὶ [ἡ] πρᾶξις. οἷον ὁρᾷ ἅμα <καὶ ἑώρακε,> καὶ φρονεῖ <καὶ πεφρόνηκε,> καὶ νοεῖ καὶ νενόηκεν, ἀλλ' οὐ μανθάνει καὶ μεμάθηκεν οὐδ' ὑγιάζεται καὶ ὑγίασται. εὖ ζῇ καὶ εὖ ἔζηκεν ἅμα, καὶ εὐδαιμονεῖ καὶ εὐδαιμόνηκεν. εἰ δὲ μή, ἔδει ἄν ποτε παύεσθαι ὥσπερ ὅταν ἰσχναίνῃ, νῦν δ' οὔ, ἀλλὰ ζῇ καὶ ἔζηκεν. τούτων δὴ <δεῖ> τὰς μὲν κινήσεις λέγειν, τὰς δ' ἐνεργείας. πᾶσα γὰρ κίνησις ἀτελής, ἰσχνασία μάθησις βάδισις οἰκοδόμησις· αὗται δὴ κινήσεις, καὶ ἀτελεῖς γε. οὐ γὰρ ἅμα βαδίζει καὶ βεβάδικεν, οὐδ' οἰκοδομεῖ καὶ ᾠκοδόμηκεν, οὐδὲ γίγνεται καὶ γέγονεν ἢ κινεῖται καὶ κεκίνηται, ἀλλ' ἕτερον [καὶ κινεῖ καὶ κεκίνηκεν]· ἑώρακε δὲ καὶ ὁρᾷ ἅμα τὸ αὐτό, καὶ νοεῖ καὶ νενόηκεν. τὴν μὲν οὖν τοιαύτην ἐνέργειαν λέγω, ἐκείνην δὲ κίνησιν. τὸ μὲν οὖν ἐνεργείᾳ τί τέ ἐστι καὶ ποῖον, ἐκ τούτων καὶ τῶν τοιούτων δῆλον ἡμῖν ἔστω.

From the above text we learn that powers are actualized, according to Aristotle, as either activities or processes. The difference between them is that processes have a beginning and an end which are different from each other, so completing the realization of the end requires qualitatively different stages in a process; while in an activity the beginning and the end are the same, in a continuous realization of the end. Since while a process is taking place it has not reached its end point yet, it can be thought of as a power in the process of being actualized, which is how Aristotle thinks about it. A process is an actuality, because the unfolding realization of its different stages is happening; but at the same time it is not fully realized, in so far as it has not reached its end yet. In that sense a change is an *actual* process in progress, realizing its remaining *potential* stages, as Aristotle explains in the *Physics*:

> The *actuality* of the potential, *qua* potential, is change (e.g., the actuality of what is alterable as alterable, is alteration; of what is increasable and its opposite, decreasable (there is no common name for both), increase and decrease; of what can come to be and can pass away, coming to be and passing away; of what can be carried along, locomotion). That this is what change is, is clear from what follows: when what is buildable, in so far as we call it such, is in fulfillment, it is being built, and that is building. (*Phys.* 201a9–18, transl. slightly modified)
>
> ἡ τοῦ δυνάμει ὄντος ἐντελέχεια, ᾗ τοιοῦτον, κίνησίς ἐστιν, οἷον τοῦ μὲν ἀλλοιωτοῦ, ᾗ ἀλλοιωτόν, ἀλλοίωσις, τοῦ δὲ αὐξητοῦ καὶ τοῦ ἀντικειμένου φθιτοῦ (οὐδὲν γὰρ ὄνομα κοινὸν ἐπ' ἀμφοῖν) αὔξησις καὶ φθίσις, τοῦ δὲ γενητοῦ καὶ φθαρτοῦ γένεσις καὶ φθορά, τοῦ δὲ φορητοῦ φορά. ὅτι δὲ τοῦτό ἐστιν ἡ κίνησις, ἐντεῦθεν δῆλον. ὅταν γὰρ τὸ οἰκοδομητόν, ᾗ τοιοῦτον αὐτὸ λέγομεν εἶναι, ἐντελεχείᾳ ᾖ, οἰκοδομεῖται, καὶ ἔστιν τοῦτο οἰκοδόμησις·

Some confusion might arise in reading the passage: it might appear that a power is potential before it is actualized, and again potential after it is actualized, as if there were unactualized and actualized potential. To avoid confusion it is important to bear in mind the distinction drawn by Aristotle between the *activation* of a power—that is, its realization—and the *completion* of the process of its realization. Thus, the power of house building becomes *actual* when *activated* at the beginning of the house-building process, and *continues to be in actuality* until all the stages of house building are completed. Although in activities the end is reached as soon as the activity occurs, and sets no limits to the duration of the activity, in the case of changes the end is complex; the process has to be initiated and continue activated until the end point of the process is reached, completing the process:

> While in some cases the exercise is the ultimate thing (e.g., in sight the ultimate thing is seeing, and no other product besides this results from sight), but from some things a product follows (e.g., from the art of building there results a house as well as the act of building), yet none the less the act [of seeing] is in the former case the end and in the latter [the act of house building is] more of an end than the mere potentiality [to build] is [even if it is less of an end than the completion of the house]. (*Met.* 1050a23–28)
>
> ἐπεὶ δ᾽ ἐστὶ τῶν μὲν ἔσχατον ἡ χρῆσις (οἷον ὄψεως ἡ ὅρασις, καὶ οὐθὲν γίγνεται παρὰ ταύτην ἕτερον ἀπὸ τῆς ὄψεως), ἀπ᾽ ἐνίων δὲ γίγνεταί τι (οἷον ἀπὸ τῆς οἰκοδομικῆς οἰκία παρὰ τὴν οἰκοδόμησιν), ὅμως οὐθὲν ἧττον ἔνθα μὲν τέλος, ἔνθα δὲ μᾶλλον τέλος τῆς δυνάμεώς ἐστιν·

The contrast is between the potentiality for building a house when nothing is being built, and the potentiality for building a house while a house is being built. The latter potentiality is the activation of the former potentiality, and has an end point that marks its full actualization. This is what the actuality of the potential *qua* potential is—the actual process of building the house. During the building process, the power to build is *as activated* (and *as actual*) as is the power to see when one is seeing. Thus, when the power is actively doing what it is in its own nature capable of doing, then the power is actualized. Prior to this it exists but in a potential state. Thus the *actuality* of a power, whether for an activity or a process, is the *activation* of that power:[22]

> That which is in the primary sense potential is potential because it is possible for it to become actual (e.g., I mean by 'capable of building' that which can build, and by 'capable of seeing' that which can see). (*Met.* 1049b12–16)
>
> τῷ λόγῳ μὲν οὖν ὅτι προτέρα, δῆλον (τῷ γὰρ ἐνδέχεσθαι ἐνεργῆσαι δυνατόν ἐστι τὸ πρώτως δυνατόν, οἷον λέγω οἰκοδομικὸν τὸ δυνάμενον οἰκοδομεῖν, καὶ ὁρατικὸν τὸ ὁρᾶν, καὶ ὁρατὸν τὸ δυνατὸν ὁρᾶσθαι·

Aristotle further distinguishes the *activation* of a power from the *realization* of the power's end. The end of a power is given in the power's definition:

> That which is capable is capable of something and at some time in some way—with all the other qualifications which must be present in the definition. (*Met.* 1047b35–1048a2)
>
> ἐπεὶ δὲ τὸ δυνατὸν τὶ δυνατὸν καὶ ποτὲ καὶ πῶς καὶ ὅσα ἄλλα ἀνάγκη προσεῖναι ἐν τῷ διορισμῷ.

As mentioned above, for Aristotle, the actuality of a power is *not* a new property that comes about.[23] Rather, it is the activation of the power, either as it is exercising its causal influence on the passive power or as the passive power is suffering that influence. For example, if a peach has the power to ripen in the heat, the ripening is the actualization of active and passive powers at play in the environment and in the peach. The ripe state of the peach that comes about is the aftermath of the activation of the powers, not their manifestation, which is the ripening process. Similarly, in the case of a builder who has the power to build a house, the built house is the output of the activation of the active and passive powers in play in the circumstances.

For Aristotle a power in potentiality is *the same power* as that power in actuality (i.e., when it is activated). In other words, the difference between potential and actual power is *not a numerical difference*. This is a very important and distinctive tenet of Aristotle's metaphysics, whose philosophical soundness shows up clearly if we consider it in relation to three debates in the recent literature on power metaphysics. In brief, these issues are: firstly, whether pure power ontologies of the kind Aristotle endorses (where there is nothing categorical anchoring the powers to reality) are committed to a world of mere potentiality; secondly, whether powers have an essentially relational nature; and thirdly, in what sense a power's directedness toward its manifestation is intrinsic to the power itself. I shall now examine each of these debates, showing in each case how Aristotle's view makes a fresh contribution, and advances the contemporary debate.

To begin with, is Aristotle's account vulnerable to the criticism that all there is or can be is potential, and that change is simply a transition from one potential state of the world to another such state? This is a problem faced by many contemporary power ontologies, sometimes referred to as the "Always packing, never travelling" problem.[24] David Armstrong formulates the problem thus:

> Given purely dispositionalist accounts of properties, particulars would seem to be always repacking their bags as they change properties, yet never taking a journey from potency to act. (1997, 80)

The problem stems from the position held by contemporary power ontologists whereby the manifestation of a power is *a new* power.[25] This position commits them to a network of powers in potentiality, as the activation of each power in potentiality is a transition to *a new* power in potentiality. Thus, nothing ever seems to be actualized. Avoiding a commitment to worlds of mere potentiality is precisely the worry that Aristotle's position avoids. On his view, and in contrast to alternative views in the contemporary literature, the transition a power makes from being in potentiality to being in actuality does not amount to bringing about *another* power in potentiality. It is rather a transition the power makes to *its own* activated state. An activated power is the very same power as the power in potentiality, but is now manifest*ing* (e.g., the power to heat actively heat*ing* something). A theory of powers that did not allow them when activated to exercise their powerfulness would be rather odd indeed. For Aristotle powers that are exercising their powerfulness are actively bringing about change, and result in a new configuration of powers. But the exercise of powerfulness is not the result, but rather the process toward the result. From this discussion it follows that for Aristotle the powerfulness of a power is not reducible to mere potentiality. (This addresses the first of the three issues in contemporary metaphysical debate mentioned above). Powerfulness is the potentiality to bring about or suffer change, but also the activity of bringing about or suffering change. Additionally, the activation of a power is neither the end of that power, nor does it render the power inert. On the contrary, the power is actively being powerful by engendering change or suffering change.

Thus, the relation between a power and its actuality is *intrinsic* to the power itself, in the way that, for example, the relation of a girl to the woman she becomes is intrinsic to that person.[26] It is a common assumption, after Aristotle, that powers are defined in terms of their actuality. Contemporary power ontologies take the manifestation of a power to be a further power, thereby establishing a network of relations whereby each power is defined in terms of its relations to something different from itself, namely other powers. By contrast, on Aristotle's view the actuality of a power is not another power that the original power is related to. (The actuality of the power to heat is the power's heating up something else—and not another power.) It follows that Aristotle's ontology is *not relational*; a power is not defined in terms of its relation to other powers. Rather, a power is defined in terms of its own state of activation, which is an intrinsic state of the power itself.

It remains now to investigate whether powers for Aristotle have an essentially relational nature on account of their dependence on other powers for their activation. To consider this point, we need to look at the conditions for activation of powers that Aristotle sets out. For Aristotle, the activation of causal powers requires two sets of conditions to obtain. On the one hand there is a variety of what we would call *enabling conditions* pertaining to the right time, the right situation, the right external conditions. Aristotle summarizes them in saying that the mover is capable of something 'at some time in some way (with all the other qualifications which must be present in the definition)' (*Met.* 1048a1–2). On the other hand, he collectively describes what triggers powers in the right circumstances into causal activity generically, in terms of 'contact' between powers:

> To act on the movable as such is just to move it. But this it does by contact, so that at the same time it [the mover] is also acted on. Hence motion is the fulfilment of the movable as movable, the cause being contact with what can move, so that the mover is also acted on. (*Phys.* 202a5–9)
>
> τὸ γὰρ πρὸς τοῦτο ἐνεργεῖν, ᾖ τοιοῦτον, αὐτὸ τὸ κινεῖν ἐστι· τοῦτο δὲ ποιεῖ θίξει, ὥστε ἅμα καὶ πάσχει· διὸ ἡ κίνησις ἐντελέχεια τοῦ κινητοῦ, ᾖ κινητόν, συμβαίνει δὲ τοῦτο θίξει τοῦ κινητικοῦ, ὥσθ' ἅμα καὶ πάσχει.

What we learn from this passage (and others already quoted) is the following. First, powers for Aristotle are *dependent* entities. As we will see in more detail later in this chapter, for Aristotle powers are co-activated with their partner-powers. For example A's power to heat (p) requires B's capacity to get hotter (p') in order to be able to achieve its manifestation, that is, heating. Hence, every power is dependent on other powers for actualizing its nature by reaching its full activation state. But dependence is not a relation; it is rather a *condition for existence.*[27] Thus, as we will see later in the chapter, powers are not for Aristotle relations or relational properties. Secondly, contact is the triggering condition, with all the other conditions mentioned in the definition determining the enabling conditions for causal efficacy to take place. It is therefore important to understand what is involved in the contact between the active power and the passive power it operates on. Aristotle tells us that: 'Things are said to be in contact when their extremities are together' (*Physics* 226b23). He further explains that, 'Things are said to be together in place when they are in one primary place and to be apart when they are in different places'[28] (*Physics* 226a21–3). So things that are in contact have their extremities in the same place. For the purposes of causation, having the extremities in the same place will have to be understood as either touching or being in proximity. (It must have been as clear to everybody in antiquity as it is to us that there is causal impact even when things are merely proximate, namely, in the same place in the sense of same spatial region.) For example, proximity to a fire is sufficient for heating, and even for catching fire. So for Aristotle 'contact' is a key factor for causal efficacy. It does entail a type of proximity or sameness of place, but more importantly, in a causal context, it has come to mean, for him, *trigger of the* change, allowing that there is some kind of 'touching' even in situations where the touching is not physical and not even reciprocal:

If anything imparts motion without itself being moved, it may touch the moved and yet itself be touched by nothing—for we say sometimes that the man who grieves us touches us, but not that we touch him. (*GC* 323a31–33)

Ὥστε εἴ τι κινεῖ ἀκίνητον ὄν, ἐκεῖνο μὲν ἂν ἅπτοιτο τοῦ κινητοῦ, ἐκείνου δὲ οὐδέν· φαμὲν γὰρ ἐνίοτε τὸν λυποῦντα ἅπτεσθαι ἡμῶν, ἀλλ᾽ οὐκ αὐτοὶ ἐκείνου.

To recapitulate, the conditions under which the actualization of powers takes place are determined in the very definition of the powers. The definition of a power specifies the *type* of power it is, namely what it is that it can bring about or suffer; the appropriate *occasion* on which the power can do this; the *way* in which it can do it; and any other *conditions* that need to obtain for it to do what it does. When all the conditions set out in the definition are met, including the appropriate pair of powers coming into *contact*, in the relevant sense of contact for the type of power they are, then *necessarily* the agent power acts on the passive power and brings about its effect:

Since that which is capable is capable of something and at some time in some way—with all the other qualifications which must be present in the definition, ... as regards potentialities of [those things that are non-rational, (e.g., fire)]...when the agent and the patient meet in the way appropriate to the potentiality in question, the one *must* act and the other be acted on...For the non-rational potentialities are all productive of one effect each. (*Met.* 1047b35–1048a8; my emphasis)

ἐπεὶ δὲ τὸ δυνατὸν τὶ δυνατὸν καὶ ποτὲ καὶ πῶς καὶ ὅσα ἄλλα ἀνάγκη προσεῖναι ἐν τῷ διορισμῷ, καὶ τὰ μὲν κατὰ λόγον δύναται κινεῖν καὶ αἱ δυνάμεις αὐτῶν μετὰ λόγου, τὰ δὲ ἄλογα καὶ αἱ δυνάμεις ἄλογοι, κἀκείνας μὲν ἀνάγκη ἐν ἐμψύχῳ εἶναι

ταύτας δὲ ἐν ἀμφοῖν, τὰς μὲν τοιαύτας δυνάμεις ἀνάγκη, ὅταν
ὡς δύνανται τὸ ποιητικὸν καὶ τὸ παθητικὸν πλησιάζωσι, τὸ μὲν
ποιεῖν τὸ δὲ πάσχειν, ἐκείνας δ' οὐκ ἀνάγκη·

*The modality is natural necessity, stemming from the nature of the pow-
ers themselves.* When Aristotle says, in the quotation above, that
'when the agent and the patient meet in the way appropriate to the
potentiality in question, the one *must* act and the other be acted
on' he is stating what is in effect a most general *law of nature*. That
is, he is stating what a power is in terms of how it behaves. When
nature follows its course, according to Aristotle, it develops as its
potentiality dictates, unless something external interferes. He says
about the natural development of an organism (e.g., an acorn) in
Book VIII of the Metaphysics:

> In the cases in which the source of the becoming is in the very
> thing which comes to be, a thing is potentially all those things
> which it will be of itself if nothing external hinders it. (*Met.*
> 1049a12–14)
>
> καὶ ὅσων δὴ ἐν αὐτῷ τῷ ἔχοντι [ἡ ἀρχὴ τῆς γενέσεως], [τοῦτο
> δυνάμει] ὅσα μηθενὸς τῶν ἔξωθεν ἐμποδίζοντος ἔσται δι' αὐτοῦ.

This is how nature operates: there are physical tendencies, which
unfold, unless something gets in their way and prevents their course.
This may happen in the case of causal interaction, or in the case of
the natural development of organisms according to their nature.
This is why Aristotle describes the latter as being such-and-such *for
the most part* in Book VI of the *Metaphysics*:

> Physics must be a theoretical science, but it will theorize
> about such being as admits of being moved, and about
> substance-as-defined *for the most part*. (*Met.* 1025b26–28)

ἡ φυσικὴ θεωρητική τις ἂν εἴη, ἀλλὰ θεωρητικὴ περὶ τοιοῦτον ὂν ὅ ἐστι δυνατὸν κινεῖσθαι, καὶ περὶ οὐσίαν τὴν κατὰ τὸν λόγον ὡς ἐπὶ τὸ πολὺ...

Both *change* and *development* are the results of unfolding potentialities, which follow their own course, for the most part, if nothing hinders.

Aristotle's characterization of this type of physical modality is a landmark in metaphysics, demarcating what has come to be thought of as physical necessity.[29] Again in the *Metaphysics*, Aristotle explains the notion of being *for the most part*, contrasting it to absolute necessity, as follows:

> Since, among things which are, some are always in the same state and are of necessity (not necessity in the sense of compulsion but that which we assert of things because they cannot be otherwise), and some are not of necessity, nor always, but *for the most part*...For instance, if in the dog-days there is wintry and cold weather, we say this is an accident, but not if there is sultry heat, because the latter is always or *for the most part* so, but not the former. (*Met.* 1026b27–35, my emphasis)
>
> —ἐπεὶ οὖν ἐστὶν ἐν τοῖς οὖσι τὰ μὲν ἀεὶ ὡσαύτως ἔχοντα καὶ ἐξ ἀνάγκης, οὐ τῆς κατὰ τὸ βίαιον λεγομένης ἀλλ' ἣν λέγομεν τῷ μὴ ἐνδέχεσθαι ἄλλως, τὰ δ' ἐξ ἀνάγκης μὲν οὐκ ἔστιν οὐδ' ἀεί, ὡς δ' ἐπὶ τὸ πολύ, αὕτη ἀρχὴ καὶ αὕτη αἰτία ἐστὶ τοῦ εἶναι τὸ συμβεβηκός· ὃ γὰρ ἂν ᾖ μήτ' ἀεὶ μήθ' ὡς ἐπὶ τὸ πολύ... οἷον ἐπὶ κυνὶ ἂν χειμὼν γένηται καὶ ψῦχος, τοῦτο συμβῆναί φαμεν, ἀλλ' οὐκ ἂν πνῖγος καὶ ἀλέα, ὅτι τὸ μὲν ἀεὶ ἢ ὡς ἐπὶ τὸ πολὺ τὸ δ' οὔ.

What characterizes the notion of being for the most part is regularity, the type of regularity that one finds in nature, under the domain of natural laws, which are not exceptionless.[30]

To recapitulate the discussion so far, causal change for Aristotle involves the mutual activation of active and passive powers, brought about by the contact between ontologically interdependent pairs of powers, such as what can heat and what can be heated. The mutual activation of interdependent powers may result either in activity (e.g. seeing) or in a process of change (e.g., being heated) All that happens in Aristotle's world is that powers in potentiality come to be activated, either as agents of change or as patients of change. What is distinctive about the view (in contrast with the versions in contemporary metaphysics) is that it takes the activation of a causal power to be the exercise of that power (i.e., an activity or process).

1.4 RELATIONS AND RELATIVES

Powers for Aristotle are not relational properties. There is no (external) relation connecting a power in potentiality to its actuality (rather, the actuality is the very same power in a different state, namely engaged in an activity). There are good reasons for not treating powers as relations, even if Aristotle does not discuss them explicitly. On the one hand, if a power is *defined* in terms of its actuality, where the definition defines the power's nature (e.g., the power to *heat*) it should be the case that the power is one with its essential nature; the essential nature of a power should not be a different entity to which the power is related. This we know from Aristotle's arguments in *Metaphysics* VIII 6. Nor should a power only *tend* towards its powerfulness—as if its powerfulness were external to the power itself—because this latter view would not make philosophical sense. That is, it would divide a power from what it is. Furthermore, there is no relation connecting mutually dependent powers. Rather, for Aristotle powers are *relatives*. Aristotle's powers are dependent on other powers in order to be activated, but ontological dependence is grounded on *monadic properties*, such as '*y* being a father' and '*x* being an off-spring', that belong to interdependent entities. Aristotle's powers are *not* related to other powers through polyadic relations, such as '*x* being the father of *y*'. Aristotle explained the ontological dependence between relatives reductively, as a *counterfactual* dependence (e.g., if there is no master there is no slave).[31] If we apply this understanding of ontological dependence to the case of causal relata, it follows that taking causal relata as ontologically interdependent amounts to the view that if there is no patient of change, there is no cause of change (there is no power to heat if there is no power for being heated up).[32] I will begin by offering what I think is the rationale for this approach, by sketching an intuition that stems from Aristotelian metaphysical principles.[33] I submit that this rationale motivates Aristotle's reductive account of relations in terms of monadic properties.

We know from Aristotle's *Categories* (chapter 1) and from the *Metaphysics* (book VII chapter 4) that even incidental properties (e.g., being pale, or being hot) have essences and definitions. Furthermore, properties cannot exist unattached, on their own, but they have to belong to a subject (see *Categories* chapter 2). If we then consider a relation between two things, for example, Marco being the father of Pietro, and we try to think of this relation as a single polyadic property that conjoins the two, Marco and Pietro, decisive difficulties follow. On the one hand, this polyadic property would belong to both subjects, since it can only exist by belonging to something(s) as subject, and both subjects have a claim to it by being conjoined by it. On the other hand, although Marco is related to Pietro as a father, Pietro is not related to Marco as a father, but as a son; hence, either the polyadic property would belong to Pietro without being true of him; or the polyadic property would have two different natures, endowing each of the two conjoined entities with different qualifications, of being a father and being a son, which is incompatible with the property being one and the same property (i.e., relation). The asymmetry of the relation introduces a plurality of natures; the relation is these natures, and this plurality undermines its oneness. Conceiving of relations as polyadic properties was not even entertained by Aristotle. For Aristotle, what we consider relations are accounted for in terms of monadic properties that are ontologically interdependent—that is, relatives. They are monadic properties of a special kind, which he called the *pros ti* (the 'toward something') type of property: such properties in themselves point toward something other than themselves. Thus, Aristotle says:

> We call *relatives* all such things as are said to be just what they are, *of* or than other things, or in some other way *in relation to* something else. For example, what is larger is called what it is *than* something else (it is called larger than something); and what is double is called what it is *of* something else (it is called double of something); similarly with all other such cases. (*Cat.* 6a36–b2)
>
> Πρός τι δὲ τὰ τοιαῦτα λέγεται, ὅσα αὐτὰ ἅπερ ἐστὶν ἑτέρων εἶναι λέγεται ἢ ὁπωσοῦν ἄλλως πρὸς ἕτερον· οἷον τὸ μεῖζον τοῦθ' ὅπερ ἐστὶν ἑτέρου λέγεται, —τινὸς γὰρ μεῖζον λέγεται,— καὶ τὸ διπλάσιον ἑτέρου λέγεται τοῦθ' ὅπερ ἐστίν, —τινὸς γὰρ διπλάσιον λέγεται.— ὡσαύτως δὲ καὶ ὅσα ἄλλα τοιαῦτα.

(Aristotle does not distinguish between relatives and relations. I take it this is for the reason given above: that neither relatives nor (asymmetric) relations can be single polyadic properties with a *single* nature belonging to each of the two relata it is true of.) What does Aristotle mean by taking relatives to be *pros ti*—toward something? He explains it as follows:

> All relatives are spoken of in relation to correlatives that reciprocate. For example the slave is called slave of a master and the master is called master of a slave (*Cat.* 6b28–30)

Πάντα δὲ τὰ πρός τι πρὸς ἀντιστρέφοντα λέγεται, οἷον ὁ δοῦλος δεσπότου λέγεται δοῦλος καὶ ὁ δεσπότης δούλου δεσπότης λέγεται...

Pros ti properties are monadic properties such that their manifestation or activation depends counterfactually on the activation of their correlatives. Someone is actually a master only if there is a slave of whom he is master, and vice versa for the slave. The relation between the reciprocating correlatives is not a linguistic or a semantic relation. It is an *ontological interdependence*, as Aristotle states clearly:

If there is no master, there is no slave either...When there is a slave there is a master; and similarly with the others [*sc.* other relatives] Also, each carries the other to destruction; for if there is not a double there is not a half, and if there is not a half if there is not a double. So too with other such cases. (*Cat.* 7b5–22)

μὴ γὰρ ὄντος δεσπότου οὐδὲ δοῦλός ἐστιν...καὶ δούλου ὄντος δεσπότης ἐστίν· ὁμοίως δὲ τούτοις καὶ τὰ ἄλλα. καὶ συναναιρεῖ δὲ ταῦτα ἄλληλα· μὴ γὰρ ὄντος διπλασίου οὐκ ἔστιν ἥμισυ, καὶ ἡμίσεος μὴ ὄντος οὐκ ἔστι διπλάσιον· ὡσαύτως δὲ καὶ ἐπὶ τῶν ἄλλων ὅσα τοιαῦτα.

So the 'pointing' nature of relatives is Aristotle's way of depicting ontological dependence. This is what binds monadic properties into reciprocal pairs for their activation (e.g., being a master and being a slave). But ontological dependence is not a polyadic relation between relata. Just as there is no polyadic connection binding a species to its genus, in spite of their ontological interdependence, similarly, for Aristotle, there is no polyadic connection binding one activated monadic property to its correlative property.[34] The same holds for the relation between matter and form, and subject and property, where Aristotle is explicit that there is no (polyadic)

entity unifying them into one.[35] The relation between the reciprocating correlatives is not a linguistic or a semantic relation. It is an
ontological relation of interdependence, as Aristotle states clearly
in the last passage quoted. So the 'pointing' nature of relatives is
Aristotle's way of depicting ontological dependence. This is what
binds relative monadic properties into reciprocal pairs (e.g., being
a master and being a slave): that the correlatives are ontologically
interdependent. The last quotation above is important for understanding Aristotle's notion of dependence, as it applies to relata. He
says that each relatum carries the other relatum 'to destruction'. He
is therefore clearly describing an existential dependence between
relata: if there is no master there is no slave. (Some dependencies
are expressed in generic terms, and some in specific terms, with the
dependencies specified respectively.)[36]

1.5 CAUSATION WITHOUT GLUE

The two pillars of Aristotle's theory of causation are his account
of powers and his reductive account of relations. In a nutshell,
for Aristotle, *causation is the activation of reciprocal causal powers.*
Aristotle considers causal powers as *relatives*; namely, the agent and
patient in a causal pair are causal relatives. In *Metaphysics* book V
Aristotle explains the term 'relative' or 'relation' as follows:

> Things are relative [*pros ti*] (1) as double to half, and treble to
> a third,...and that which exceeds to that which is exceeded;
> (2) as that which can heat to that which can be heated, and
> that which can cut to that which can be cut, and *in general the
> active to the passive*; (3) as the measurable to the measure, and
> the knowable to knowledge, and the perceptible to perception.
> (*Met.* 1020b26–32, my emphasis)

Πρός τι λέγεται τὰ μὲν ὡς διπλάσιον πρὸς ἥμισυ καὶ τριπλάσιον πρὸς τριτημόριον,...καὶ ὑπερέχον πρὸς ὑπερεχόμενον· τὰ δ' ὡς τὸ θερμαντικὸν πρὸς τὸ θερμαντὸν καὶ τὸ τμητικὸν πρὸς τὸ τμητόν, καὶ ὅλως τὸ ποιητικὸν πρὸς τὸ παθητικόν· τὰ δ' ὡς τὸ μετρητὸν πρὸς τὸ μέτρον καὶ ἐπιστητὸν πρὸς ἐπιστήμην καὶ αἰσθητὸν πρὸς αἴσθησιν.

Causal examples such as heating and being heated are included in the above among relatives such as double and half, and they are collectively grouped under the description of being active and being passive. It follows that generally, for Aristotle, the mover and the movable—namely, the active and the passive powers in causal interactions—are engaged in a causal relation which, according his theory of relations, involves two monadic properties rather than a polyadic one. In the causal cases, the two monadic properties are the powers themselves, namely the active power and the passive power. Using the example just given, it would be the heating power and the power to be heated, the cutting power and the power to be cut, the power of perception to the power of being perceived, and generally the active and the passive powers. According to Aristotle's account of relations, then, the active and passive powers are monadic properties that are ontologically interdependent.

We saw that Aristotle explained the ontological dependence between relata as an existential dependence (e.g., nobody is a slave if there is no master). Similarly the ontological dependence between the causal relata entails that there is no mover if there is no movable. But here the question arises whether the ontological dependence determines the potential or the activated state of the powers in question. Clearly, if there is nothing that can be affected, then the mover will not bring about any effect; there is no actual moving— changing—if there is nothing that can be moved—changed. For instance, if nothing can be heated, no heating will take place either.

But can there be a mover in potentiality, even if there is nothing that could be moved? Could there be, for example, a knife in a world where nothing could be cut? We already saw that the definition of a power mentions the end toward which the power is directed: what the power is capable of bringing about (*Met.* 1047b35–1048a8). But if there is nothing that can be so affected, how can there be a power whose nature is to bring about that effect? Aristotle believes in some form of the Principle of Plenitude—namely, that what is possible will happen.[37] If so, then it follows that he believes that the end of each power in potentiality must be realizable. So, there could be no mover, even in potentiality, in a world where it was not possible for it to move anything. Hence, we must assume that the ontological dependence between active and passive powers applies to their potential state, as much as to their activated state.[38]

Causation is thus accounted for by Aristotle in terms of pairs of causal powers (an active and a passive one) that come to be activated in mutual dependence on each other. This mutual dependence binds the cause and effect together, but without reifying a relation between them. This latter conclusion follows from Aristotle's theory of relatives that we have examined in the preceding section. What makes Aristotle's theory of causation unique in the history of philosophy is that it is grounded in his account of relations in terms of monadic properties, which are ontologically interdependent. On this view, powers depend for their activation on the activation of their mutual partner-powers. Because of their mutual dependence for activation, partner-powers realize their natures in activities that are *co-determined, co-varying, and co-extensive in time.* Thus, on this account there is *reciprocity* in causation. Consider the causal scenario when A causes B to become hotter. On Aristotle's account, A's power to heat is activated; its manifestation is hea*ting* B up. But this can take place only if B's power to be heated is activated too and manifests itself in B's getting hotter. A's heating and B's being heated are mutually dependent in a variety of ways and each activity lasts as long as the other lasts. In the *De Anima* Aristotle wonders why the senses do not perceive themselves since they perceive other things made of perceptible elements and they themselves are so composed of such elements (*DA* 417a1–7). He concludes that 'the power of sense is parallel to what is combustible. For that never ignites itself spontaneously, but requires an agent which has the power of starting ignition' (*DA* 417a7–10). The external agent is perception's partner-power, which activates it. By developing an account of causation as the activation of causal partner-powers, Aristotle puts forward a realist theory of causation that does *not* reify the interaction of the causal partners into a relation.[39]

That causation is the mutual activation of causal powers is a view that is gaining consensus in contemporary metaphysics.[40] However, there is an important feature to causation that is left out in the contemporary views of this kind, namely *agency*; and its omission leaves important metaphysical work undone. Aristotle's analysis of the interaction between mutually activating causal powers is different from those advanced in the contemporary debate, in that it does justice to the intuition that there is agency in causation. Aristotle draws a distinction between the causal agent and patient, associating agency with what brings about change and patiency with what changes. Accounts that do not draw this distinction provide no argument that causation needs to be symmetric with respect to change; and furthermore, they would not be able to explain the possibility of the exercise of a power that does not itself change (unless by change they understand the mere manifestation of a power). By 'change' I mean that the resulting power (property) is different from the original one, as in the case of heating. Aristotle does not consider the mere exercise of a power a change (e.g., when the floor is sustaining my weight, the weight does not change but it is causally exercised on the floor).

I will now turn to examine the nature of the causal *agency* that an active power exercises on a passive power. There are two aspects of causal agency that reveal its nature. The first is what it brings about, and the other is how it achieves it. In thinking about the interaction between causal agent and patient, it might be natural or intuitive to think of it as a *transmission* of powerfulness. The idea that causation happens because of the passing around or transmission of properties can be traced back to an ancient Greek conception known in the literature as the Contagion Model of causation. Aristotle too talked of the transmission of the form of the agent's power onto the patient's power.[41] But, even for Aristotle, as we will see, this is a figurative way of describing the power interaction. The transmission of powerfulness is a way of describing what is brought about by causation, *as if* the patient received the powerfulness of the agent. Nothing is actually transferred from the agent to the patient; what takes place is not the transmission of anything. On Aristotle's view, all there is to powers 'interacting' is their *mutual activation*; there is no exchange between them, no transmission of anything, and no relation bridging the two. The interdependence of the relative powers translates into their mutual *qualitative transition* to exercising their powerfulness, which is what their causal interaction consists in. Mutual manifestation is the simultaneous transition of each of the partner powers to their activated states (e.g., heating and being heated).[42]

Let us now look more closely at Aristotle's talk of causation in terms of transmission, and at how we can gain a better insight into causation itself. In the *Physics*, Aristotle describes what the mover does to the movable in terms of *transmission of the form* of the mover to the movable:

The mover will always transmit a form, either a 'this' or such or so much, which, when it moves, will be the principle and cause of the motion (e.g., the actual man begets man from what is potentially man.). (*Phys.* 202a9–12)

εἶδος δὲ ἀεὶ οἴσεταί τι τὸ κινοῦν, ἤτοι τόδε ἢ τοιόνδε ἢ τοσόνδε, ὃ ἔσται ἀρχὴ καὶ αἴτιον τῆς κινήσεως, ὅταν κινῇ, οἷον ὁ ἐντελεχείᾳ ἄνθρωπος ποιεῖ ἐκ τοῦ δυνάμει ὄντος ἀνθρώπου ἄνθρωπον.

The transmitted form might be a substantial form, as in the case of the transmission of the form of a human being to the menstrual fluids in the generation of an embryo; or it might be a quality, a such, as for instance of heat or of weight, etc. So, in general terms, the causal action of the active power on the passive one consists in the transmission of a form from an agent to a patient. The transmitted form is then the cause; the privation of the form in the patient is what allows for the form's reception, and the physical process facilitating the transmission of the form is what grounds the causal change (e.g., in building the movements of the builder's hands facilitate the transmission of the form of the house to the construction materials; for a fire, contact facilitates the transmission of the form to the object heated). Aristotle wants to find a way to explain the change that is brought about by the active power, and this is one way in which talk of transmission may be helpful. In the example above, the generation of a new human being is accounted for by the transmission of the form of a human being, which is the principle and the cause of the motion. The form transferred is the form that determines the end (τέλος) of the potentiality in the moving power's definition. Thus a parent has the potentiality to generate a human being, and a painter the potentiality to generate a painting on canvas. These are the ends that the movers' powers are directed towards, in their potential state (e.g., the ends that the parent and the painter have respectively). They express what the powers can bring about when actualized.

What does it mean to say that the form of the moving power is transmitted? Once again, Aristotle's explanation of causation in terms of the transference of a form from the active power to the passive one should *not* be taken as a literal description. Aristotle is *not* reifying the form of the power into an active agent of its own, over and above the power itself. There is no homunculus-form that is transmitted from the parent to the offspring. There are only motions transmitted from the parent to the menstrual fluids by the sperm that is implanted in them; but the transmitted motions have a form (they are 'shaped'); thus the heat in the parent's sperm generates the motions in the fluids, which gradually shape the embryo, as Aristotle tells us explicitly.[43] Similarly, there is no form of a statue that is literally transferred from the sculptor to the marble; a sculptor transfers the form of a figure in her mind to the marble through the movements of her hands and chisel. Nevertheless, talk of transmitted forms might be the best way available to Aristotle to describe collectively the type of effect that the respective moving powers have on the passive ones. The movements generated from the heat of the sperm in the first case, and from the hands of the sculptor in the second, bring about changes of particular types, which are determined by the kind of active power that is acting on the passive one. The resulting change is *as if* the sperm transferred a form onto the menstrual fluids, which 'en-formed' them and shaped them into an embryo; and *as if* the sculptor transferred a form onto the marble, which 'en-formed it' into a statue. There ain't no magic; Aristotle's account is realistic and intuitive. Physical macro-changes emerge from micro-changes brought about by the fundamental powers (i.e., the hot, the cold, the wet, and the dry, as we have seen), which affect their passive correlates. Even if one took Aristotle to be saying that, literally, there is a (reified, matter-less) form that is transmitted to the passive power, this would still *not* explain how causation takes place. We would want to know how that form does it; what causal efficacy a form can have on a passive power. Assuming Aristotle is looking for an answer as to *how* one power affects another, adding a further item to the causal series would not offer an explanation. It would only continue the regress generated in the search for the mechanism of causal efficacy. Then how does causal efficacy operate? Even if macro-powers depend on micro-powers to bring about their effects, how do micro-powers exert their causal efficacy on other micro-powers? As we have seen, Aristotle avoids the regressive series of introducing further intermediaries by assuming the *efficacy* of an active power on a passive one; all that happens is that 'when the agent and the patient meet in the way appropriate to the potentiality in question, the one *must* act and the other be acted on' (*Met.* 1048a6–7; see also pp. 21–4). This is the level at which the readiness of active and passive powers in appropriate circumstances engenders causal efficacy. There is no further underlying mechanism to uncover. Here we reach the explanatory rock bottom in Aristotle's theory. The transference of the form of the active power to the passive one is not a description of the mechanism of causal efficacy, but only of the type of qualitative change that takes place in the passive power. Aristotle has identified a ground-level activity that cannot be explained by more primitive ontological tools.[44]

Aristotle's view can thus be contrasted, despite apparent similarities, with the 'passing around' model for causation put forward by Mumford and Anjum (2011). They develop this model as an answer to the "Always packing, never travelling" argument discussed before (pp. 19–21). They introduce the model thus:

> On reflection, the idea of causation as a passing around of powers, especially for a pandispositionalist, starts to look extremely attractive (Mumford 2009). Some examples will illustrate this. You come in from the cold and sit by the fire. You sit by the fire because it is hot, which for the pandispositionalist means that it

has the power to warm your body. Causation occurs when the fire warms your body, changing it from cold to hot. Armstrong retorts that such causation, for pandispositionalism, consists in the mere passing around of powers. In the present case, that would mean that *the heat of the fire, which consisted in it having the power to warm some other object, has been passed on to you. But that sounds quite right.* (2011, 5–6, my emphasis)

The difficulty I have with the position advocated by Mumford and Anjum is that the notion of the 'passing around of powers' can explain the transfer of energy between objects (e.g., heat) but not cases where the causal effect also involves qualitative change. For example, the broken vase that received the hammer's blow has not become more powerful in the way the body near the fire has become hotter; rather, it shattered. 'Passing around force' does not describe being in pieces, by contrast to 'passing around heat', which describes being hot. This is important because it shows what we can and what we cannot explain further in causation. The transfer of parcels, whether of energy or particles or matter, cannot be all there is to causation, because *transference does not explain qualitative change.* Aristotle explains what happens in causation not as a transmission, at the bottom level, but as the mutual activation of interdependent powers. On the other hand, the language of transmission is helpful in giving us a way of talking of the activation of the agent *qua* agent as the *transmission* of the form, and of the activation of the patient *qua* patient as the *reception* of that form (resulting in the effect). In other words, the language of transmission helps capture the difference between the activation of the active and passive powers involved in a causal interaction. The difference needs to be expressed ∂/ somewhat; Aristotle makes this point in the *Physics* thus:

It is contrary to reason to suppose that there should be one identical actualization of two things which are different in kind. Yet there will be, if teaching and learning are the same, and agency and patiency. (*Phys.* 202b1–3)

ἀλλ' ἄλογον δύο ἑτέρων τῷ εἴδει τὴν αὐτὴν καὶ μίαν εἶναι ἐνέργειαν· καὶ ἔσται, εἴπερ ἡ δίδαξις καὶ ἡ μάθησις τὸ αὐτὸ καὶ ἡ ποίησις καὶ ἡ πάθησις.

To briefly recapitulate some of the conclusions reached so far regarding Aristotle's account of the activation of causal powers in interaction: their actualities are essentially different activities—we might call them *causing* and *suffering* respectively, where the suffering is the activation of the passive power, while the causing is the activation of the active power involved in the causal interaction.[45] The causal effect is the actuality or activation of the passive power, which is a *change*.[46] Given that in causation both the active and the passive powers are activated, and each has its own type of actuality, one might want to press the question of why on this account the causal change (i.e., the effect) is identified with the actuality of the *passive* power. This is because in Aristotle's account the passive power is activated as a recipient of change (i.e., it changes) while the active one is activated as an agent of change. This division of roles between active and passive powers is not further explained by Aristotle, but I believe is required.

I would like to briefly note here, without argument, a difference I find in the way Aristotle thought of causation and the way contemporary science does. Aristotle thought there is qualitative change, which incorporated quantitative change (i.e., as qualitative change with respect to amount). Thus when there is, for example, loss of body heat, Aristotle would explain this as a two-way qualitative change (i.e., two processes of causal interaction: the hot body warms up the air in its environment, while the cold air cools down the body). According to contemporary science, this causal process would be explained as a quantitative change—an exchange of energy between the body and the air around it. Ultimately, contemporary science aims to reduce all change to quantitative energy or particle exchanges. I submit qualitative change cannot be *fully* reduced to quantitative change. If this is right, Aristotle's power ontology would prove explanatorily stronger in explaining change because qualitative influence between powers would accommodate quantitative change, but not the opposite way around.

That causation has a direction is a generally shared intuition.[47] The orthodox view on the direction of causation has been that it reduces to the direction of time: causes occur prior to their effects. But the temporal view has fallen into disfavor of late,[48] again,[49] and a number of alternatives have been suggested. Aristotle's account does justice to the intuition that causation has a direction—not reducible to the direction of time. For Aristotle a power aims at a state other than its present one. The distinction between agent and patient in causation is pivotal to accounting for the direction of causation, and thus its *asymmetry*.[50] Thus, to go back to the picture sketched in *Physics* III 3, for Aristotle thinking (at least figuratively) of the operation of the mover on a movable as transmission of form from the mover to the movable is a way of underpinning causal direction metaphysically.

On the other hand, there is no reason why causing could not be in two directions at once, where both powers act as agents and patients of change (e.g., as in the case of a cube of ice in a glass of lemonade, when the one is cooling and the other is getting hotter). Aristotle acknowledges, for example in *Physics* 202a5–12, that in most causal interactions in nature the change is mutual. The agent changes the patient and the patient changes the agent. Being an agent or a patient of change are roles the powers play; in most cases, Aristotle thinks that each power is at the same time both active and passive, since powers operate on each other. The occurrence of mutual change in causation is not evidence against Aristotle's agent-patient model of causation. Cases of causal interaction in which both agent and patient undergo a change are to be understood simply as *two pairs of simultaneous interactions*. For example, where two playing cards rest against each other, each playing card acts on the other, and each of them suffers the other's agency.

Aristotle's language of transmission of form is helpful for presenting another of the fundamental features of causation, that is, its *incompleteness*. As we have seen, causal interaction begins with contact between the agent and patient (*Physics* 202a5–7, see section 1.3). The contact facilitates the 'transmission' of the form from the mover to the movable. Transmission is a process that takes place in time. While it lasts the transmission has not been completed. The unfolding of the stages of transmission marks the incompleteness of the causal process (e.g., building a structure). Once the transmission is completed, the causal interaction is not taking place any more. The agent is not acting on the patient, which now possesses the transmitted form. So the process of realization of the agent's capacity to transmit the form and the patient's capacity to receive the form is the causal process, which lasts until the transmission is completed. The activity takes place through time, during which period the process is driven by the not yet fully fulfilled powers of the agent to transmit the form and of the patient to receive it. So the causal process of transmission is actual while these powers are active, prior to the time at which they are fully completed. In that sense, the causal process is actual only while the powers that drive it are still transmitting the form (i.e., while the transmission is still incomplete). Aristotle writes that 'Motion is thought to be a sort of actuality, but incomplete, the reason being that the potential whose actuality it is, is incomplete' (*Phys.* 201b31–33, translation slightly modified).[51]

Finally, thinking (figuratively) of the operation of the active power upon the passive one in terms of transmission is helpful in bringing out further features of Aristotle's account of causation, some of which are particularly relevant to his theory of perception, as we will see in chapter 1. Transmissibility requires (i) that there is a suitable patient for receiving the form; (ii) that at the time of transmission the form is present in the agent *in actuality*; (iii) that the form is possessed by the agent in a way that is suitable, given the circumstances in which transmission has to take place, and the type of patient who will receive it (namely, the agent power of that type can function in its environment); (iv) that there is contact between mover and moved (as discussed on, pp. 21–4). Conditions (ii) and (iii) require further investigation. That the form has to be present in the agent in actuality at the time of transmission is captured by Aristotle in a clear example: 'The *actual* man begets man from what is potentially man' (*Physics* 202a10, added emphasis). In some cases, the agent possesses the form in actuality in unusual ways, and possibly in more than one way when the transmission occurs. Consider a sculptor having the form of the statue in mind, which is a way of possessing the form in a non-transmissible way, in her imagination, and also having the form embodied in the movement of her hands through which she sculpts the statue, which is a way of possessing the form in a transmissible way. Or further consider the mathematics teacher having the demonstration of a theorem in mind, and having it written on the blackboard. By analogy to the case in which the mathematics teacher has the demonstration of a theorem in mind, in the case of color Aristotle holds that an object in the dark has color only in first actuality; this is the object's potentiality to have visible color. The color property is the same, even before the color becomes visible:

> Every color has in it the power to set in movement what is actually transparent; that power constitutes its very nature. That is why it is not visible except with the help of light; it is only in

the light that the color of a thing is seen. (*DA* 418a31–b3; my emphasis)

πᾶν δὲ χρῶμα κινητικόν ἐστι τοῦ κατ' ἐνέργειαν διαφανοῦς, καὶ τοῦτ' ἐστὶν αὐτοῦ ἡ φύσις. διόπερ οὐχ ὁρατὸν ἄνευ φωτός, ἀλλὰ πᾶν τὸ ἑκάστου χρῶμα ἐν φωτὶ ὁρᾶται.

As we will see in chapter 3, it is clear that it is the same property that is in the dark, capable of acting on the transparent, as when activated by acting on the transparent. The object possesses *visible* color—that is, color in second actuality—only when it is illuminated—activating the transparent: 'without the help of light color remains invisible' (*DA* 419a9). The color is visible in such conditions because it can be seen only when it is in second actuality. When the color is actually seen, it actualizes its potentiality for visibility. This is in a sense its third actuality, but Aristotle never uses this expression. Yet, it is again the same property that becomes actually seen, as we saw in the quote above: it is the color of the object that is seen. (I will not continue to use the expression 'third actuality' in order not to complicate further my discussion of the text or of other commentators on perception. Rather, I will consider visible color as the first actuality, and seen color as the second actuality of the power.) Analogously with sound, there are unperceived disturbances in the air that could be heard if a perceiver was present, and there are such disturbances that are also perceived (i.e., soundings). An object's sounding lasts only while a perceiver hears it, and the hearing lasts only as long as the sounding:

> It is possible to have the capacity to hear and not to hear, and that which can produce sounds is not always doing so. But when that which can hear is hearing and that which can produce sound is producing it, then *hearing in actuality and sounding in actuality come to be at the same time*, and one might call

the one hearing and the other sounding. (*DA* 425b28–426a1, my translation and emphasis).

ἔστι γὰρ ἀκοὴν ἔχοντα μὴ ἀκούειν, καὶ τὸ ἔχον ψόφον οὐκ ἀεὶ ψοφεῖ, ὅταν δ᾽ ἐνεργῇ τὸ δυνάμενον ἀκούειν καὶ ψοφῇ τὸ δυνάμενον ψοφεῖν, τότε ἡ κατ᾽ ἐνέργειαν ἀκοὴ ἅμα γίνεται καὶ ὁ κατ᾽ ἐνέργειαν ψόφος, ὧν εἴπειεν ἄν τις τὸ μὲν εἶναι ἄκουσιν τὸ δὲ ψόφησιν.

Since the actualities of the sensible object and of the sensitive faculty are one in actuality, while different in their modes of being, actual hearing and actual sounding *appear and disappear from existence at one and the same moment,* and so actual savor and actual tasting, etc., while as potentialities one of them may exist without the other. But the earlier philosophers of nature did not state the matter well, thinking that there is without sight nothing white nor black, nor flavor without tasting. For in one way they were right but in another wrong; for since the perception and the perceptible are so spoken of in two ways, as potential and as actual, the statement holds of the latter, but it does not hold of the former. This ambiguity they wholly failed to notice. (*DA* 426a15–26, my translation and emphasis)

ἐπεὶ δὲ μία μέν ἐστιν ἐνέργεια ἡ τοῦ αἰσθητοῦ καὶ τοῦ αἰσθητικοῦ, τὸ δ᾽ εἶναι ἕτερον, ἀνάγκη ἅμα φθείρεσθαι καὶ σώζεσθαι τὴν οὕτω λεγομένην ἀκοὴν καὶ ψόφον, καὶ χυμὸν δὴ καὶ γεῦσιν, καὶ τὰ ἄλλα ὁμοίως· τὰ δὲ κατὰ δύναμιν λεγόμενα οὐκ ἀνάγκη. ἀλλ᾽ οἱ πρότερον φυσιολόγοι τοῦτο οὐ καλῶς ἔλεγον, οὐθὲν οἰόμενοι οὔτε λευκὸν οὔτε μέλαν εἶναι ἄνευ ὄψεως, οὐδὲ χυμὸν ἄνευ γεύσεως. τῇ μὲν γὰρ ἔλεγον ὀρθῶς, τῇ δ᾽ οὐκ ὀρθῶς· διχῶς γὰρ λεγομένης τῆς αἰσθήσεως καὶ τοῦ αἰσθητοῦ, τῶν μὲν κατὰ δύναμιν τῶν δὲ κατ᾽ ἐνέργειαν, ἐπὶ τούτων μὲν συμβαίνει τὸ λεχθέν, ἐπὶ δὲ τῶν ἐτέρων οὐ συμβαίνει. ἀλλ᾽ ἐκεῖνοι ἁπλῶς ἔλεγον περὶ τῶν λεγομένων οὐχ ἁπλῶς.

To sum up and generalize, transmissibility requires that the form is possessed by the agent in a way that is suitable, given the circumstances in which transmission has to take place, and the type of patient that will receive it. Transmission is *context relative*. Consider the teacher who possesses knowledge of a theorem, but only in a language that her pupil would not understand. Possessing knowledge of the theorem does not make her into a teacher (of the theorem) until she embodies this knowledge in the spoken English words that transmit it to the student. Secondly and for the same reason, namely that the form must be transmissible to a particular type of patient and in a particular set of circumstances, no type of transmission is more privileged than others; none has more claim to be called causation than any other. This means that no type of possession of the form by the agent is more privileged than others. Thus, whether the lesson is in a lecture or in an article, neither is more genuinely the lesson than the other. The teacher possesses the lesson in different ways—in her memory, her lecture, and the article. All of them are transmissible forms, each fitting different circumstances in which transmission could take place. This has important consequences for Aristotle's theory of perception, as we will see in chapter 3.

1.6 THE CAUSAL POWERS MODEL IN *PHYSICS* III 3

In light of the above discussion, we are now in a position to understand Aristotle's programmatic stance at the beginning of *Physics* III 3: accounting for motion/change[52] does not require appealing to any new, primitive category of being:

> There is no such thing as motion over and above the things. It is always with respect to substance or to quantity or to quality or

to place that what changes changes. But it is impossible, as we assert, to find anything common to these which is neither 'this' nor quantity nor quality nor any of the other predicates. Hence neither will motion and change have reference to something over and above the things mentioned; for there is nothing, over and above them. (*Physics* 200b32–201a3, my emphasis)

οὐκ ἔστι δὲ κίνησις παρὰ τὰ πράγματα· μεταβάλλει γὰρ ἀεὶ τὸ μεταβάλλον ἢ κατ᾽ οὐσίαν ἢ κατὰ ποσὸν ἢ κατὰ ποιὸν ἢ κατὰ τόπον, κοινὸν δ᾽ ἐπὶ τούτων οὐδὲν ἔστι λαβεῖν, ὡς φαμέν, ὃ οὔτε τόδε οὔτε ποσὸν οὔτε ποιὸν οὔτε τῶν ἄλλων κατηγορημάτων οὐθέν· ὥστ᾽ οὐδὲ κίνησις οὐδὲ μεταβολὴ οὐθενὸς ἔσται παρὰ τὰ εἰρημένα, μηθενός γε ὄντος παρὰ τὰ εἰρημένα.

This is in line with Aristotle's commitment not to reify causation into a relation. Instead of introducing new metaphysical building blocks to explain motion (and more generally causation), Aristotle makes use of his three well known principles: the form, the priva-tion of form, and the substratum that remains through change. In addition, he appeals to his distinction between being in potential-ity and being in actuality, which is a primitive distinction of ways in which things are,[53] and plays a crucial role in accounting for the connection between cause and effect, as we will see in what follows. Aristotle describes his account of causation in terms of causal powers in some detail in *Physics* III 3, where he looks at the interaction between a mover and a movable in the case of motion (κίνησις). We thus learn more about the relation of dependence binding together active and passive powers. Aristotle puts flesh on the bones of his account of the dependence between active and passive powers in a causal pair during their activation. During the causal interaction, the mover moves in actuality, and the mov-able is actually moved. These two actualities are not casually coincident. The occurrence of the first requires the occurrence of the second. The relation between the two actualities is explored dialectically, in what I call the Actualities of Motion Dilemma. In brief, Aristotle considers two possibilities: that the two actualities of the mover and the movable are different, and that they are one and the same. If they are different, either both actualities occur in one of the two, either the mover or the moved, or one occurs in each. If both the actualities occur in one of them, then, first, one of them will not have its own actuality realized in it (e.g., the actuality of the mover will occur in the moved, not in the mover)— but how could that be, that the actuality of the mover will be in the moved? And secondly, whatever has both actualities in it will change in two different ways in relation to one form.[54] If on the other hand the actuality of the mover is in the mover, and the actuality of the movable is in the movable, then either the causal agency of the mover will impact on the mover itself, but not on the movable, or it will impact on nothing, in which case it is not being a mover in actuality. Finally, if the actualities of the mover and the moved are the same, then we reach absurdity, since agency and patiency cannot be the same. In what follows, I will first give an argument analysis of the Dilemma in its entirety, and then selectively discuss the claims that are the most relevant for the reconstruction of Aristotle's account of causation.

The Actualities of Motion Dilemma

In the structured representation of the argument below, the convention I follow is to indent under the conclusion the premises or the sub-arguments pertinent to the support of that conclusion.[55] The premises justifying or objecting to a conclusion are grouped at the same level of indentation. I indicate in parentheses the premises I have supplied for completeness of the argument, in addition to what is found in Aristotle's text.

C The realization of the agent's and the patient's capacities are neither the same nor different. (Supplied).

P 1 Because it is impossible that the realization of the agent's capacity is different from the realization of the patient's capacity. (Supplied).

P 2 Because if the realization of the agent's capacity is different (in number) from the realization of the patient's capacity, one of the following disjuncts is true:

(**2.1**) either both are realized in the patient;

(**2.2**) or both are realized in the agent;

(**2.3**) or one is realized in the agent and one in the patient (e.g. the realization of the agent's capacity takes place in the agent and the realization of the patient's capacity takes place in the patient). (See *Phys.* 202a25–7); (**2.2**) and (**2.3**) are supplied.)[56]

P 3 But none of the disjuncts is true.

P 4 Because (**2.1**) is impossible. Namely, it is impossible that the realization of the agent's capacity and the realization of the patient's capacity are both in the patient (Supplied).

P 5 Because if the realization of the agent's capacity and the realization of the patient's capacity are both in the patient, then both consequences follow:

(**5.1**) the agent's capacity will not be realized in the subject that has the capacity, the agent;

(**5.2**) the same subject, the patient, will undergo the realization of two [opposite] capacities at the same time in relation to one form. (See 202a33–6.)

P 6 But (**5.1**) is nonsense (202a36).

P 7 And (**5.2**) is impossible (202a36).

P 8 And *mutatis mutandis* for (**2.2**). (See 202a29–30.)

P 9 And it is impossible that the realization of the agent's capacity takes place in the agent, and realization of the patient's capacity takes place in the patient (Supplied).

P 10 Because if the realization of the agent's capacity and the realization of the patient's capacity are each in each, then one of the following disjuncts is true:

(**10.1**) either every agent will also be acted upon;

(**10.2**) or the agent, having causal efficacy, will not be causally efficacious. (See 202a28–b1).

P 11 But (**10.1**) is false, and leads to infinite regress (Supplied).

P 12 And (**10.2**) is false (Supplied).

P 13 And it is impossible that the realization of the agent's capacity is one and the same with the realization of the patient's capacity (202a36–b2).

P 14 Because then agency and patiency would have the same actuality, and so acting and being acted upon would be the same thing. (See 202b2–5 for the example).

P 15 But agency and patiency are not the same actuality (Supplied.).

P 16 Because agency and patiency are different in essence (Supplied).

P 17 Because the agent's capacity to act and the patient's capacity to suffer are essentially different things. (See 202a20 and 201b1.)

P 18 And the essence of an actuality is the same as the essence of its capacity (Supplied).

P 19 And it is nonsense that two things different in essence (e.g. the agent's acting and the patient's being acted upon) have one and the same actuality. (202a36–b2).

P 20 Because the actuality of something is the instantiation of its essence. (Supplied.)

In discussing the Dilemma, I shall be concerned mainly with the way Aristotle understands the relation of mover to movable (which is not reified by Aristotle). I will first identify the questions he thinks need to be addressed, and then examine the solutions he gives, thereby developing his own theory of causation. I will begin by considering the role of the form (εἶδος), which is the principle and cause of the motion in Aristotle's account of causation. There are three interrelated subthemes to be investigated. First, there is the transmission of the form from the mover to the movable (202a9–12). Secondly, the actuality of the mover and the actuality of the moved are in relation to one form, the transmitted one.[57] And finally, these two actualities are of different types.[58]

In view of what has been said about the transmission of the form so far, we are in the position to understand the transmission of the form as a way of describing collectively the type of change that is effected by the mover on the moved. The form that is the principle and cause of the motion is the form that is transmitted from the mover to the movable. For example, the causal efficacy of fire consists in its transmitting the form of heat to the pot. It follows that the motion suffered by what is movable consists in the reception of the form that is transmitted to it. So the mover's being a mover and the movable being moved will be achieved in relation to one form. But since the mover transmits and the movable receives the form, their achievements are of different types,[59] because they relate to the same form differently. Thus, in figurative terms, the actuality of the mover as a mover is the transmission of the form, and the actuality of the movable as movable is the reception of that form.

The second issue that arises out of the Dilemma of the Actualities of Motion is the distinction Aristotle makes between the subjects the actualities *occur in*, and the subjects they *belong to*. Here Aristotle's metaphysical intuitions are tested to the extreme, and he finally opts for an account that opens new ground in the area of causation. Aristotle asks where the actualities of the mover as mover—the action—and of the movable as movable— the passion— are (i.e. whether they are in the mover or in the movable (ἐν τίνι; 'in what?', 202a25)). By asking in what the action of the agent and the passion of the patient are, he distinguishes in one and the same question two metaphysical relations: 'belonging to a subject' and 'occurring in a subject'.[60] We need to examine why this distinction arises here, and how it can be understood, for this distinction will play an important role, especially in Aristotle's theory of perception. Let us first look at Aristotle's own attempt to justify the distinction. He writes: 'Since then they are both [the agent's action and the patient's passion] motions, we may ask: in what are they?' (202a25). He then proceeds:

> It is not absurd that the actualization of one thing should be in another. Teaching is the activity of a person who can teach, yet the operation is performed in something—it is not cut adrift from a subject [the teacher], but is of one thing [the teacher] in another [the learner]. (*Phys.* 202b5–8)
>
> οὔτε τὸ τὴν ἄλλου ἐνέργειαν ἐν ἑτέρῳ εἶναι ἄτοπον (ἔστι γὰρ ἡ δίδαξις ἐνέργεια τοῦ διδασκαλικοῦ, ἔν τινι μέντοι, καὶ οὐκ ἀποτετμημένη, ἀλλὰ τοῦδε ἐν τῷδε)

In the first brief quotation Aristotle makes a general point: he tells us that in relation to motions we can ask where they take place. Thus, my walk can take place in the park, and my tanning at the seashore. But in neither case am I doing something (at least in any way significant) to, or changing that in which my motion takes place. My walk and my tanning are external to the park and the seashore. They are 'in' them in a local sense, which must not be what Aristotle means here, if he is not to conflate, for example, my tanning taking place in the seashore from its taking place in me, who tans.[61] The second passage clarifies the type of distinction that Aristotle has in mind. He concentrates on one of the two actualities, the agent's, and says that teaching is performed by the teacher in something. If this is to be more illuminating than the first passage, we must take Aristotle to be saying something other than that teaching takes place in a classroom. Indeed, he does tell us that teaching takes place in the learner. But how is this to be understood and generalized? A clue as to what Aristotle means by talking of where an action takes place can be found in a sub-argument in the Dilemma (**P 9–12**), in the following dialectical move:

> [Suppose] the agency is in the agent and the patiency in the patient. [Then] ... the motion will be in the mover, for the same account will hold of mover and movable. Hence either every mover will be moved, or, though having motion, it will not be moved. (*Phys.* 202a26–31)
>
> ἢ ἡ μὲν ποίησις ἐν τῷ ποιοῦντι, ἡ δὲ πάθησις ἐν τῷ πάσχοντι...ἡ κίνησις ἐν τῷ κινοῦντι ἔσται (ὁ γὰρ αὐτὸς λόγος ἐπὶ κινοῦντος καὶ κινουμένου), ὥστ᾽ ἢ πᾶν τὸ κινοῦν κινήσεται, ἢ ἔχον κίνησιν οὐ κινήσεται.

The key ideas in this argument are that where the activity of the mover as a mover is will also be where the motion is; and the thing the motion is in is set in motion. Aristotle's justification for the first claim, that motion follows the activation of the mover as mover, is that the rationale in the case of the mover must be the same as in the case of the movable. Because if, as per the initial hypothesis, the action of the mover moves the movable, then it must be that the action of the mover generates motion. But if the action of the mover is in the mover, the generated motion will, for that reason, also be in the mover. But then the mover will be in motion, for otherwise 'though having motion, it will not be moved', which is treated as absurd and closes this branch of the argument. So the motion is where the actuality of the mover as mover is, and whatever the motion is in, it sets that thing in motion. In that case we can interpret the question 'ἐν τίνι;' ('in what?', 202a25) as asking 'where does the motion bring about the change?'. Teaching is in a learner, as heating is in a colder object, because it is these objects that are set in motion by the movers. So the actuality of the mover as mover is in the patient, generating the motion in it. The way it is in the patient is like the way the form is in matter.[62]

On the other hand, the actuality of the patient as patient is always in the patient, because the patient always suffers the motion that comes about. The picture which emerges from the distinction of the two metaphysical relations, 'belonging to a subject' and 'occurring in a subject', is that there is a motion that is the coincidence of two activities, the agent's and the patient's, in the patient.[63] Immediately following the Actualities of Motion Dilemma, Aristotle denies three of its premises:

[1] It is not absurd that the actualization of one thing should be in another.

[2] There is nothing to prevent two things having one and the same actualization.

[3] Nor is it necessary that the teacher should learn, even if to act and to be acted on are one and the same, provided they are not the same in respect of the account which states their essence . . . but in respect of that to which they belong (ᾧ ὑπάρχει ταῦτα), the motion. (*Phys.* 202b5–21, translation slightly modified)

This leads Aristotle directly to the discussion of his own position, which he had already sketched, just before entering the Dilemma, as follows:

> The solution of the difficulty is plain: motion is in the movable. It is the fulfillment of this potentiality by the action of that which has the power of causing motion; and even the actuality of that which has the power of causing motion is not other than the actuality of the movable; for it must be the fulfillment of both; for, it is on the movable that it [the mover] is capable of acting. Hence there is one and the same actuality of both. (*Phys.* 202a13–18, translation slightly modified)
>
> Καὶ τὸ ἀπορούμενον δὲ φανερόν, ὅτι ἐστὶν ἡ κίνησις ἐν τῷ κινητῷ· ἐντελέχεια γάρ ἐστι τούτου [καὶ] ὑπὸ τοῦ κινητικοῦ. καὶ ἡ τοῦ κινητικοῦ δὲ ἐνέργεια οὐκ ἄλλη ἐστίν· δεῖ μὲν γὰρ εἶναι ἐντελέχειαν ἀμφοῖν· κινητικὸν μὲν γάρ ἐστιν τῷ δύνασθαι, κινοῦν δὲ τῷ ἐνεργεῖν, ἀλλ' ἔστιν ἐνεργητικὸν τοῦ κινητοῦ, ὥστε ὁμοίως μία ἡ ἀμφοῖν ἐνέργεια.

I will outline Aristotle's position before discussing it in detail. Causal interaction consists in the activation of both the active and passive powers involved in the interaction (e.g. being able to teach and being able to learn); it is figuratively described as transmission of the form— indicating the type of activity that is engendered by the active power and suffered by the passive power. The activation of these powers is a process (e.g., the movements of the sculptor's arms and chisel on the wood) that, at one and the same time, constitutes the causing and effecting. The process is both a causing and an effecting, which are different, interdependent, activated asymmetric powers. Their asymmetry lies in the fact that the active power is realized in the bearer of the passive powers, producing an effect in what is acted upon.

The challenge is to explain the nature of the special 'bond' between the two powers (or their bearers) engaged in causal interaction. Aristotle's solution is to make the motion of the causally interacting substances *the same*. Their motion, being one and the same but belonging to both substances, binds the two substances together. But how can the motion of the agent be the same as the motion of the patient?

> It is contrary to reason to suppose that there should be one actualization [ἐνέργεια] of two things which are different in kind. Yet, there will be if teaching and learning are the same, and agency and patiency. To teach will be the same as to learn, and to act the same as to be acted on—the teacher will necessarily be learning everything that he teaches, and the agent will be acted on. (*Phys.* 201a35–202b5)
>
> ἀλλ' ἄλογον δύο ἑτέρων τῷ εἴδει τὴν αὐτὴν καὶ μίαν εἶναι ἐνέργειαν· καὶ ἔσται, εἴπερ ἡ δίδαξις καὶ ἡ μάθησις τὸ αὐτὸ καὶ ἡ ποίησις καὶ ἡ πάθησις, καὶ τὸ διδάσκειν τῷ μανθάνειν τὸ αὐτὸ καὶ τὸ ποιεῖν τῷ πάσχειν, ὥστε τὸν διδάσκοντα ἀνάγκη ἔσται πάντα μανθάνειν καὶ τὸν ποιοῦντα πάσχειν.

Aristotle does not draw back from his solution in view of this problem, but is led to innovate. He will keep the oneness of the motion, but account for its twoness in a metaphysically novel way, which follows different principles from his essentialism about substances. Aristotle tells us that the motion that is in the movable, brought about by the mover,

> ...is the fulfillment of this potentiality [of the movable as movable] by the action of that which has the power of causing motion [the mover]; and the actuality of that which has the power of causing motion [the mover] is not other than the

actuality of the moveable; for it must be the fulfillment of both. (*Phys.* 202a14–16)

ἐντελέχεια γάρ ἐστι τούτου [καὶ] ὑπὸ τοῦ κινητικοῦ. καὶ ἡ τοῦ κινητικοῦ δὲ ἐνέργεια οὐκ ἄλλη ἐστίν· δεῖ μὲν γὰρ εἶναι ἐντελέχειαν ἀμφοῖν·

The terms translated as 'fulfillment' and 'actuality' are ἐντελέχεια and ἐνέργεια respectively, which are used interchangeably in this context.[64] Clearly, so described, the solution faces the *prima facie* objection we encountered above—that teaching will be the same as learning, and that the teacher will learn what she teaches. So Aristotle proceeds to refine his answer by a series of examples. Before looking at the examples, it may be helpful to say that he is only elucidating the view he has already stated, and not altering this view or proposing a new theory. This is surprising since one would have expected his answer to use different terminology in view of the clarification he makes. But Aristotle does not change the terminology of his solution, despite the fact that he has the opportunity to do so when he repeats it (at *Phys.* 202b–9). Indeed, his solution, enriched by the examples, does avoid the objection, as I shall argue below. But one would have expected a re-description of his solution that did not retain the objectionable sameness of the two actualities, which his solution does not require and is misleading for the reader. As we do not get a re-description, we must conclude that Aristotle is using the terms ἐντελέχεια and ἐνέργεια broadly here, to mean by actualization the *activity* in which the agent and patient are mutually engaged, rather than the natures of their activities. Aristotle gives four examples to elucidate his view. He sets up the problem by stating the *explanandum* first:

A thing is capable of causing motion because it can do this, it is a mover because it actually does it. But it is on the movable that it is capable of acting. (*Phys.* 202a16–7)

κινητικὸν μὲν γάρ ἐστιν τῷ δύνασθαι, κινοῦν δὲ τῷ ἐνεργεῖν, ἀλλ' ἔστιν ἐνεργητικὸν τοῦ κινητοῦ.

The action of the mover can be realized only by acting on the movable. This requires Aristotle to explain how the mover's capacity is bound up with the movable. Following his statement of the problem, he restates his solution and elucidates it with the first two examples:

> Hence there is one and the same actuality [ἐνέργεια] of both [the mover and the movable] alike, just as one to two and two to one are the same interval, and the steep ascent and the steep descent are one. (*Phys.* 202a18–20)[65]
>
> ὥστε ὁμοίως μία ἡ ἀμφοῖν ἐνέργεια ὥσπερ τὸ αὐτὸ διάστημα ἓν πρὸς δύο καὶ δύο πρὸς ἕν, καὶ τὸ ἄναντες καὶ τὸ κάταντες.

Aristotle explains the sameness involved in these examples: 'For these are one and the same, although their definitions [λόγος] are not one. So it is with the mover and the moved' (*Phys.* 202a20). This is important but incomplete. It is important because it blocks the objection that teaching would be the same as learning, by stating that they have different essential natures. But if they have different essential natures they are not one and the same entity described in two different ways. Whatever it is that is one and the same between the two intervals or between the ascent and descent must have two different definitions/natures. The majority of the commentators, ancient and modern, who read λόγος as 'account/ description' rather than 'definition', take the examples to introduce a single common entity in each case (e.g., the unit value one, or the inclined road—or the non-directional relation between the extremes).[66] By contrast with the majority view, my reading of Aristotle's examples and explanation takes λόγος at 202a20–21 to mean 'definition'.

The ontological complex of the two directional intervals and their ground, or the complex of the two routes and their ground, are not any of the familiar types of entity in Aristotelian ontology (although their components are). Aristotle is here engaging in a novel exploration of ontological dependence, not of matter and form, or subject and property, or potential and actual, but of two interdependent natures. When Aristotle says that there is a single actuality (ἐνέργεια) of both the mover and the movable (as there is between the two intervals or the two routes), he must mean that the mover and the movable are so related in their activity as to be one in some sense, but not one in the definitions that describe what each of them does or suffers. What makes the definitions of the vector lines from 1 to 2 and from 2 to 1 two are their opposite directions; but what is it that makes these vector lines one? It is the non-directional interval between one and two that is the same for both vector lines. The interval would not be the same, for example, between vector lines 1 to 2 and 4 to 3 (on a line). Similarly with the uphill and downhill routes: they are different because of their opposed directions, but are both the same stretch of land, as opposed to two routes on different sides of the hill that share no common stretch of land. Although these examples and this explanation go some way towards explaining what Aristotle means by claiming that the actuality of the mover and the movable is the same, his position is not as explicit as in the explanation we shall find in his next set of examples, to which I now turn. After the Dilemma, Aristotle states his own position, resolving the puzzles encountered in the course of the Dilemma itself. On the issue we are examining here, he writes:

> Nor is it necessary that the teacher should learn, even if to act and be acted on are one and the same, provided that they are not the same in respect of the account [λόγος] which states their essence [<τὸ> τί ἦν εἶναι] (as raiment and dress), but are

the same in the sense in which the road from Thebes to Athens and the road from Athens to Thebes are the same, as has been explained above. (*Phys.* 202b10–14)

οὔτ' ἀνάγκη τὸν διδάσκοντα μανθάνειν, οὐδ' εἰ τὸ ποιεῖν καὶ πάσχειν τὸ αὐτό ἐστιν, μὴ μέντοι ὥστε τὸν λόγον εἶναι ἕνα τὸν <τὸ> τί ἦν εἶναι λέγοντα, οἷον ὡς λώπιον καὶ ἱμάτιον, ἀλλ' ὡς ἡ ὁδὸς ἡ Θήβηθεν Ἀθήναζε καὶ ἡ Ἀθήνηθεν εἰς Θήβας, ὥσπερ εἴρηται καὶ πρότερον;

The use of the 'technical' expression, coined by Aristotle himself, for essence, <τὸ> τί ἦν εἶναι, settles the issue as to whether by 'account', λόγος, he means description or definition of nature.[67] This is further supported by his immediate example of things that have the same account, namely raiment and dress. 'Raiment' and 'dress' are indeed one thing, under two names or descriptions, but with one definition which expresses its essence. In *Topics* I 7, 103a25–7, Aristotle says that whatever is one in essence is one in the primary sense (κυρίως), and indeed we find there the very same example of the 'raiment' and 'dress' to illustrate this type of oneness; this is not the case with the two routes, but it would be if the descriptions were 'the road from Athens to Thebes' and 'the road we travelled on last week'—from Athens to Thebes. The route from Thebes to Athens differs in definition from the route from Athens to Thebes since they are not, as Aristotle tells us, like raiment and dress. The reference back to what 'has been explained above' in the last quotation is to the passage just examined, 202a19–20, on the relation of the uphill route to the downhill one that differs in account, λόγος; hence there, too, Aristotle intends λόγος to be the definition of essence. There is further evidence that here λόγος is the definition of essence, and not a mere description. This comes in an unexpected metaphysical observation that Aristotle makes in the lines immediately following. This observation also makes it evident that Aristotle's aim in the two passages we are examining is to introduce a sense of qualified sameness, a sense different from identity, by making such statements as that mover and movable are 'one and the same', or that one 'actuality...must be the fulfillment of both', or that 'to act and to be acted on are one and the same':[68]

> For it is not the case that all the same properties belong to [ταὐτὰ πάντα ὑπάρχει] those things which are in any way the same; rather, this is the case only for those things to be which is the same [τὸ εἶναι τὸ αὐτό]. (202b14–6, my translation)
>   οὐ γὰρ ταὐτὰ πάντα ὑπάρχει τοῖς ὁπωσοῦν τοῖς αὐτοῖς, ἀλλὰ μόνον οἷς τὸ εἶναι τὸ αὐτό.

The expression ταὐτὰ πάντα must refer to attributes of substances, and not to the substratum underlying a substance; for it would be extremely unnatural for Aristotle to say that the underlying substratum belongs to (ὑπάρχει) a substance. Furthermore, although he only talks of things to be which are the same (literally, that have the same being, τὸ εἶναι τὸ αὐτό), I take it that he means things whose constitution is the same. One could take this to be limited only to forms, since their being exhausts their constitution and so the same being entails the same properties. But one could take it more liberally to mean 'embodied being', so that substances whose embodied form is the same have the same properties.[69] There are other possible readings, but for our purposes the safe reading of mere forms gives us a neat contrast to the cases we are examining. What it is to be an agent is different from what it is to be a patient; their definitions are different (202a20, 202b22), and with them their kind (202b1). The definitions stating their essence are different (202b12), but 'to act and to be acted on are one and the same' (202b11). Aristotle's examples have already prepared us for understanding this statement. There is a kind of sameness that the route from Athens to Thebes has with the route from Thebes to Athens, because these routes are realized on the same road. The line from 1 to 2 is realized on the same interval as the line from 2 to 2. In all such cases, their ground of realization is one and the same, although the two powers differ in kind, and thus their actualities differ in kind, too.[70] Aristotle finally states this explicitly:

> To generalize, teaching is not the same in the primary sense [κυρίως] with learning, nor is agency with patiency, but that to which those belong [ᾧ ὑπάρχει] [scilicet is the same for both], namely the motion [κίνησις]; for the actualization [ἐνέργεια] of this [teaching] in that [learning] and the actualization [ἐνέργεια] of that [learning] through the action of this [teaching] differ in definition. (Phys. 202b19–22, translation slightly modified)[71]

> ὅλως δ᾽ εἰπεῖν οὐδ᾽ ἡ δίδαξις τῇ μαθήσει οὐδ᾽ ἡ ποίησις τῇ παθήσει τὸ αὐτὸ κυρίως, ἀλλ᾽ ᾧ ὑπάρχει ταῦτα, ἡ κίνησις· τὸ γὰρ τοῦδε ἐν τῷδε καὶ τὸ τοῦδε ὑπὸ τοῦδε ἐνέργειαν εἶναι ἕτερον τῷ λόγῳ.

The motion to which teaching and learning belong is the *substratum* of the two actualities of the activated powers. It is the interaction between the two substances that activates both powers—e.g. the active power to teach and the passive power to learn (202a13 and 202a16, a18). Teaching causes learning. Neither can happen without the other. The teacher is not teaching if the learner is not learning, and the learner[72] is not learning if the teacher is not teaching. The two powers—to teach and to learn—can be activated only together. Their interdependence is captured by the fact that they are activated by one and the same activity, which cannot be separated into two. Both of them therefore characterize that activity, essentially, which in this case is an instance of teaching and learning. The activity bears the two forms in the way that matter bears the essential form in a substance, being en-formed by it. Only here, the two forms come together in mutual interdependence; the activity is essentially both teaching and learning.[73] This is possible only because the activity is composed of the activities of two different 'powerful' entities (e.g., substances). The active and passive powers in each causal pair are interdependent in different ways, such as being co-existent and co-variant, which is secured by their mutual dependence on the underlying activity. Thus, for example, the physical movement of the carpenter's hands and chisel on the hardwood constitute the carpenter's carving, and the log's being shaped into a statue.[74]

To recapitulate and generalize, when causation occurs there is a *common activity* that consists of the activation of the active power and the activation of the passive power, both of which happen *simultaneously,* and which are *different types* of activity.[75] The activity *takes place* where the change occurs: in the bearer of the passive power. In the case of the interaction of an active and a passive power, for instance when water dissolves salt, the change happens in the salt, which passively dissolves under the agency of water. This change is the common activity of the two powers, which renders water a solvent and the salt a solute. (In Aristotle's perceptual example, as we will see in chapter 2 the activity is the hearing of the sounding, consisting of the ear hearing and the sound sounding.)

CONCLUDING REMARKS

Aristotle will address the problem of the structure and the functionality of the faculty of perception as a metaphysical problem, and will resolve it through metaphysical innovation. His innovation is given in his account of causation in terms of powers. The main characteristics of his solution are the following. Causation is an activity involving two powers, which belong to different substances or parts of substance(s). This causal activity consists of the activities of each of the two powers that are mutually activated. Each of the activated powers engenders activation of a different type, but the two types are complementary partner activities. In consequence, the activity between the two powers is a composite (third) activity exemplifying two different types of sub-activity. Thus, the mutually activated powers make up a complex causal activity of agency and patiency, which sustain each other in existence. The Aristotelian 'activity' or 'activation' of a power should not be understood as necessarily involving movement (e.g., in the way that carving a statue or writing does). Heating for example involves only *qualitative* change, even if the change spreads gradually through the heated body. The activation of the power to heat does not consist in the propagation of heat in the heated body but only in the increase in temperature, which is not a movement.

As we saw, Aristotle does not introduce relations in his ontology, but addresses the need for relations through monadic relatives. One of the obstacles to admitting relations in ontology is the nature of asymmetric relations, which has been and remains a problem in metaphysics, because one and same entity cannot have different natures to 'impart' to asymmetric relata. In his account of causation we find Aristotle innovating, by positing *a single activity of two different natures*—agency and patiency. Why then not asymmetric relations with dual natures, if causal activities can have dual natures and be single, but two in being? The answer is that causal activities are composed of activity-components. Specifically, they consist of the activated (correlative) active and passive powers. The types of being characterizing what a composite entity is can vary, since composition does not require definitional unity of its form—which is what substantial and incidental forms have in Aristotle's categorial ontology. The unity of a composite could be merely physical, not derived from formal unity, but merely from the mechanism of the composition (e.g., a glass of oil and water is one by composition of stuff; having dinner on a flight is a composition of activities). In the case of powers, the mechanism of composition of the causal activity is the mutual activation of partner powers, and the resulting (composed) activity is respectively two in being.

Notes

1. It follows that for Aristotle the senses are infallible—at least when perceiving their special sensibles (see, e.g. *Metaphysics* 1010b19–21). The infallibility of the special senses, with reference also to Aristotle's account of illusion and hallucination, will be addressed in chapters 2 and 3.
2. At the end of his account of efficient causation in terms of powers in the *Physics* Aristotle remarks that "A similar definition will apply to each of the other kinds of motion" (202b29); perception is a case of motion (i.e., change of the sense organ of the perceiver) as will be discussed in chapter 2.
3. The use of the term 'power' is well established in scholarly discussions of Aristotle's psychology; for a recent example, see, T.K. Johansen, *The Powers of Aristotle's Soul* (2012). Establishing a common framework of discussion for Aristotle's theory of powers and contemporary power ontologies is important for reasons that will emerge in the chapter. I share Esfeld's consideration, made in a different context, that while from a strictly philological point of view using modern terminology to discuss Aristotle's theory of perception might be questionable, "when it comes to Aristotle's significance for today's philosophy, the interest is in what we can learn from the study of his texts for those points that continue to be an issue today" (2000, 321).
4. For the distinction between first and second actuality see *DA* II.1 (412a10–11, 21–27; cf. II.5 417a22–29, 417b2–16).
5. *DA* II.1 (412a10–11, 21–27; cf. II.5 417a22–29, 417b2–16).
6. Properties are not subject to change. The property of heat cannot not become the property of cold. Since properties themselves do not change, when change occurs it is the entity qualified by a property that is changing, by acquiring a new property in place of the former one, (e.g., when the hot is replaced by cold, it is what is hot that changes, not the property of being hot, which is in fact lost). Of course, language cannot match the richness of qualitative variation in the world with correspondingly different descriptions. Instead language has to employ generalization, which may mislead us into thinking that properties survive change.
7. See *GC* 330a24–29.

8. See GC 337a2–6: 'All the other things—the things, I mean, which are reciprocally transformed in virtue of their qualities and their powers (e.g., the simple bodies)—imitate circular motion. For when Water is transformed into Air, Air into Fire, and the Fire back into Water, we say the coming-to-be has completed the circle, because it reverts again to the beginning'.

9. I call this metaphysical position Power Structuralism. The position was first put forward in my research statement submitted to the *European Research Council* in December 2009 (award number 263484).

10. The qualification that change might be brought about in something else, or in the bearer of the causal power itself *as if it were another thing*, is aimed at including in the account complex entities which have the capacity to bring about a change in a part or the whole *of themselves* (e.g., an athlete training herself).

11. In contemporary parlance, Aristotle holds a *pure* power ontology. Contrast this with contemporary views in which a power has a categorical basis (e.g., Armstrong, 2004, 138–9; 2000, 13–4; 1997, 80; Crane 1996). Although I reached my interpretation independently, I have found additional support for it in Broackes' 'Aristotle, Objectivity, and Perception'. Broackes argues that there is no categorical basis in Aristotle's powers thus:

> A radiator will heat things because it is actually hot: the action is due to its actuality. But that does not in itself I think require Aristotle to give a nondispositional basis to heat. There is nothing in Aristotelian doctrine to say that it is deeper or hidden actualities that give rise to powers.... Heat—and similarly lightness, weight, and cold—might for all that has been said be powers ultimate and ungrounded. (Broackes 1999, 86; see also footnote 45, page 79).

12. For example, Bird (2007), Holton (1999), Shoemaker (1984), Mellor (1974).

13. The commitment to an ontology of powers only, with no categorical properties, has brought about in some quarters the worry that is expressed, for example, in the Domino argument as formulated by John Heil:

> Despite its appeal in some quarters, many philosophers have been struck by the thought that a properties-as-powers view leads to a debilitating regress. Suppose As are nothing more than powers to produce Bs, Bs are nothing more than powers to produce Cs, Cs are nothing more than powers to produce Ds... and so on for every concrete spatio-temporal thing. How is this supposed to work? Imagine a row of dominos arranged so that, when the first domino topples, it topples the second, which topples the third, and so on. Now imagine that *all there is* to the first domino is a power to topple the second domino, and *all there is* to the second domino is a

power to be toppled and a power to topple the third domino, and so on. If all there is to a domino is a power to topple or be toppled by an adjacent domino, *nothing happens: no domino topples because there is nothing—no thing—to topple.* (Heil 2003, 98, my emphasis).

I believe there are difficulties with the framing of this example, which surface as paradoxes in its conclusion. The framing difficulties derive from the description of a domino as nothing but the power to topple or to be toppled. But given this assumption, nothing more is required in order to generate the concluding paradox (i.e., no assumption about the nature of powers is needed for the paradox). The reason is that the 'toppling', that is the concept used to describe the type of power in the example, makes an implicit reference to a structure that is external to the power—it is not the power (of being toppled) that is toppled. But saying that something has the power to be toppled or to topple *and* that there is nothing more to it than these powers generates a paradox, because we attribute to this item powers that presuppose the very external structure that is denied of the item. Even if each of these powers had a categorical base or aspect to their natures, and were not just powerfulness, the paradox would remain unaffected since there would still be no domino to be toppled. There is therefore no reason given by the domino argument for thinking that a power has something more to its nature than powerfulness.

14. Of course the criterion of being a cause that is the *originative* source of change would require to be relativized to a context, for otherwise one could trace back endlessly origins of change. Aristotle does not mention this issue in the passage quoted above, but it is a consideration he is sensitive to, as we see from his subsequent discussion of matter and the introduction of the concept of *proximate* matter:

It seems that when we call a thing not something else but 'of' that something else (e.g., a casket is not wood but of wood, and wood is not earth but made of earth…), that something is always *potentially (in the full sense of that word) the thing which comes after it in this series.* For example, a casket is *not* earthen nor earth, but wooden; for wood is potentially a casket and is the matter of a casket. (*Met.* 1049a18–23; my emphasis)

In causal series of changes (e.g., when the wood becomes a casket) *adjacent* items are one potentially the other. The earth is not potentially a casket, because there is an intermediate step between earth and casket in the series of changes from earth to wood to the casket. So it is the wood that is strictly speaking potentially the casket in the present context, despite the fact that the wood comes from earth, and hence the casket comes from earth. Correspondingly, in any given change, the origin of the change (i.e. its cause) will be taken to be the immediate cause of this particular change in question, rather than an antecedent one in the causal history of this change.

15. See Plato, *Theaetetus* 152a–160e.
16. See, for example Martin 1992, Martin 2008, and Martin's contribution to Crane 1996; Mumford and Anjum (2011); Heil 2003.
17. I discuss this further in section 1.3.
18. Contemporary metaphysicians who hold a distinction similar to Aristotle's between active and passive powers are, for example, Shoemaker (1998) who talks of 'forward-' and 'backward-looking conditional powers'.
19. See section 1.3.
20. Contrast with, for example, Mumford and Anjum: 'The manifestation of a power will...be itself a *further* power or cluster of powers' (2011, 5, my emphasis).
21. In our common sense conception of change, both process and activity count as changes. What Aristotle wishes to capture by treating only process as change is that activity does not alter the constitutional makeup of the active agent, but only puts the existing constitution to work. See also my 'Aristotelian Powers At Work; Reciprocity Without Symmetry in Causation' in Jon Jacobs (ed.) *Putting Powers to Work*, forthcoming OUP.
22. By contrast, the actuality of the outcome resulting from a change (e.g., the actuality of a house) is something other than—beyond—the change itself.
23. This is an important difference between Aristotle's account of powers and the contemporary ones (e.g., Bird (2007). On the latter, the manifestation of a power is a *new* power that comes about (e.g., an ice cube's power to cool the lemonade in the glass is manifested in the new—lower—temperature of the lemonade). It is an important difference because it allows Aristotle's ontology not to fall prey to the "Always packing, never travelling" argument. It also has very important consequences with respect to Aristotle's theory of perception, as we shall see in chapter 3.
24. The expression "always packing, never travelling" is first used by Molnar (2003, 173).
25. For example, see Bird: 'The essence of a potency involves a relation to something else; if inertial mass is a potency then its essence involves a relation to a stimulus property (impressed force) and a manifestation property (acceleration)'. (2007, 107)
26. C. B. Martin (2008) also takes the directedness of a power toward its manifestation to be intrinsic to the power, but his position differs from mine in that he does not make the manifestation as well intrinsic to the power; see for example his Two-Triangles model:

You should not think of disposition partners jointly *causing* the manifestation. Instead, the coming together of the disposition partner *is* the mutual manifestation: the partnering and the manifestation are identical. This partnering-manifestation identity is seen most clearly with cases such as the following. You have two triangle-shaped slips of paper that, when placed together appropriately, form a square. It is not that the partnering of the triangles *causes* the manifestation of the square, but rather that the partnering *is* the manifestation. (2008, 51, emphasis in the original)

This is an important difference between Aristotle's view and Martin's, in that for him, although the directedness is intrinsic to what has it (the powers), what it is directed toward (the manifestation) is not intrinsic to what has it (the power itself). With reference to the example in the quote above, the square is not intrinsic to either of the triangles that constitute it. By contrast, on my view the power that is directed towards heating is activated when it is in fact heating something. Heating is the exercise of the powerfulness of the power to heat, which is a state attained by the power to heat.

27. The view has the following corollary: because powers depend on further powers to actualize what they are, they are not quiddities. We cannot swap their powerfulness and expect their natures to remain the same. Hence, epistemologically, the natures of powers are on our side of the veil of ignorance. See for reference Bird 2007, chapter 4.

28. Aristotle defines place as 'the innermost motionless boundary of what contains' (*Physics* 212a20–21).

29. I take it that this is what Mumford and Anjum hold too, when they write:

Dispositionality is a primitive, unanalyzable modality that is intermediate between pure possibility and necessity…because of its special modal nature, no analysis that fails to invoke it can succeed. It will be subject to counterexamples because it will attempt to reduce dispositionality to something else, such as necessity, which thereby misses the subtlety and flexibility of dispositionality. In particular, it would miss the key element that dispositions can be subject to prevention and interference. This modal feature is essential to dispositionality: it is what makes it distinct from everything else (2011, 193).

30. Aristotle did not talk of laws of nature. Yet, it is clear from the normativity expressed in the passage quoted above, that the definition of a power determines the conditions whose satisfaction is the instantiation of laws of nature. This point too is further developed in my 'Aristotelian Powers At Work; Reciprocity Without Symmetry in Causation' in Jonathan Jacobs (ed.) *Putting Powers at Work*, forthcoming with OUP.

31. See *Cat.* 6b28–30.

32. Additionally, in my view, the ontological dependence between active and passive powers applies to their potential state, as much as to their activated state. On the other hand, the manifestation partners need not be actual, so long as they are possible.

33. Aristotle himself does not explain what motivates his approach.
34. A species is ontologically dependent on its genus, and yet there is no entity as it were stretching between them; the same holds for relata even if their ontological interdependence is different in kind than the genus-species one.
35. See *Metaphysics* 1045b8–16; b21–22.
36. For a helpful discussion of existential dependence and its particular or generic formulations see Lowe http://plato.stanford.edu/entries/dependence-ontological/ accessed on 20/02/2014.
37. See Makin (2006, 84).
38. Note that this does not undermine Aristotle's realism with respect to perceptible qualities. For color in its first actuality for example the correlative power is light. There can be colors without perceivers. And the same holds for all perceptible qualities. See also chapter 3.
39. For a discussion of nonefficient causation in Aristotle see Marmodoro 'Potentiality in Aristotle's Metaphysics', in K Engelhard and M Quante (eds.) *The Handbook of Potentiality*, Springer, forthcoming.
40. See e.g Heil (forthcoming) and Mumford and Anjum (2011).
41. See *Physics* 202a9–11.
42. In contemporary physics, virtual particles are posited as *force-carriers* to explain how elementary particles act on one another. (Force-carriers are what we might call *pure quantities of power*.) Thus, elementary particles exert forces on each other by exchanging such virtual particles (e.g., the gauge bosons). One might think that, by introducing virtual particles to *carry* forces from particle to particle (e.g., to carry the electromagnetic force or the weak force) contemporary physics has solved the problem of causal *efficacy* by replacing causal efficacy with *addition* or *subtraction* of force in the *constitution* of the particles (e.g., more, or less, weak force), thereby avoiding qualitative interaction between particles—but this is not the case. Virtual particles of different types interact with one another *qualitatively* too. For instance, vector bosons can be produced by quark-antiquark annihilation. In such cases, I contend, the qualitative change is not further explained in elementary physics beyond that such change occurs in these circumstances. Similarly, on the Aristotelian account I want to motivate, the activation of partner powers is not further reducible to any activity.
43. See Aristotle, *Generation of Animals* II.2–3.
44. I hold this to be at the limit of our understanding of the nature of causation, and not just how Aristotle saw it, although I will not argue for this claim here.
45. "Effecting" is a term introduced in the contemporary debate of causation by Heil (forthcoming in Jacobs (ed.) *Putting Powers to Work*, OUP); but Plato (in the *Theaetetus*) and Aristotle (in the *De Anima* and in the *Physics*) used it first.

46. The change may be a *process*, such as becoming hotter; or an *activity*, such as seeing; see pp.

47. While there is general agreement that causation has a direction, people do disagree on what underpins metaphysically causal direction (see, e.g., Schaffer (2007) for an excellent account of the spectrum of positions): http://plato. stanford.edu/entries/causation-metaphysics/, accessed February 20, 2014. Those who, like Heil, deny agency in causation and claim that caution is symmetric are left without a way of accounting for causal direction.

48. Schaffer reckons six main arguments in the literature regarding the relation between the causal and temporal directions, and four conclude that they do not coincide. See http://plato.stanford.edu/entries/causation-metaphysics/, accessed February 20, 2014.

49. The first period of disfavor was under the influence of Aristotle's theory.

50. I argue for why it is metaphysically valuable to hold on to the intuition that causation is asymmetrical in 'Aristotelian Powers at Work: Reciprocity Without Symmetry in Causation' in Jonathan Jacobs (ed.) *Putting Powers to Work* forthcoming with OUP.

51. ἥ τε κίνησις ἐνέργεια μὲν εἶναί τις δοκεῖ, ἀτελὴς δέ· αἴτιον δ' ὅτι ἀτελὲς τὸ δυνατόν, οὗ ἐστιν ἐνέργεια.

52. Aristotle's definition of κίνησις (see, e.g. *Physics* 201a9–10; 201a27–9; 201b4–5; 202a13–4) is fairly broad, and it allows for a great variety of cases to come under the mover-movable relation, including such cases as aging or ripening, which we would consider untypical cases of causation. But it includes uncontroversial instances of causation, such as building, heating, doctoring, etc.

53. 'We have distinguished in respect of each class between what is in fulfilment and what is in potentiality' (*Physics* 201a9–10).

54. For example it will become more and less hot at the same time.

55. The argument analysis is reprinted from Marmodoro 'The Union of Cause and Effect in Aristotle; Physics III 3' *Oxford Studies in Ancient Philosophy*, Oxford: Oxford University Press (2007, 230–31).

56. Later translations (the Arab-Latin one), and commentaries (e.g. Themistius) take (2.2) to be part of the original Aristotelian text; Simplicius has it as a variant at 202a26. Ross (1979, 540), after Philoponus (1987, 370, line 20), comments that 'the fuller reading is the result of a later endeavor to make a formally complete disjunction without regard to the actual course of discussion … Aristotle evidently omits as patently impossible the view that both activity and passivity are embodied in the agent'.

57. This tenet is presupposed by the rhetorical question Aristotle asks: 'How will there be two alterations of quality in *one* subject towards *one* form?' (202a35–6). See **P (5.2)** in the Dilemma.

58. See *Physics* III 3, 202b1–5. Here Aristotle distinguishes teaching from learning, not because the content of the lesson is different, but because the one activity is teaching, and the other is learning, the same lesson. Contrast, for

example Themistius (1900, 78, 9–23), who in his interpretation confuses the content of teaching and learning and the common underlying substratum for both. Themistius talks about the very same theorem being taught and learned as an example of the common substratum of teaching and learning, and assimilates it to the stretch of path for the roads from Athens to Thebes and from Thebes to Athens. But this mistakes what is common in the forms of moving and being moved with what underlies the activities of moving and being moved.

59. 'It is contrary to reason to suppose that there should be one identical actualization of two things which are different in kind. Yet there will be, if teaching and learning are the same, and agency and patiency' (202b1–3). See **P 15** in the Dilemma.

60. Being 'in a subject' in the context of *Physics* III 3 should not to be understood along the lines of inherence in the *Categories* as, for instance, red inheres in an apple. The reason is that the *Categories'* inherence in the substance entails belonging to that substance as subject; whereas, as we shall see, here, for example, heating something belongs to the fire but occurs in the pot.

61. Contrast Hussey *ad locum* who holds that 'there is nothing to suggest that anything other than a local sense of "in" is intended' (Hussey, 1983, 65).

62. See *Physics* IV 3, 210a20–1.

63. Before we come to this, a clarification is needed regarding whether the mover itself is in motion. Aristotle distinguishes the motion of the mover, due to necessary contact with the movable, from the motion in the movable due to the mover's causal efficacy. The first is in the mover and the second in the movable. In the sub-argument of the Dilemma examined above (pp.), the falsehood that closes one of the branches is that 'every mover will be moved' (202a30). See (**P 10.1**) in the Dilemma, This follows from the assumption that the mover's actuality, as a mover, is in the mover itself. Then, due to their self-imposed causal efficacy, all movers would move, which is treated as a falsehood, and so it is denied that the mover's actuality is in the mover. But although 'every mover will be moved' is treated as a falsehood in the Dilemma, Aristotle has earlier stated that 'every mover is moved' (202a3). The difference between the statements is that the second ranges over movable movers only, while the first ranges over all movers, including God, who is immovable, which falsifies the statement. During the causal interaction the mover and the moved become actually such without this involving an additional change in either of them than the ones mentioned above. Of course this argument does not block the possibility of self-directed motion, as in the case of a doctor healing herself, where the mover and moved are the same.

64. Gill offers a very informed discussion of the etymology of ἐντελέχεια, its possible translations, and the debated issue of its synonymy with ἐνέργεια. Gill devotes particular attention to the textual observation that: 'Aristotle's argument...proves that the ἐντελέχεια of the agent and the patient is one, but in

the argument Aristotle does not explicitly claim that motion is the ἐντελέχεια of both'. Gill finds it an 'attractive suggestion' to explain the textual observation thus: 'the claim would be that the ἐντελέχεια of the teacher and the learner is the same but what it is to be that ἐντελέχεια for the teacher is an activity, namely a teaching of the teacher in the learner, and a change in the learner, namely a learning of the learner by the teacher'. But she dismisses this as Aristotle's view in light of 202b19ff, because she finds no indication of an ontological asymmetry between agency as activity and patiency as change (Gill, 1980, 134–35).

65. The first example is ambiguous. On the one hand the interval from one to two can be taken to be the same as the interval from two to one, being either an arithmetical unit of value one, or a geometrical magnitude of value one. On the other hand, the two intervals can be taken to be different, such as vectors with opposite directions, or the positive and negative values of the number one. I take the example in the latter way because, as we shall see, the metaphysics of the two intervals require them to have different essential natures, as opposite vectors do, or as the positive and negative unit values do; whereas taken in the former way the two intervals are one and the same, described in two different ways—from one to two, and from two to one. The ancient and medieval commentators interpret this example in two ways, both of which belong to the one-entity-two-descriptions family of interpretations. They vacillate (often indiscriminately) between two readings within the one-entity-two-descriptions family: either one interval described in two different ways in terms of its end points, or one relation described from the point of view of either relatum. Reading the example as one interval described differently in terms of its end points is found for example in: Simplicius (446, 31–2); Philoponus (1897, 370, line 7; 375, line 26; 376, line 5); Aquinas (*Physics*, 147). Reading the example as one relation that has two *relata*, and accordingly two descriptions (e.g., the relation of procreation, with father and son as the two *relata*, and 'being the father of' and 'being the son of' as the two descriptions), is found for example in: Simplicius (439, 34bis-37; 448, 30ff; on this reading of Simplicius see also C. Luna, 'La relation chez Simplicius', in *Simplicius, sa vie, son oeuvre, sa survie*, Actes du colloque international de Paris (28 Sept.-1 Oct. 1985), De Gruyter, Berlin-New York, 1987. Averroes (*Aristotelis De Physico Auditu Libri Octo* (Venezia 1562–74), 92v. I–L; 94r. E; 95r. A); Aquinas (*Physics*, 145; to be contrasted with 147). I believe that the reason for the commentators' vacillation between the two readings is that at 202b17–9 Aristotle describes the example, speaking loosely, both as an interval (διάστασις) between two points, and as the relation of distance (τὸ διίστασθαι) of either point from the other, as if they were equivalent ways of formulating the example. The modern commentators do not fall prey to this possible confusion, but yet most of them follow

the one-entity-two-descriptions interpretation. See, for example Ross (1979, 361; 362; 540); Gill (1980, 140; 143); Waterlow (1982, 182; 191), Hussey (1983, 69–70). Waterlow and Hussey share the view that Aristotle has some insight into Frege's distinction between sense and reference. I shall come below to the arguments they offer in support of their interpretation.

66. I have already discussed above the position of the ancient and medieval commentators in note 67. I will limit myself here to presenting two recent and very interesting accounts that have been offered for the same entity view; one is by Waterlow (1982, 180–82), and the other by Hussey (1983, 66).

Waterlow (and also Kosman, 1975, 499–519 at 514) in analyzing the analogous case of hearing and sounding identifies the multiply described entity as a single event, a single change that is both teaching and learning:

His [Aristotle's] argument proceeds on the following assumption: the only reason anyone could have for supposing that being a changer (an actual changer) entails change in that changer, rests on a false view of the difference regarding these (in some given instance, such as teaching and learning) as different concrete events, that one could be misled into thinking that the changer as such undergoes a change. But once it is seen that these are different ways of describing the same event, the problem disappears, leaving only one change, which is to be located in the patient . . . The point of crucial importance that Aristotle emphasizes again and again . . . is that X's teaching is not a different concrete event from Y's learning. These are one and the same actuality under two descriptions (1982, 180–2).Waterlow associates this single event that is the entity to which the two descriptions apply with 'a neutral verb-stem determinable by active and passive voices . . . we may say (a) that teaching is a predicate of Y as well as of X; and (b) that "teaching" applies to Y in a determinate form (the passive) which is perfectly consistent with the statement "Y does not teach"' (1982, 182). I am arguing here that the ontology of causation for Aristotle is more complex than that of one event under two descriptions.Hussey, who also holds the one-entity-two-descriptions view, considers that Aristotle's 'positive argument to show that "the changes [of the agent and patient] are the same" may be that an operation must be something that happens over a period of time, and that if we look at the minimal case of change, in which the agent is completely unaffected, there is "nothing happening" except the change of the patient. Hence, the operation of the agent must be the change' (1983, 66). According to the analysis I am developing here, the change is not one in so far as two essential natures are involved in its occurrence: agency and patiency. The change involves the transference of a form, and Aristotle finds this to be an irreducibly complex activity of give and take; there are no two distinct activities, nor only one: an indivisible physical process grounds two essential natures of action and passion. So even in the minimal case described in the quote above, the agent transmits and the patient suffers the form. The changes in the agent depend on what is required in each instance for the form to be possessed by the agent in a transmissible mode, which is the causally active factor.

67. No doubt is recorded in the modern editions on the expression τί ἦν εἶναι at 202b12; only the two immediately preceding articles τὸν <τὸ> have had a less firm transmission in the manuscripts, as Ross documents in the apparatus *ad locum*: we find only τὸν in IJ; only τὸ in E, and neither in F. It was easy for one or the other article to drop by haplography during the transmission process. Bonitz prints both articles τὸν τὸ as part of the text. Ross chooses to print <τὸ> as a *lacuna* to be completed by sense.

68. ἐντελέχεια γάρ ἐστι τούτου [καὶ] ὑπὸ τοῦ κινητικοῦ. καὶ ἡ τοῦ κινητικοῦ δὲ ἐνέργεια οὐκ ἄλλη ἐστίν (202a14–5); μία ἡ ἀμφοῖν ἐνέργεια (202a18); οὔτε μίαν [scilicet ἐνέργειαν] δυοῖν κωλύει οὐθὲν τὴν αὐτὴν εἶναι (202b8–9).

69. Of course, if being picks out only the universal form the entailment would not follow. Aristotle says in *Metaphysics* V 6:

> Some things are one in number, others in species, others in genus, ...; in number those whose matter is one, in species those whose definition is one.... The latter kinds of unity are always found when the former are (e.g., *things that are one in number are also one in species, while things that are one in species are not all one in number*). (1016b31–6, my emphasis)

So for our present passage, 202b14–6, we need to assume embodiment—if this is the particularizing principle, securing the numerical identity of the individuals. If one attributes to Aristotle a different particularizing principle than matter, then that principle will be in play in the present passage.

70. Because the agent's and the patient's capacities are *essentially different*, the one being the capacity of transmitting the form and the other being the capacity to receive the transmissible form, the realization of the two different capacities is also essentially different. Charles shows on the basis of investigation of various passages of the *Physics* that:

> A process is one in number only if it is one in essence...but the essence of each thing is defined when one says what it is to be that thing (1017b21–3). If so, processes are one in number only if the definitions of what it is to be that thing are identical... Aristotelian processes are essentially realizations of given capacities of given subjects: their essential properties include the subject of change and the end point of the type of change (i.e. its goal). They are distinct if they do not share all essential properties...It follows that in III 3 teaching and learning must be numerically distinct processes since they differ in essence. (Charles, 1984, 10; 11; 18).

71. Since there is disagreement between the interpreters on the translation of this passage, I report here the original text:

ὅλως δ' εἰπεῖν οὐδ' ἡ δίδαξις τῇ μαθήσει οὐδ' ἡ ποίησις τῇ παθήσει τὸ αὐτὸ κυρίως, ἀλλ' ᾧ ὑπάρχει ταῦτα, ἡ κίνησις·

As Hussey notes, there are two ways of understanding the passage:

(i) 'the change in which these things are present (i.e., of which it is true that it is an acting-upon and a being-acted-upon) is the same as being acted upon'

(ii) 'the change in which these things are present (i.e., of which it is true that it is both an acting-upon and a being-acted-upon) is the change' (1983, 72)

The latter (ii) is the way in which the majority of the interpreters, including myself, read the passage (e.g. Philoponus (1987, 383, lines 21–2), Ross (1979, 362), and Gill (1980, 137). Hussey, though, opts for (i) (1983, 6), and so does Charles (1984, 14). For, Hussey remarks, in (i) the 'extra point is made that "change is indeed the same in definition as the being-acted-upon (for change has been defined as the actuality of the changing thing)"'. Hussey does not develop this point further, but Charles does, as he grounds on these lines his interpretation of the chapter, differing from that of the majority. I shall devote the discussion here to the arguments in support of, and against, translation (i), and discuss Charles' interpretation. Both Hussey and Charles acknowledge that on linguistic grounds both readings (i) and (ii) of the passage are equally possible; the reasons why they prefer reading (i) to (ii) are mostly interpretative. Charles says:

I reject this translation (sc. the equivalent to Hussey's (ii)) because (a) it gives up the essential connection on which Aristotle elsewhere insists between the process and the suffering (202a14–6, b25–7); (b) it postulates a process which is non-directional (and non-relational) and thus conflicts with Aristotle's general view of the essences of processes as the realization of goal-directed capacities (201a16–8); (c) the grammar of 202b19–22 seems to require that the clause 'the process is the same in the primary sense' takes over both the notion in the primary sense from b20, and also the grammatical object with which it is the same in this sense: namely, the learning, suffering. (1984, 14–5)

In answer to (a) I submit that it is not true that by taking κίνησις as the ground of the instantiation for action and passion, 'the essential connection...between the process and the suffering' is given up; rather, more than one essential connection is allowed, namely the relation to agency and also to patiency. In answer to (b), in my interpretation, the nature of motion is to be found, not in the underlying physical activity, but in the two beings that this activity grounds, agency and patiency. Neither of its natures is truer of the motion than the other, any more than either direction of the route between Athens and Thebes is truer of the underlying road than the other. Aristotle's definition of change does not favor the one over the other. Change is no more the unfolding actuality of the potentiality of the patient as a patient, than it is the unfolding actuality of the potentiality of the agent as an agent. In answer to (c) I wish to defend my reading of the text on the ground that it is actually the most natural: it takes 'being one in the primary sense' to be retaining the same meaning throughout, and working as a predicate that has as its logical subjects on the one hand teaching and learning (as a pair) and action and passion (as a pair), and on the other hand 'that to which these things belong, namely the underlying process'.

72. In the context of this argument Aristotle takes 'learner' to range only over those who are taught.

73. Hussey offers a very different account of the sameness of the motion of the agent and the patient. He says:

What then *is* Aristotle's positive argument to show that the changes [of the agent and the patient] are the same? It might be just that an operation must be something that *happens* over a period of time, and that if we look at a minimal case of change, in which the agent is completely unaffected, there *is* "nothing happening" except the change-(Intransitive) of the patient. Hence, the operation of the agent must be the change-(Intransitive). (1983, 66)

I do not agree that, because the agent's transitive change of the patient happens over time, within a small period of time the agent does not suffer any change. To put it in Aristotelian terms, some but not all of the form that is being transmitted will be transmitted within a short interval.

74. Thus, in contrast to other contemporary power-based accounts of causation such as Heil's, Martin's, and Mumford and Anjum's, for Aristotle causation involve *two* manifestations, namely the manifestation of the active power of the agent and the manifestation of the passive power of the patient. See following note.

75. There is an interesting parallel between the metaphysics of the common activity of two powers and the metaphysics of a relation between two relata (in the contemporary non-Aristotelian) conception of a relation. A single instance of a relation belongs to two relata, each of which is differently

characterized by it; thus, a single instance of a relation renders Carol a mother and Linda a daughter. Similarly in Aristotle, a single activity enables the ear to hear and the sound to sound. But there is also a difference in their metaphysics: what is common between two subjects in contemporary theory is the entity (e.g., a relation) that characterizes each relatum differently; while what is common between two powers (or their bearers) in Aristotle is an *activity-substratum* that constitutes different activities in each power (e.g., hearing, sounding).

Chapter 2

Aristotle's Causal Powers Theory of Perception

INTRODUCTION

There is clear textual evidence that Aristotle endorses a causal theory of perception; the interpretation of the theory however has generated much debate. This chapter will contribute to the ongoing debate a fresh interpretation that brings Aristotle's power ontology to bear on his account of perception. For Aristotle perception takes place when the perceiver and the object of perception causally interact, and their respective powers come to be actualized. It thus requires an agent capable of being affected and an object capable of affecting him/her.[1] These capabilities are why a bee perceives the fragrance of a rose and a stone does not: the stone is incapable of being affected. The power that activates perceiving, the perceptible quality, comes from without the sense organs. The perceiver experiences the perceptible, and the perceptible makes itself manifest to the perceiver, as a result—and for the duration—of their mutual interaction. In perception the perceiver's sense organ is made to be like the perceptible object, by taking on somehow its perceptible qualities.[2] What does Aristotle mean by these claims? This chapter sets out Aristotle's fundamental assumptions with respect to the number, nature and operation of the five senses humans are endowed with.

2.1 THE FACULTY OF PERCEPTION

Perceiving is an activity of the soul. Aristotle investigates the nature of the soul (ψυχή) and its activities primarily in the *De Anima* and in a collection of short treatises known as *Parva Naturalia*. His approach is guided by two powerful insights (which might however feel foreign to us). First Aristotle conceives of the soul as the principle of functional organization of all the activities of a living natural body. Thus, the domain of his inquiry into the nature of the soul is much broader than the remit of modern psychology, and spans all living beings: not merely humans, but also plants and animals. Secondly, what guides Aristotle's psychological inquiry is his general interest in the explanation of the phenomena we experience, or those we associate with the soul. His psychological theory addresses questions such as: How is the soul related to the body? Is the soul immortal? Can the mental be explanatorily reduced to the physical? What accounts for the actions of living beings? Aristotle sees these and related questions as part of his more general investigation into the nature of things, searching for what makes something what it is and for accounts of change. It is therefore not surprising that in his account of the soul Aristotle applies concepts drawn from his broader metaphysical theory: both his power ontology and his hylomorphism. On Aristotle's hylomorphic account of reality all things, manmade or nature-made, can be analyzed into two constituents: the form, which is the principle of functional organization, and the matter in which such a principle is implemented.[3] Substantial forms (e.g., being a man) account for what things are, and incidental forms (e.g., being pale) account for a substance's qualitative change. Thus, Aristotle understands the soul as the substantial form of an organic body, and the body as the matter of the soul. The soul-body relation is only a special case of the general form-matter relationship. For example, the round shape of a ball is different from the matter the ball is made of, but cannot exist as such without being implemented in matter. By analogy, the soul is different from the body, but cannot exist without the body. The difference between an organism and the ball is that the soul *qua* organizational principle determines the nature of the matter of the body all the way down, by transforming the menstrual fluids provided by the mother into flesh and bones in the generation of a new organism. By contrast, neither the shape of a ball nor its function determines its matter all the way down, for a ball can be made of different materials. If the soul is the principle of organization of the body's activities, the study of the soul includes the study of all such activities and of the relevant psychic faculties. Aristotle distinguishes the following faculties: nutrition, perception, intellect, and desire. The faculty of nutrition is common to all natural living beings; animals have perception in addition[4]; and humans alone have intellect. I turn now to how the (human) faculty of perception operates via the five senses.

2.2 THE FIVE SENSES

For Aristotle the world is given to our experience as diversified by five fundamental types of perceptible qualities: colors, odors, sounds, tastes, and the tangibles. These qualities are *real causal powers*—powers to interact with the perceptual powers of the perceiver.[5] It is because the world is diversified by five fundamental types of qualitative features that animals, and humans in particular, are endowed with five senses to perceive these. The power to perceive, defined more generally, is the ability of the senses to be causally acted upon by perceptible objects in the world.[6] This ability to be acted upon by a perceptible quality is found only in matter. This is why animals need sense organs. The sense organs are the seat of the faculties of perception, one organ for each faculty; for example 'the eye is the matter of sight' (*DA* 412b20). In *De Anima* II 1 Aristotle explicitly says that the sense organs stand to the faculties of perception as matter to form, or as potentiality to actuality.[7]

From this thesis, that it is because there are five types of qualities that we have five faculties of perception, follows a central assumption in Aristotle's account of the senses: each type of perceptible quality in the world (i.e., each type of *special sensible*) individuates a different sense: a *special sense* (sight for color, hearing for sound, etc.), with its own sense organ. Aristotle writes,

> In dealing with each of the senses we shall have first to speak of the sensibles which are perceptible by each...I call by the name of special sensible of this or that sense that which cannot be perceived by any other sense than that one...in this sense color is the special object of sight, sound of hearing, flavour of taste (*DA* 418a6–13)
>
> Λεκτέον δὲ καθ' ἑκάστην αἴσθησιν περὶ τῶν αἰσθητῶν πρῶτον...λέγω δ' ἴδιον μὲν ὃ μὴ ἐνδέχεται ἑτέρᾳ αἰσθήσει αἰσθάνεσθαι...οἷον ὄψις χρώματος καὶ ἀκοὴ ψόφου καὶ γεῦσις χυμοῦ.

For example, Aristotle uses this individuation criterion explicitly in the following argument:

> Since bloodless animals do not breathe, they must, it might be argued, have some novel sense [in place of smelling which depends on breathing] not reckoned among the usual ones. Our reply must be that this is impossible, since it is scent that is perceived; a sense that apprehends what is odorous and what has a good or bad odor cannot be anything but smell. (*DA* 421b19–23, translation slightly modified)

ὥστε τὰ ἄναιμα, ἐπειδὴ οὐκ ἀναπνέουσιν, ἑτέραν ἄν τιν᾿
αἴσθησιν ἔχοι παρὰ τὰς λεγομένας. ἀλλ᾿ ἀδύνατον, εἴπερ τῆς
ὀσμῆς αἰσθάνεται· ἡ γὰρ τοῦ ὀσφραντοῦ αἴσθησις καὶ δυσώδους
καὶ εὐώδους ὄσφρησίς ἐστιν.

So the perceptible quality, in this case odor, individuates the sense
of smell; if it is odor that is perceived, it is the faculty of smell
through which the perceiving is done.[8]

What is it that we perceive? When talking about the object
of perception Aristotle appears to vacillate between taking the
object of perception to be the perceptible *quality*, and taking it
to be the *entity* in world possessing that perceptible quality.[9] My
take on this issue is that the shift does not matter to Aristotle, for
he thinks that the object of a sense is something external which
stimulates the sense: it is any *instance* of the perceptible quality
corresponding to that sense. Instances of forms or qualities can
be individuated at will, by abstraction. An instance of a form is
the property itself spatiotemporally located; or the subject that
immediately possesses that property (for example, in the case of
color, the surface of an object); or the object that possesses that
property. All of these items involve the instantiation of the relevant quality, which makes them perceptible by that sense, and
thus its objects. Because the objects that possess a perceptible
quality are perceptible *as possessors of that quality*, there is no
further nature of each such object that is revealed by its being
perceptible as such. Thus, the objects of a sense are instances of
a perceptible quality, *whatever* it is that is individuated as instan-
tiating the quality, namely either the property-instance itself or
the whole object that possesses that instance. Aristotle writes:

> The object of sight is the visible, and what is visible is (a) color
> and (b) a certain kind of object [i.e., the visible kind] which

can be described in words but which has no single name…Whatever is visible is color and color is what lies upon what is in its own nature visible [e.g., a surface]; 'in its own nature' here means not that visibility is involved in the definition of what thus underlies color, but that that substratum contains in itself the cause of visibility. (*DA* 418a26–30, translation slightly modified)

Οἳ μὲν οὖν ἐστιν ἡ ὄψις, τοῦτ' ἐστὶν ὁρατόν, ὁρατὸν δ' ἐστὶ χρῶμά τε καὶ ὃ λόγῳ μὲν ἔστιν εἰπεῖν, ἀνώνυμον δὲ τυγχάνει ὄν…τὸ γὰρ ὁρατόν ἐστι χρῶμα, τοῦτο δ' ἐστὶ τὸ ἐπὶ τοῦ καθ' αὑτὸ ὁρατοῦ· καθ' αὑτὸ δὲ οὐ τῷ λόγῳ, ἀλλ' ὅτι ἐν ἑαυτῷ ἔχει τὸ αἴτιον τοῦ εἶναι ὁρατόν.

From the analysis I have developed above, it follows that even when the object of the sense is taken to be the perceptible quality (rather than the object possessing it), it is the quality as embedded in a spatiotemporal location, rather than the quality in abstraction, that can stimulate the sense organ and hence is the object of that sense.

Perception takes place when the perceiver and the object of perception causally interact, and is an alteration of the perceiver's sense organ by the object of perception.[10] Here is how Aristotle defines it:

Perception consists in being moved and acted upon…for, it seems to be a sort of quality change (*DA* 416b33–35, my translation; see also 418a3–6).

ἡ δ' αἴσθησις ἐν τῷ κινεῖσθαί τε καὶ πάσχειν συμβαίνει… δοκεῖ γὰρ ἀλλοίωσίς τις εἶναι.

The issue of what is the nature of the 'alteration' the sense organ undergoes has divided ancient and modern scholars and requires careful discussion, which I postpone to section 2.6. First I want to focus on one of the cornerstones of Aristotle's account of perception, the claim that there is a one-to-one correspondence among the type of an instantiated perceptible quality, the type of the corresponding alteration of the sense organ, and the type of the content of the resulting perceptual experience (e.g., a correspondence between the types of: this desk's color, the modification of my sense organ of sight stimulated by this instance of color, and the content of my experience of the color). Aristotle puts it this way:

> It is impossible that what is one and the same [i.e., a sense] should be moved at one and the same time with contrary movements in so far as it is undivided, and in an undivided moment of time. For if what is sweet be the quality perceived, it moves the sense in this determinate way, while what is bitter moves it in a contrary way, and what is white in a different way. (*DA* 426b29–427a9)[11]
>
> ἀλλὰ μὴν ἀδύνατον ἅμα τὰς ἐναντίας κινήσεις κινεῖσθαι τὸ αὐτὸ ᾗ ἀδιαίρετον, καὶ ἐν ἀδιαιρέτῳ χρόνῳ. εἰ γὰρ γλυκύ, ὡδὶ κινεῖ τὴν αἴσθησιν ἢ τὴν νόησιν, τὸ δὲ πικρὸν ἐναντίως, καὶ τὸ λευκὸν ἑτέρως.

Additionally, in *Sense and Sensibilia* we read that:

> In one and the same faculty the perception actualized at any single moment is necessarily one, only one stimulation or exertion of a single faculty being possible at a single instant…. Hence, it is not possible to perceive two distinct objects simultaneously with one and the same sense (*SS* 447b17–19, translation slightly modified).
>
> ἀλλὰ κατὰ μίαν δύναμιν καὶ ἄτομον χρόνον μίαν ἀνάγκη εἶναι τὴν ἐνέργειαν· μιᾶς γὰρ ἡ εἰσάπαξ μία χρῆσις καὶ κίνησις, μία δὲ ἡ δύναμις.

This description of the principle, and of what motivates it, lends itself to a general physical interpretation.[12] One and the same physical thing cannot suffer different and even incompatible changes at the same time.[13] This is relevant to perception because for Aristotle we become aware of a perceptible quality (e.g., of blue) as the sense organ of sight becomes somehow affected by the external quality, resulting in its becoming *like* that quality.[14] But it is important to note that the general justification for the principle comes from Aristote's power ontology as applied to his theory of perception: *the activity of a single power at an instant is a single type of activity.* The correspondence principle follows from this. Each sense is a perceptual power, with a distinctive type of activity that defines it; this is why the power of sight cannot be activated by seeing and, for example, hearing.

Aristotle associates *infallibility* with the perception of the special sensibles by their special sense, saying for example that:

> Each sense has one kind of object which it discerns, and never errs in reporting that what is before it is color or sound (though it may err as to what it is that is colored or where that is, or what it is that is sounding or where that is). Such objects are what we propose to call the special object of this or that sense. (*DA* 418a14–17)
>
> ἀλλ' ἑκάστη γε κρίνει περὶ τούτων, καὶ οὐκ ἀπατᾶται ὅτι χρῶμα οὐδ' ὅτι ψόφος, ἀλλὰ τί τὸ κεχρωσμένον ἢ ποῦ, ἢ τί τὸ ψοφοῦν ἢ ποῦ. τὰ μὲν οὖν τοιαῦτα λέγεται ἴδια ἑκάστης.

Thus, for example, sight cannot be mistaken about whether it is perceiving color or not. The argument (which Aristotle does not supply) must be that this is so because it is only color that can stimulate the sense organ of sight, so sight cannot be mistaken about that.[15] Anything beyond the type of sensible it is might be subject to misperception. Yet it is not clear from the text whether Aristotle thinks the agent can misperceive *which* color she is perceiving. He does allow that the agent can be mistaken about the type of object she is perceiving (other than it being a *colored* object). He does not comment on whether the perceiver can misperceive the particular color, or sound, etc. If the argument for the infallibility of perception is the one I supplied above, then it does not apply to the identity of the perceptible quality (i.e., which particular color or which sound one is perceiving). The reason is that different colors can stimulate the sense organ of sight, and so the agent can infallibly perceive color, and yet be mistaken about the hue or shade of it.[16] But on the picture sketched so far, even if perception of the sensibles that are the special objects of the special senses is infallible, it will reveal to the perceiver relatively little about the world. It will scarcely tell one anything about the world's furniture. It will give one awareness only of colors, sounds, etc., and only in simple perceptual contents. Of course Aristotle is aware that a full theory of perception is required to account for much more information about the world than this.

2.3 THE POWER(S) TO CAUSE PERCEPTUAL EXPERIENCES

Perception for Aristotle is an instance of causation, which, as we saw in chapter 1, he explains as the activation of a passive and an active power, 'held together' as it were by mutual dependence, but not by a reified relation.[17] In the case of perception the two causal powers are the perceptible quality of an object and the corresponding power of the perceiver to experience that type of property. On Aristotle's view the perceptible quality of the object is the active power; the perceiver's perceptual power is the passive one. In perception the perceptible quality *activates* the sense organ of the perceiver, whose perception would otherwise be only potential. Aristotle explains:

> We use the word 'perceive' in two ways, for we say that what has the power to hear or see, 'sees' or 'hears', even though it is at the moment asleep, and also that what is actually seeing or hearing, 'sees' or 'hears'. Hence 'sense' too must have two meanings, sense potential, and sense actual. Similarly 'to be a sentient' means either to have a certain power or to manifest a certain activity. (*DA* 417a10–14)
>
> τὸ αἰσθάνεσθαι λέγομεν διχῶς (τό τε γὰρ δυνάμει ἀκοῦον καὶ ὁρῶν ἀκούειν καὶ ὁρᾶν λέγομεν, κἂν τύχῃ καθεῦδον, καὶ τὸ ἤδη ἐνεργοῦν), διχῶς ἂν λέγοιτο καὶ ἡ αἴσθησις, ἡ μὲν ὡς δυνάμει, ἡ δὲ ὡς ἐνεργείᾳ. ὁμοίως δὲ καὶ τὸ αἰσθητόν, τό τε δυνάμει ὂν καὶ τὸ ἐνεργείᾳ.
>
> '[S]ense' and 'the sensible object' are ambiguous terms (i.e. may denote either potentialities or actualities). (*DA* 426a23–24)
>
> διχῶς γὰρ λεγομένης τῆς αἰσθήσεως καὶ τοῦ αἰσθητοῦ, τῶν μὲν κατὰ δύναμιν τῶν δὲ κατ' ἐνέργειαν.

In activating the sense organ of the perceiver, the perceptible quality does not change the sense, but only 'energizes' it into action, by analogy with what happens (e.g., when one plays a note by plucking a guitar's string, without changing physically the string itself). In the *De Anima* Aristotle explains that in perception the sense organ gets engaged in the activity of perceiving the perceptible, thus:

> In the case of sense clearly the sensitive faculty already was potentially what the object makes it to be actually; the faculty is not affected or altered. This must therefore be a different kind of movement; for movement is an activity of what is imperfect,

activity in the unqualified sense (i.e. that of what has been per-fected) is different. (*DA* 431a4–8)

φαίνεται δὲ τὸ μὲν αἰσθητὸν ἐκ δυνάμει ὄντος τοῦ αἰσθητικοῦ ἐνεργείᾳ ποιοῦν· οὐ γὰρ πάσχει οὐδ' ἀλλοιοῦται. διὸ ἄλλο εἶδος τοῦτο κινήσεως· ἡ γὰρ κίνησις τοῦ ἀτελοῦς ἐνέργεια, ἡ δ' ἁπλῶς ἐνέργεια ἑτέρα, ἡ τοῦ τετελεσμένου.

In perception the perceptible qualities of the objects in the world get activated too, as they are causal powers of objects. Recall now that causal powers are *pros ti* or relatives; so perceptible qualities are also relatives. In the *Categories* (as we have seen in chapter 1) Aristotle explains that perception and the perceptible differ from other relatives in that they are not by nature simultaneous (as, for example, slave and master are), but the perceptible is *prior to* per-ception.[18] Aristotle in fact holds that ~~that~~ perceptible qualities are *necessarily prior* to perception, and justifies this by appealing to their causal role in relation to the perceivers' experience of them. For Aristotle objects have perceptible qualities (e.g. sounds, colors, etc.) whether they are perceived or not. These qualities are of this or that type, independently of the perceiving sense.[19] For example, in the *Metaphysics* Aristotle writes:

> For in point of fact perception is not of itself, but of something else besides the perception that is necessarily prior to the per-ception; for that which effects change is prior by nature to that which is changed. (*Met.* 1010b35–36)[20]
>
> οὐ γὰρ δὴ ἥ γ' αἴσθησις αὐτὴ ἑαυτῆς ἐστίν, ἀλλ' ἔστι τι καὶ ἕτερον παρὰ τὴν αἴσθησιν, ὃ ἀνάγκη πρότερον εἶναι τῆς αἰσθήσεως·

There is plenty of textual evidence for Aristotle's commitment to the real existence in the world of the perceptible qualities of objects. I highlight here some additional key passages where the commitment is evident. In *De Anima* II 8, 420a17, Aristotle claims that sound 'is external and not private' (ἀλλότριος καὶ οὐκ ἴδιος); in *DA* II 5, 417b20–1 he reiterates and generalizes the point by claiming that the visible and the audible, which produce the activity of perception, are external, like the rest of the objects of perception,[21] and he repeats the point that the objects are external at 417b28–9. Another statement of Aristotle's commitment to the real existence of perceptible qualities, whether perceived or not, is to be found in the *De Sensu*. He there raises the following question:

> One might ask: if every body is infinitely divisible, are its sensible qualities—color, savor, odor, sound, weight, cold or heat, heaviness or lightness, hardness or softness—also infinitely divisible? Or, is this impossible? (*DS* 445b3–7 translation)[22]
>
> Ἀπορήσειε δ' ἄν τις, εἰ πᾶν σῶμα εἰς ἄπειρον διαιρεῖται, ἆρα καὶ τὰ παθήματα τὰ αἰσθητά, οἷον χρῶμα καὶ χυμὸς καὶ ὀσμὴ καὶ ψόφος, καὶ βαρὺ καὶ κοῦφον, καὶ θερμὸν καὶ ψυχρόν, καὶ σκληρὸν καὶ μαλακόν, ἢ ἀδύνατον.

Aristotle's solution is that perceptible qualities, when embodied in infinitesimally small quantities of matter, are real and potentially perceptible, but not actually so:

> It is owing to this difference [between potential and actual] that we do not [actually] see its ten-thousandth part in a grain of millet, although sight has embraced the whole grain within its scope; and it is owing to this, too, that the sound contained in a quarter-tone escapes notice, and yet one hears the whole strain, inasmuch as it is a continuum; but the interval between the extreme sounds [that bound the quarter-tone] escapes the

ear [being only potentially audible, not actually]. So, in the case of other objects of sense, extremely small constituents are unnoticed; because they are only potentially not actually [perceptible e.g.] visible, unless when they have been parted from the wholes. ... But yet this [small object] is to be considered as perceptible: for it is both potentially so already [i.e., even when alone], and destined to be actually so when it has become part of an aggregate. (445b31–446a14, translation modified)

καὶ διὰ τοῦτο τὸ μυριοστημόριον λανθάνει τῆς κέγχρου ὁρωμένης, καίτοι ἡ ὄψις ἐπελήλυθεν, καὶ ὁ ἐν τῇ διέσει φθόγγος λανθάνει, καίτοι συνεχοῦς ὄντος ἀκούει τοῦ μέλους παντός· τὸ δὲ διάστημα τὸ τοῦ μεταξὺ πρὸς τοὺς ἐσχάτους λανθάνει. ὁμοίως δὲ καὶ ἐν τοῖς ἄλλοις αἰσθητοῖς τὰ μικρὰ πάμπαν· δυνάμει γὰρ ὁρατά, ἐνεργείᾳ δ' οὔ, ὅταν μὴ χωρὶς ᾖ· καὶ γὰρ ἐνυπάρχει δυνάμει ἡ ποδιαία τῇ δίποδι, ἐνεργείᾳ δ' ἤδη ἀφαιρεθεῖσα. χωριζόμεναι δ' αἱ τηλικαῦται ὑπεροχαὶ εὐλόγως μὲν ἂν καὶ διαλύοιντο εἰς τὰ περιέχοντα, ὥσπερ καὶ ἀκαριαῖος χυμὸς εἰς τὴν θάλατταν ἐγχυθείς. οὐ μὴν ἀλλ' ἐπειδὴ οὐδ' ἡ τῆς αἰσθήσεως ὑπεροχὴ καθ' αὑτὴν αἰσθητὴ οὐδὲ χωριστή (δυνάμει γὰρ ἐνυπάρχει ἐν τῇ ἀκριβεστέρᾳ ἡ ὑπεροχή), οὐδὲ τὸ τηλικοῦτον αἰσθητὸν χωριστὸν ἔσται ἐνεργείᾳ αἰσθάνεσθαι. ἀλλ' ὅμως ἔσται αἰσθητόν· δυνάμει τε γάρ ἐστιν ἤδη, καὶ ἐνεργείᾳ ἔσται προσγενόμενον. ὅτι μὲν οὖν ἔνια μεγέθη καὶ πάθη λανθάνει, καὶ διὰ τίν' αἰτίαν, καὶ πῶς αἰσθητὰ καὶ πῶς οὔ, εἴρηται. ὅταν δὲ δὴ ἐνυπάρχῃ τούτῳ τοσαῦτα ὥστε καὶ ἐνεργείᾳ αἰσθητὰ εἶναι, καὶ μὴ μόνον ὅτι ἐν τῷ ὅλῳ ἀλλὰ καὶ χωρίς, πεπερασμένα ἀνάγκη εἶναι τὸν ἀριθμόν, καὶ χρώματα καὶ χυμοὺς καὶ φθόγγους.

Aristotle's realism with respect to perceptible qualities is however not without qualification. In what follows I will argue that for Aristotle things are not sweet or loud or bright independently of perception. But nor are they made such by perception. Aristotle's realism is more complex and subtle. When perceptible qualities are perceived, they reach their *second and fullest actuality*, which is only a *change in metaphysical status* of the qualities themselves, rather than an identity-change of the properties. (This thesis will be expounded and argued for in chapter 3).

2.4 ARISTOTLE'S CAUSAL POWERS THEORY OF PERCEPTION

Aristotle describes the causal interaction between the object of perception and the perceiver in a much-debated passage of *De Anima*, in these terms:

The actuality of the perceptible and of the perceptual experience is one and the same, although their being is not the same. I mean, for example, the sound in actuality and hearing in actuality; for it is possible that that which has the capacity to hear does not hear, and that which can produce sounds is not always doing so. But when that which can hear is hearing and that which can produce sound is producing it, then hearing in actuality and sounding in actuality come to be at the same time, and one might call the one hearing and the other sounding (*DA* 425b26–426a1, my translation and emphasis)

ἡ δὲ τοῦ αἰσθητοῦ ἐνέργεια καὶ τῆς αἰσθήσεως ἡ αὐτὴ μέν ἐστι καὶ μία, τὸ δ' εἶναι οὐ τὸ αὐτὸ αὐταῖς· λέγω δ' οἷον ὁ ψόφος ὁ κατ'ἐνέργειαν καὶ ἡ ἀκοὴ ἡ κατ' ἐνέργειαν· ἔστι γὰρ ἀκοὴν ἔχοντα μὴ ἀκούειν, καὶ τὸ ἔχον ψόφον οὐκ ἀεὶ ψοφεῖ, ὅταν δ' ἐνεργῇ τὸ δυνάμενον ἀκούειν καὶ ψοφῇ τὸ δυνάμενον ψοφεῖν, τότε ἡ κατ' ἐνέργειαν ἀκοὴ ἅμα γίνεται καὶ ὁ κατ' ἐνέργειαν ψόφος, ὧν εἴπειεν ἄν τις τὸ μὲν εἶναι ἄκουσιν τὸ δὲ ψόφησιν.

The above text is of crucial importance because it is there that Aristotle states his views on the ontological status of perceptible qualities and how perception comes about, but it also contains a formidable interpretative challenge. How are we to understand the claim that *two essentially different entities* (the perceptible quality and the corresponding experience) have *one and the same actuality*? *Prima facie*, this statement flies in the face of all we know about Aristotle's essentialism. According to Aristotle's well-known views, different types of activity each have their own nature, or essence, which determines their respective actualities. In what sense, then, could two different activities share the same actuality? To explain this and other puzzling claims in the passage above, we need to draw on his account of causation in the *Physics* (see chapter 1). It is Aristotle himself who directs us there.[23] When talking about perception and perceptible properties in *De Anima* III 2, he does not expound on his subtle realism[24] and his metaphysical account of it, but explicitly refers back to his arguments in *Physics* III 3. In the *De Anima* he writes:

> *If it is true that the movement (i.e. the acting, and the being acted upon) is to be found in that which is acted upon*, both the sound and the hearing so far as it is actual must be found in that which has the capacity of hearing; for it is in the passive factor that the actuality of the active or motive factor is realized; that is why what causes movement is at rest (*DA* 426a2–6, translation slightly modified, my emphasis)
>
> εἰ δή ἐστιν ἡ κίνησις (καὶ ἡ ποίησις καὶ τὸ πάθος) ἐν τῷ κινουμένῳ, ἀνάγκη καὶ τὸν ψόφον καὶ τὴν ἀκοὴν τὴν κατ᾽ ἐνέργειαν ἐν τῷ κατὰ δύναμιν εἶναι· ἡ γὰρ τοῦ ποιητικοῦ καὶ κινητικοῦ ἐνέργεια ἐν τῷ πάσχοντι ἐγγίνεται· διὸ οὐκ ἀνάγκη τὸ κινοῦν κινεῖσθαι.

The conceptual connections between the *Physics* and the *De Anima* are evident also in the following passages (which will be investigated in later sections of this chapter):

The actuality of the perceptible and of the perceptual experience is one and the same, although their being is not the same. (*DA* 425b26–27, my translation)

ἡ δὲ τοῦ αἰσθητοῦ ἐνέργεια καὶ τῆς αἰσθήσεως ἡ αὐτὴ μέν ἐστι καὶ μία, τὸ δ' εἶναι οὐ τὸ αὐτὸ αὐταῖς·

Since the actualities of the sensible object and of the sensitive faculty are one in actuality, while different in their modes of being (*DA* 426a15–17, my translation)

ἐπεὶ δὲ μία μέν ἐστιν ἐνέργεια ἡ τοῦ αἰσθητοῦ καὶ τοῦ αἰσθητικοῦ, τὸ δ' εἶναι ἕτερον.

Motion is in the movable. It is the fulfillment of this potentiality by the action of what has the power of causing motion; and *the actuality of that which has the power of causing motion is not other than the actuality of the movable; for it must be the fulfillment of both.* A thing is capable of causing motion because it can do this, it is a mover because it actually does it. But it is on the movable that it is capable of acting. Hence *there is a single actuality of both alike.* (*Phys.* 202a13–18, my emphasis)

Καὶ τὸ ἀπορούμενον δὲ φανερόν, ὅτι ἐστὶν ἡ κίνησις ἐν τῷ κινητῷ· ἐντελέχεια γάρ ἐστι τούτου [καὶ] ὑπὸ τοῦ κινητικοῦ. καὶ ἡ τοῦ κινητικοῦ δὲ ἐνέργεια οὐκ ἄλλη ἐστίν· δεῖ μὲν γὰρ εἶναι ἐντελέχειαν ἀμφοῖν· κινητικὸν μὲν γάρ ἐστιν τῷ δύνασθαι, κινοῦν δὲ τῷ ἐνεργεῖν, ἀλλ' ἔστιν ἐνεργητικὸν τοῦ κινητοῦ, ὥστε ὁμοίως μία ἡ ἀμφοῖν ἐνέργεια.

It is thus clear that *Physics* III 3 and *De Anima* III 2 discuss two different instances of causation, to which the same metaphysical account applies. In a nutshell, in the interpretation I am arguing for, Aristotle takes the distinctive view that the activation of *both* powers takes place in the sense organ of the perceiver (on the model of mover and moved, and teaching and learning in *Physics* III 3—see chapter 1).

> For as the acting-and-being-acted-upon is to be found in the passive, not in the active factor, so also the actuality of the sensible object and that of the sensitive subject are both realized in the latter. (*DA* 426a9–11)
>
> ὥσπερ γὰρ καὶ ἡ ποίησις καὶ ἡ πάθησις ἐν τῷ πάσχοντι ἀλλ᾽ οὐκ ἐν τῷ ποιοῦντι, οὕτω καὶ ἡ τοῦ αἰσθητοῦ ἐνέργεια καὶ ἡ τοῦ αἰσθητικοῦ ἐν τῷ αἰσθητικῷ.

The perceptual qualities of objects and the corresponding capacities of the perceiver to experience such qualities are 'tied' together by multiple dependencies.[25] This is because for Aristotle the perceiver is the ground for the fullest realization of the perceptible qualities of objects. In chapter 1 we examined the following mutual dependencies: (i) the activation of the one cannot take place without the activation of the other; (ii) their activations are temporally co-extensive;[26] (iii) there is co-variation between the manifestation of the perceptible quality and the perceiver's experience of it. Aristotle expresses all these dependencies by saying that the actuality of the two powers is *one*: 'The actuality of the perceptible and of the perceptual experience is one and the same' (*DA* 425b26–27, my translation).[27]

The two powers involved in perception are intimately engaged with each other, as the one activates the other. Yet they are essentially different (one can even be physical, while the other is mental). Also, Aristotle is concerned to clarify that their inter-engagement does not determine what subject each power belongs to; they belong to different subjects. The activated perceptible quality (e.g., sounding) is a property *of the object,* not of the perceiver; even if its activation takes place in the perceiver.[28] As we will see in what follows, this is a very important tenet in securing Aristotle's realist stance regarding perceptible qualities. Thus, he writes:

> Nor is it necessary that the teacher should learn, even if to act and to be acted on are one and the same, provided they are not the same in respect of the account which states their essence (as raiment and dress), but are the same in the sense in which the road from Thebes to Athens and the road from Athens to Thebes are the same, as has been explained above. (*Phys.* 202b10–14)

> οὔτ' ἀνάγκη τὸν διδάσκοντα μανθάνειν, οὐδ' εἰ τὸ ποιεῖν καὶ πάσχειν τὸ αὐτό ἐστιν, μὴ μέντοι ὥστε τὸν λόγον εἶναι ἕνα τὸν <τὸ> τί ἦν εἶναι λέγοντα, οἷον ὡς λώπιον καὶ ἱμάτιον, ἀλλ' ὡς ἡ ὁδὸς ἡ Θήβηθεν Ἀθήναζε καὶ ἡ Ἀθήνηθεν εἰς Θήβας, ὥσπερ εἴρηται καὶ πρότερον.

Similarly here also:

> A thing is capable of causing motion because it *can* do this, it is a mover because it actually *does* it. But it is on the movable that it is capable of acting. Hence there is a single actuality of both alike, just as one to two and two to one are the same interval, and the steep ascent and the steep descent are one—for these are one and the same, although their definitions are not one. So it is with the mover and the moved. (*Phys.* 202a16–20)

> κινητικὸν μὲν γάρ ἐστιν τῷ δύνασθαι, κινοῦν δὲ τῷ ἐνεργεῖν, ἀλλ' ἔστιν ἐνεργητικὸν τοῦ κινητοῦ, ὥστε ὁμοίως μία ἡ ἀμφοῖν ἐνέργεια ὥσπερ τὸ αὐτὸ διάστημα ἓν πρὸς δύο καὶ δύο πρὸς ἕν,

καὶ τὸ ἄναντες καὶ τὸ κάταντες· ταῦτα γὰρ ἓν μέν ἐστιν, ὁ μέντοι
λόγος οὐχ εἷς· ὁμοίως δὲ καὶ ἐπὶ τοῦ κινοῦντος καὶ κινουμένου.

From these passages (and the analysis of *Physics* III 3 given in
chapter 1) we learn that for Aristotle the sameness of teaching
and learning does not *identify* teaching with learning; it does not
entail that the teacher is learning. (Hence their sameness need
not determine sameness of agents either—i.e., of the teacher and
the learner). Similarly, the sameness of the ways from Athens to
Thebes and from Thebes to Athens does not entail that someone
who is on the road from Athens to Thebes is going to Athens.
Rather, the sameness is sameness of substratum—it is the same
road that constitutes the two different ways, to Thebes and to
Athens. It is correspondingly the same activity that constitutes
the teaching and learning; the same activity is (an instance of)
teaching by the teacher, and (an instance of) learning by the pupil.
Just as the travellers engage differently with the road when going
to Thebes to the way they engage with it when going to Athens,
similarly the teacher engages differently with her lecture than
the pupil does. Hence, the teacher teaches and the pupil learns.
Yet there is an important difference between the various cases
Aristotle presents (the road from Athens to Thebes, the magnitude case, and the teaching and perception cases). The difference
is that the activities of the two powers engaged in perception and
in teaching are simultaneous; while this is not so in the other two
cases. For instance, one can walk from Thebes to Athens without
anyone walking from Athens to Thebes; but one cannot see if
nothing is seen. The reason for the difference is that the other two
cases share a *material substratum*, whereas in the perception and
the teaching cases the two powers share an *activity* as a substratum, where the activity results from the interaction of the powers.
Therefore, the *activity-substratum*, which requires the activation

of the perceptible and perceiving powers, exists only when the two powers are actively engaged with one another, and not otherwise. Hence, the perceiving and being perceived obtain only during their mutual interaction. As we have seen above, Aristotle makes the point thus:

> Since the actualities of the sensible object and of the sensitive faculty are one in actuality, while different in their modes of being, actual hearing and actual sounding appear and disappear from existence at one and the same moment, and so actual savor and actual tasting, etc., while as potentialities one of them may exist without the other. (*DA* III 2, 426a15–19, my translation)
>
> ἐπεὶ δὲ μία μέν ἐστιν ἐνέργεια ἡ τοῦ αἰσθητοῦ καὶ τοῦ αἰσθητικοῦ, τὸ δ' εἶναι ἕτερον, ἀνάγκη ἅμα φθείρεσθαι καὶ σῴζεσθαι τὴν οὕτω λεγομένην ἀκοὴν καὶ ψόφον, καὶ χυμὸν δὴ καὶ γεῦσιν, καὶ τὰ ἄλλα ὁμοίως· τὰ δὲ κατὰ δύναμιν λεγόμενα οὐκ ἀνάγκη·

For Aristotle it is only in the context (and for the duration) of the causal interaction with a perceptual system that the perceptual qualities of an object's surface can be realized. The perceiver's perceptual system, though external to the colored object, is a necessary realization-ground for the perceptual qualities of the object. To understand this dependence on external conditions, consider a car. It can reach its maximum speed on a flat road surface. The causal interaction between the car and the road is the realization ground for the speed of the car. The flatness of the road is (in this case) a necessary external condition for the car to realize its speed potential in the course of the causal interaction between car and road. Take a further analogy: the same blow of the hammer will be actualized differently if it impacts on a wall, on water, or on plastic.

What is actualized is a different physical phenomenon in each case (e.g., a dent, a splash, a bounce). The actualized end of the power of the blow is different in each case, but this does not make the power different.[29] Yet, a perceptual quality is a property of the external object's constitution, despite its dependence on external conditions for its realization. It is a constitutive property of the object, whose actualization is grounded on a causal interaction with the perceiver. The dependence on a perceiver does *not* render the actuality of colorfulness of the color any more *subjective,* or *mental,* than the actuality the color attains by interacting with light. Using an example from contemporary (or Democritean) physical theory, when some gas is released into a cubic container, the cubic shape of the volume of gas supervenes on the location of the individual gas molecules that are in causal interaction with the container. This shape of the volume of gas lasts while the gas's causal interaction with the external conditions persists. Yet, the cubic shape is a constitutive property of the volume of gas. Likewise, the perceptual quality is a constitutive property of the object's surface, although it is actualized on the ground of, and for the duration of, the causal interaction of the properties of the object's surface with the vision system of the perceiver.[30]

The specificity and explanatory value of the interpretation I am defending is further brought to light if contrasted with the alternative but related interpretations defended recently by Alan Silverman (1989) and Justin Broackes (1999). Silverman holds that the dependence of the perceptible qualities of objects on our perceptual systems is *not essential* to the perceptibles, but rather merely necessary, following from their essence. He writes:

[T]he sense taking on of the sensible form is what Aristotle describes as the actualization of distinct potentialities of the sense and of the sensible: the form of the sensible taken *on is not identical* with the essence of the sensible but it is rather a necessary accident of that essence (that is, the 'sensible form' of red taken on in sensation stands to the essence of red as being receptive of grammar stands to the essence of man (*Top.* 102a18–22). (1989: 271, my emphasis)[31]

As I argued above, there are many coefficients that come into the actualization of a power, and variation in any of these coefficients changes the effect of the power in each context. For instance there is variation even in the activation of the transparent light by a color, depending on the intensity of the light. Hence, there can be no precision in the definition of the essence of a power, determining what is essential and what is a necessary accident. Although it is not explicit in the text, Aristotle is clearly operating with some notion of the 'usual conditions' under which the essence of a power is determined.[32] Evidence for this is the fact that he is not strict about what he takes to be the essence of a power. For instance, a color is at times defined as aiming at the activation of the transparent (*DA* 418a31–b2), and at other times as aiming at the activation of the sense organ (*DA* 424b5–6). I therefore do not think we have a strict criterion for determining which end is essential to a power and which is merely a necessary accident of it.

Broackes has advanced an interpretation similar to Silverman's in distinguishing the essence of a perceptible power from its visibility. He writes:

> Color defines the nature of sight, which in turn allows us to call it the seeable; but it has a more basic nature than that of being the seeable. *De Anima* itself marks the priority of color to sight, near the start of chapter 7: *color is the cause of vision, but it is no part of its definition that it be visible.* (1999, 61, my emphasis)

Broackes does not describe visibility as a necessary accident of color (as Silverman does), but explains it as being grounded on the activation of the transparent by the color of the object:

> So what of (o), the suggestion that colors are powers to produce perception? ... How can Aristotle talk in *DA* 3.2 as if the activity of color is to be perceived, if he also believes that colors are, fundamentally, features capable of full existence in the absence of perceivers? ... Suppose we use the predicate 'red$_p$' for things with the power to produce perceptions of red when normally viewed, and the predicate 'red$_g$' for things with the objectively characterizable ground of that power (e.g. a certain degree of transparency); and suppose we talk similarly with respect to other colors and color in general. Colors$_p$ are powers, in actuality precisely when producing perception. By contrast, colors$_g$ are not powers, and there is no need to say that their actuality is to be perceived. Yet the two are closely connected: something will have a color$_p$ iff it has a color$_g$, and Aristotle could easily have applied the word 'color' (or χρῶμα) to both these things. If something like this is right, we would have a nice explanation of the variety in Aristotle's characterization of color. (o) will be a plausible account of colors$_p$, (3) [where (3) is Aristotle's explanation of the relation of the transparent to color: 'The color of an object is (a) the ratio of white to black in it, or of light to dark—or, more generally, (b) its degree of transparency (cf. 439b8–10)] a plausible account of colors$_g$. (1999, 67)

My response to Silverman's interpretation applies to Broackes' as well; it is clear that Aristotle moves from one characterization of color to the other quite readily in his writings. On the other hand, Broackes uses this interpretation to explain in further detail the metaphysical impact of color on the sense organ, with which I have a difficulty to register:

> This distinction also helps resolve a puzzle in Aristotle's talk of actualities and potentialities. In accordance with the general theory of causation, in perception a thing which is 'already' actually f makes the sense-organ, which was potentially f, actually f (*DA* 2.5, 418a4; 2. 11, 424a1–2); *De Anima* 3.2, however, seems to imply that the sense-object is in activity only while it is being perceived... An attractive solution is now available: the rose is actually red$_g$ before affecting the eye... yet it [the rose] counts as actually red$_p$ only after affecting the eye (in that only then is its power to look red in activity). When the theory of causation demands that actual redness be propagated though the medium and to the eye, this can only be redness$_g$: one could hardly demand the propagation of redness$_p$ in activity without securing that every eye that saw red was somehow itself seen to be red. (1999, 67–8)

Whereas Broackes holds that generally colors$_g$ are not powers, he describes the rose's red$_g$ *as if* it was a power. I believe this problem stems from the fact that Broackes implicitly attributes *two* properties to a red object: red$_g$ and red$_p$. The result is that he is forced to make red$_g$ the color that gives rise to the perception of red; he talks of the form of red$_g$ as 'propagated through the medium and to the eye' (1999, 68), since the eye is not red$_p$ before perception occurs, so as to transmit red$_p$'s form. This move, however, raises two problems for Broackes' reading; it treats red$_g$ as a power, which Broackes does not want to do; and it presents red$_g$ as both the cause of red$_p$ and as the ground of red$_g$ and red$_p$. Although I agree with Broackes that Aristotle's position in *De Anima* III.2 is that redness$_p$ is in activity only while it is being perceived, I disagree with the implication that there are two properties involved, red$_g$ and red$_p$. On my reading of Aristotle, red$_g$ and red$_p$ are simply the same power. This interpretation is supported by what Aristotle writes in the *De Anima*:

> The earlier students of nature were mistaken in their view that without sight there was no white or black, without taste or savor. This statement of theirs is partly true, partly false: 'sense' and 'the sensible object' are ambiguous terms (i.e., may denote either potentialities or actualities): the statement is true of the latter, false of the former. (*DA* 426a20–25)
>
> ἀλλ' οἱ πρότερον φυσιολόγοι τοῦτο οὐ καλῶς ἔλεγον, οὐθὲν οἰόμενοι οὔτε λευκὸν οὔτε μέλαν εἶναι ἄνευ ὄψεως, οὐδὲ χυμὸν ἄνευ γεύσεως. τῇ μὲν γὰρ ἔλεγον ὀρθῶς, τῇ δ' οὐκ ὀρθῶς· διχῶς γὰρ λεγομένης τῆς αἰσθήσεως καὶ τοῦ αἰσθητοῦ, τῶν μὲν κατὰ δύναμιν τῶν δὲ κατ' ἐνέργειαν, ἐπὶ τούτων μὲν συμβαίνει τὸ λεχθέν, ἐπὶ δὲ τῶν ἑτέρων οὐ συμβαίνει.

As I understand Aristotle's position is that, were no perceiver to see it, a rose would not be actively red (as it is actively red when we see it), but the rose is in fact potentially red independently of being seen. For Aristotle the color, say, that an object 'achieves' while being perceived is a high degree of activation of the *object's* color, rather than a mere representation of the object as colored. More generally, for Aristotle perceptible qualities are in the world such as we perceive them, but only while we perceive them, because they require a perceiver in order to reach their fullest actualization. A shorthand way to characterize Aristotle's position is as *subtle perceptual realism*. (The point of contrast with *robust realism* lies in the fact that the perceptible qualities are not fully activated at all times, but only when perceived by the perceiver). I will return to a fuller discussion of Aristotle's subtle perceptual realism in chapter 3.

2.5 ALTERNATIVE INTERPRETATIONS OF *DE ANIMA* III 2

My interpretation of Aristotle's causal powers theory of perception has drawn support especially from *De Anima* III 2, which is a pivotal text for understanding Aristotle's theory of perception. It is also a text that, not surprisingly, has exercised—and divided—the commentators since antiquity. In what follows, I will discuss three alternative views of how the passage has been understood, and discuss the difficulties raised by each. This will lend, albeit indirectly, additional support to the view I have been defending in the previous sections of this chapter. The three views I will examine are those of Aryeh Kosman (1975), Thomas Johansen (1998), and Victor Caston (2002).[33] I will focus on their proposed interpretation of the already quoted central claim in *De Anima* III 2:

> The actuality of the perceptible and of the perceptual experience is one and the same, although their being is not the same (*DA* 425b26–27, my translation).

Kosman's key idea is that in perception a *numerically one* event occurs: an activity that is *at once* the realization (an 'acting out'; see 1975, 506) of both the nature of the perceived property and the nature of the perceptual experience. However, an important difficulty for this line of interpretation is that Aristotle treats activities as belonging to substances, rather than as entities in their own right; thus, how can one activity characterize both the subject of experience and the object in the world? Would it be a mental or a physical activity? Kosman is elusive in calling it 'hearing/sounding' (*sic* 1975, 514). What does the slash-sign signify? Is it supposed to be explanatory? In which way? By way of clarifying his interpretation, Kosman illustrates it with the diagram below (reproduced from 1975, 514):

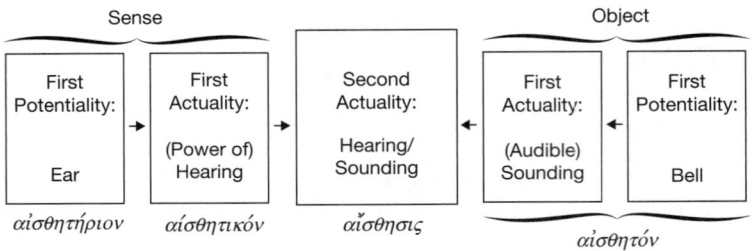

Figure 2.1

Yet, even when visually represented as above, the account that Kosman proposes no more than states the problem rather than solving it. How can the actuality of the mental (the perceptual experience) and the actuality of the physical (the object's perceptible quality) be *one thing*? Kosman adds that,

What it is to see is not the same as what it is to be seen, but when seeing and being seen take place, *there is only one event* which occurs. Eyes and objects thus exhibit first actualities *whose realization in second actuality is one and the same thing* (compare the ability of the builder to build and of the bricks to be built into a house, or the respective powers of learner and teacher). *This realization is the activity of sensing, being sensed itself, in which the sense is acting out its nature qua sensitive, and the sensed object is acting out its nature qua sensible...*On the subjective side is the ear and its (power of) hearing, and corresponding to them on the objective side, the bell and its (unheard) sounding; both hearing and sounding are realized in the same second actuality which is *one and the same actual hearing/sounding*. (1975, 513–4, my emphasis)

From this passage we see that Kosman's interpretation leaves unexplained the metaphysical relation that 'what it is to see' and 'what it is to be seen' bear to the single event that occurs when they occur. Yet this is the main metaphysical innovation in Aristotle's account of perception, and the main challenge for his interpreters. Without an explanation of this, we have no understanding of how perception takes place. In addition Kosman shifts between sounding and being heard, and coloring and being seen as if they were two pairs of synonymous expressions. This is evident in the following paragraph, for example, where Kosman's first example involves seeing and being seen and the second hearing and *sounding*, instead of *being heard*:

> What it is to see is not the same as what it is to be seen, but when seeing and being seen take place, there is only one event which occurs... [B]oth hearing and sounding are realized in the same second actuality which is one and the same actual hearing/sounding. (1975, 513–4)

Kosman moves freely from identifying the second actuality with the sound's *being heard* to identifying it with its *sounding*. And yet, on Kosman's account the bell is sounding even when it is not being heard. So, how can he switch from 'sounding' to 'being heard' as if they were interchangeable expressions? Finally, the claim that sounding might occur without being heard raises the question of what Aristotle thinks is co-instantiated with the hearing of the sound. Simply saying that the one sounding is and the other is not heard does not help us understand their ontological difference.

I turn next to Johansen's account. Johansen explains the relation of the actualities of the perceiving experience and the perceptible quality on the model of 'the potentiality of the hot to heat up... [being] actualized *together with* the potentiality of the cold to be heated up' (1998, 266, my emphasis). Being 'actualized together' however does not explain the metaphysical oneness of the perceptible quality and the perception of it; Johansen adds more content to his interpretation by further explaining their oneness in terms of *co-location* (presumably, in the relevant sense organ of the perceiver), thus:

> The actuality of the sense-object and the actuality of the sense-faculty are one and the same *because they happen in the same place.* (1998, 254, my emphasis)

Yet, one would want to learn more from Johansen about how co-location justifies oneness of actualities, as many things may be co-located but not causally related or ontologically dependent or co-existent in time, etc. In other words, the relation of co-location is metaphysically too loose to account for the various dependencies that tie perceptible qualities and perceptual experiences together (see above sections 2.3 and 2.4). Additionally, coincidence in space cannot justify coincidence in time, as Johansen seems to assume; so if we took Johansen's line of interpretation we would commit Aristotle to a *non sequitur.* Johansen returns to the explanation of the oneness of the actualities of the perceptible qualities and their corresponding perceptual experiences with what seems to be a different approach:

> But if you are interested in how it is that the actuality of sounding can be said to *coincide* with the actuality of hearing whilst also causing the actuality of hearing, then here is your answer: sound is an active potentiality to cause hearing. The reason why the actuality of sounding coincides with the actuality of hearing is that hearing is the passive potentiality *corresponding with* the sound's active potentiality. That is just like the way in which the potentiality of the hot to heat up is actualized together with the potentiality of the cold to be heated up.

There is nothing special going on in perception here. (1998, 266, my emphasis)

Note that the claim that '[t]he actuality of the sense-object and the actuality of the sense-faculty *are one and the same*' (1998, 254) differs crucially from the claim that 'the actuality of sounding *can be said to coincide* with the actuality of hearing' (1998, 266). Being *one and the same* is not the same as *coinciding*. Perhaps this slide is unintentional and due to an attempt to accommodate both Aristotle's claim of oneness and the strength of one's general intuitions about the difference between sensible property and perceptual experience. Alternatively, Johansen might positively mean to interpret 'being one and the same' as 'being coincident'. But if the latter is what he proposes, there are reasons not to endorse it. In the relevant passage of the *De Anima* Aristotle asserts the oneness of the actualities, and then proceeds to make their oneness do explanatory work for their coincidence in time. Aristotle writes: 'The actuality of the perceptible and of the perceptual experience is one and the same, although their being is not the same' (*DA* 425b26–27), and then proceeds to argue that,

> Since the actualities of the sensible object and of the sensitive faculty are one in actuality, while different in their modes of being, actual hearing and actual sounding appear and disappear from existence at one and the same moment, and so actual savor and actual tasting. (*DA* 426a15–18)

Additionally, as we have seen in the above quotation, on Johansen's interpretation there is nothing metaphysically "special" characterizing the case of hearing and sounding, or perception in general. Indeed, Johansen suggests that the case of hearing and sounding is metaphysically on a par with the case of x actively heating up y and y

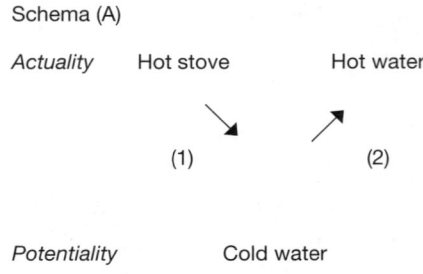

Figure 2.2

being heated up by x. He takes the two schemas below (reproduced from his 1998 book, page 264) to represent the same metaphysics. Johansen comments on the schema thus:

> Here the arrow from 'Hot stove' to 'Cold water' (1) represents the action of the hot on the cold. The arrow from 'Cold water' to 'Hot water' (2) represents the *change* that the water undergoes from hot to cold. (1998, 264–5 my emphasis)

Let us focus on the metaphysical relation of heating up to being heated. Are these the same activity or different? Johansen would need them to be the same activity if he is to use them to explain, through the active and the passive, the *oneness* of the actuality of the sensible and the sensitive. If schemas (A) and (B) above represented the same metaphysics, Johansen would be saying that the actualities of the sensible object and of the sensitive faculty are one actuality as the *active* and the *passive* forms of the same action. But this cannot be right, as we have also seen in examining Kosman's views.

My more general concern is with the breadth of ontological implications of the active-passive relation. On the one hand, the active and the passive could be describing a Cambridge change. For instance, I can think of my deceased grandfather who will thereby be thought of by me, without changing. But on the other hand, the

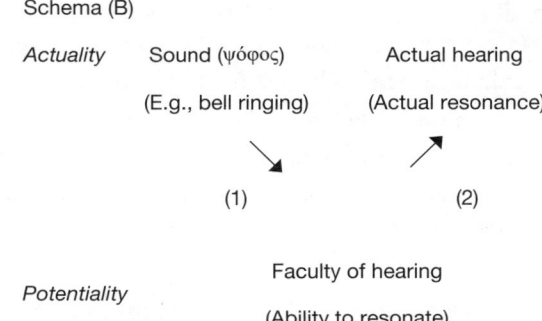

Figure 2.3

active and passive can be used to describe a real change, as that of a teacher teaching and the pupil learning, as Aristotle does in *Physics* III 3.[34] Here what the teacher is doing differs from what the pupil is suffering. Aristotle is emphatic that if the teaching was acting on the teacher (rather than on the pupil) the teacher would be learning, which he thought absurd. Hence Aristotle does not consider teaching the same as learning, but thinks that the teacher does one thing and the learner another. So explaining that the actuality of the senses and what is sensed are the same as the active and the passive forms of one and the same activity leaves the problem unanswered, because the active-passive does not always describe a single activity; there is a variation in the range of the active-passive with respect to Cambridge or real change, and consequently, variation with respect to the oneness of the active and passive activities.

Concluding our overview of interpretations with Caston's position, he explains the metaphysics of hearing and sounding with the model of 'articulated structure' (2002, 777) which, he argues, Aristotle uses for accounting how we perceive that we perceive.[35] For Caston, perceiving that we perceive is an example of articulated structure, where *a single token* mental state instantiates *different content types*. He describes his model thus:

There is a higher-order content—perceiving *that we perceive*—as well as the first-order content of the original perception. But this is independent of how many token mental states are involved...[Aristotle] believes that no other token state is required to make the original state conscious. The original state instantiates *both* lower—*and* higher-order contents. (2002, 777)[36]

Caston extends his metaphysical model from the case of perceiving and perceiving that we perceive to the case of hearing and sounding in *DA* III 2; his example is seeing azure and looking azure:

According to Aristotle, there is a single token event that is *both* an activity of azure *and* an activity of sight—it instantiates both *types* of activity. (2002, 785)

While I share Caston's approach to the texts in question, Caston seems to *assume* the oneness of the object's and the perceiver's activities, and from this he derives the claim that the two are in the perceiver (he does not explain in which sense of 'in') and that they have co-extensive life spans. He writes:

The object's activity, in contrast, is the same as the perception of the object *and so* is present 'in' the perceiver (ἐν τῷ αἰσθητικῷ, 426a9–11), coming into being and perishing 'at the same time as' the perception (ἅμα φθείρεσθαι καὶ σῴζεσθαι, 426a15–26). (2002, 783)

I argued in two journal publications (2006) and (2007) for a different direction of explanation: in my interpretation, it is because the two activities, which are not identical, have a common ground of realization, which happens to be in the perceiver, that they are bound by mutual dependences (including co-extension in time). The best way of pointing out the difference between Caston's and my readings of the ontology of perceiving and being-perceived is the following. Caston takes perceiving and being-perceived to be a single state or event that *instantiates* two types, whereas I see it as a single activity that *consists of* two types in the way that an asymmetric relation consists of two types, which qualify its relata (e.g., the asymmetric relation 'being shorter than' qualifies one relatum as taller and the other as shorter).

CONCLUDING REMARKS

In this chapter we examined the foundations of Aristotle's theory of perception, with particular reference to key texts such as *De Anima* III 2. The chapter introduced the five special senses; an account of how the sense organs are causally impacted upon by the perceptible properties; and the one-to-one correspondence principle holding between the type of an instantiated perceptible quality, the type of the corresponding alteration of the sense organ, and type of the content of the resulting perceptual experience. Additionally, this chapter presented the arguments that motivate Aristotle to posit that the perceptible qualities of objects are real properties of theirs. The next chapter will investigate the unique type of realism Aristotle is committed to in perception.

APPENDIX: HOW DO THE SENSES 'TAKE ON' PERCEPTIBLE QUALITIES?

When Aristotle writes that 'what can perceive is potentially such as the object of sense is actually' (*DA* II 5, 418a3–4), he seems to commit himself to the claim that a sense organ in one way or another becomes *like* its object when it perceives it. How are we to understand this likeness? The issue has divided commentators; it will be helpful to lay out the main views under discussion. Such views are alternative ways of thinking of the interaction between the object of perception and the sense organs of the perceiver—which I explained in this chapter as a mutual activation of causal powers. They will also be relevant to the discussion of the role of the medium in perception, which I address in chapter 3.

At opposite ends of the spectrum there are two well-known interpretations. According to one of them, Aristotle believes that psychological changes are always grounded in underlying physical changes, including perception. According to the other, perceiving is not grounded in anything further, but instead constitutes a basic form of animal interaction with the world.[37] On the former approach, which has become known in the literature as the 'literalist' reading, what it takes for a person to perceive is for her to *come to exemplify* the perceptible qualities that causally impact on her sense organs. So, for example, on this approach a person perceives redness when she has an eye made of suitably gelatinous stuff such that when it is exposed to a color in its environment it becomes, in virtue of this exposure, itself red. So on this interpretation, *likeness* between the sense organ and the object of perception is shared-property exemplification.[38] The sense organ undergoes a real change in perception. Sorabji (1974) was the first contemporary proponent of this approach[39]; a representative quotation from his work follows:

> The organ is colored during the perceptual process (425b22–25)... This coloration is a *physiological process*, which could in principle, even if not in practice, be seen by other observers, using ordinary sense-perception... Four passages [*scilicet DA*

424a7–10; 425b22–24; 427a8–9; 435a22–24] suggest a *literal* taking on of color... One advantage of assuming a literal taking on of color is that this explains how shapes and sizes can be received in the organ. The colored patches in the eye-jelly have shapes and (small-scale) size. (1974, 71, my emphasis)

By contrast, others understand Aristotle as claiming that no physiological or material change takes place during perception—perception is purely a 'spiritual' change (to use Thomas Aquinas' expression to refer to this view). What does it mean to say that the sense organs undergo a spiritual change in perception? This interpretation assumes that Aristotle did not conceive of biological matter as being inanimate, contrary to how we conceive of it, following on the sharp Cartesian division between material substance and mental substance. Rather, for Aristotle perceptual powers, as well as other mental powers, are primitive properties of biological matter. Perceptual powers are as primitive as the weight or the warmth of biological matter.[40] Thus, in perception these primitive powers of the animate biological matter that makes up the sense organ are simply activated. Among the Greek commentators of late antiquity, Philoponus had already cast doubt on the literalist interpretations (*in DA* 303.3). Non-literalist interpretations extend at least as far back as Brentano (1867), who had been inspired by the still earlier approach of Aquinas. In contemporary times Burnyeat has been the most adept defender of the spiritualist approach.[41] The following quotations are representative of his view:

The physical material of which Aristotelian sense-organs are made does not need to undergo any ordinary physical change to become aware of a color or a smell. One might say that *the physical material of animal bodies in Aristotle's world is already pregnant with consciousness, needing only to be awakened to red or warmth* ... What produces the perception of red or of middle C is not light striking the retina or the movement of air striking the ear; it is red and middle C. All of which is further grounds for thinking that the unordinary change produced by this unordinary agency, the taking on of sensible form, is not red in your eye or middle C in your ear, in the sense that the Sorabji reading requires, but simply awareness of red and middle C. (1992, 19–20, my emphasis)

We are forced to conclude that the organ's becoming like the object is not its literally and physiologically becoming hard or warm but a noticing or becoming aware of hardness or warmth. All these physical-seeming descriptions—the organ's becoming like the object, its being affected, acted on, or altered by sensible qualities, its taking on sensible form without the matter—all these are referring to what Aquinas calls a 'spiritual' change, a *becoming aware* of some sensible quality in the environment. (1992, 21, my emphasis)[42]

The advantages and disadvantages of the two approaches have been discussed in great depth in the literature; see for example Shields (2007, 293–98), and Caston (2004, 265–300). In view of the difficulties that both lines of interpretation have been shown to face, in more recent years Aristotelian scholars have been working on developing alternatives. I will here consider three representative ones, in order of publication: *the encoding model,* in Scaltsas (1996); *the same proportions model,* Caston (2004); and *the same structure model,* in Shields (2007).

Scaltsas (1996) argues that Aristotle takes each sense organ to have a physiology that allows it to be a mean, and receive stimuli which do not physically change the organ, but are in some way 'registered' in the organ's form. A natural model for such a sense organ would be the chord of a lyre. Scaltsas points us to Aristotle's view that to have the capacity to perceive, is to 'have a mean [μεσότητα]…[or] a first principle [ἀρχὴν] of a kind such as to receive the forms of objects of perception' (*DA* 424b 1–2, my translation). On the basis of this definition, Scaltsas argues that,

> [Aristotle] does not explain what it is to receive a form in the principle of the sense organ, but he does the next best thing, viz., he gives an example of something with a principle and a mean. The example is that of a lyre, in which the tension of the chords secures their consonance (συμφωνία) and correct pitch (τόνος, 424a31–32). This example gives us a rudimentary model of what Aristotle has in mind when talking of a sense organ having a principle. We can think of the sense organ as a lyre whose chords are tuned in accordance with a principle of consonance and correct pitch. The lyre model will provide a way of understanding what it is to receive the form in the principle rather than in the matter. What the lyre-model provides is the possibility of explaining that *more than physical change occurs in perception.* Striking the strings of a lyre does produce a physical change, namely, the movement of the strings, but that is not all that occurs. *What more, or what else, occurs depends on the relation between the movement of the strings and the concordant chord…* [T]he harmonious sound that is produced…results from the consonance and pitch of the strings. (1996, 28, my emphasis)

This is the line of interpretation I follow with respect to the activation of the sense organ in perception. The disturbance caused by a perceptible quality in the sense organ does not bring about a (persisting) change in the sense organ. Rather, the sense organ, which has its own form, registers the disturbance brought about by the perceptible quality by a blending interaction between its own form and the disturbance suffered. We can think of this blending of forms by elaborating the example above. Consider a tuned lyre, and a soprano singing an aria. The vibrations caused by the aria will resound in the chords of the lyre. This reverberation is a blend of the form of the aria and the form of the attuned chords of the lyre. Such a blend of forms, one encoded in the disturbance deriving from the perceptible, and the other of the sense organ, constitutes the experience by the perceiver of the perceptible. (As we will see in the following chapters, the process is in fact somewhat more complex, insofar as the form of the common sense is also involved in the perceptual experience, but this only adds complexity without changing the phenomenon.)

A different line of interpretation is offered by Caston (2004), who argues that what happens in perception is *transduction*, that is *conversion* of qualitative proportions from one type of matter to another. He writes:

> Perceptible qualities are thus defined as proportions of a specific pair of contrary qualities along the same range. So while crimson and spicy might share the same numeric proportion, they will still be proportions of different contraries: one is a proportion of white and black, the other a proportion of sweet and bitter... something might take on the proportions of a given perceptible quality, such as crimson... but in *different* contraries, and so it need not produce a replica of the perceptible quality... there is a clear and precise sense in which the organ becomes like the object and has its form within it, without receiving the matter and hence without producing a replica... *The organ takes on the defining ratio of the perceptible quality, without exemplifying it in the same contraries*... (2004, 314, my emphasis)... The resulting states of the organ... *concretely embody* the proportions of the qualities of the object in their own contraries. (2004: 315, my emphasis)... That is just what it is for a form to be received without the matter: information about the object is transmitted by preserving

only certain aspects of its form, thus effecting a transduction. (2004, 316)[43]

Caston offers a detailed interpretation of the 'translation' of the form of the perceptible into the 'language of the form' of the sense organ, in terms of the proportion of the contraries in the forms. This may well have been the mechanism in terms of which Aristotle conceived of the reception of the form of the perceptible by the form of the sense organ. Although in principle this is compatible with the position I have adopted above, it is a more specific conception of the reception of the form than the one I gave; conversely, my own allows for more diversity and complexity in the type of reception of the form. For brevity of comparison, the difference between his account and mine can be summarized thus: on the one hand, one can think of the reception of the form of the perceptible along the lines of the transduction of the proportion of opposites in it into the same proportion of opposites in form of the sense organ; on the other, one can think of the reception of the form as being more complex (e.g., as when voice resonance is produced in the reverberating chords of a lyre)— which resonance, need not be explainable in terms of sameness of proportions of opposites in the voice and the chords.

Finally, Shields (2007) too analyzes the sense organs' reception of perceptible qualities in terms of proportions of opposites, focusing on the following description by Aristotle of the reception process: 'the sense is affected by what is colored or flavored or sounding not insofar as each is what it is, but insofar as it is of such and such a sort and according to its form' (DA 424a22–24). Shields explains Aristotle's claim thus:

> The idea here corresponds to the way in which a new synagogue, a scale model used for fund-raising before the

temple was built, and a two-dimensional blueprint are isomorphic. Although neither a blueprint nor a model is itself
a (non-homonymous) synagogue, each is isomorphic with
the other. Importantly, the blueprint *represents* the building though it is in a two-dimensional medium. In this way of
thinking of perception, the perceiver comes to perceive the
object not by realizing the sensible quality, but by *coming to be
in a state representing it*, by manifesting an isomorphism caused
to occur by the object perceived. Thus, the eyes do not become
crimson when a perceiver views a Mr. Lincoln hybrid tea rose;
nor do the ears become somehow cacophonous when listen-
ing to Shostakovich's ballet *The Age of Gold*. Rather, *one comes
to share the structure of these objects, without exemplifying them*.
(2007, 297, my emphasis)

Here too the correspondence is taken to be an isomorphism,
although not explicitly of the proportion of the opposites. In my
own interpretation, the reception of the form of a perceptible by the
form of the sense organ is proportionate, without necessarily being
isomorphic.

Notes

1. In addition, an appropriate medium is required. The nature and the role of the
   medium are discussed in chapter 3.
2. See e.g. *DA* 418a3–6 and *DA* 424a1–2.
3. For my own interpretation of Aristotle's views on the matter-form relationship, see Marmodoro (2013) 'Aristotle's hylomorphism without reconditioning', *Philosophical Inquiry*, Volume 37, Issue 1/2, 2013
4. As the faculty of perception is common between humans and animals,
   Aristotle develops an account of complex perceptual content such that its
   complexity is not the result of the intervention of a higher intellectual faculty
   (which animals don't possess). Animals will not have all the types of complex
   content that humans have, but they must be able to, for example, choose on a

particular occasion one fruit rather than another because of what they smell, or to look for food because they smell it.

5. This conception of perceptible properties as real causal powers commits Aristotle to a very interesting type of perceptual realism, which will be investigated in chapter 3.

6. For which things count, for Aristotle, as perceptible objects, see this section, below. For what being causally acted upon consists in, see section 2.4 of this chapter.

7. Johansen (1998) argues that the top-down account in *Physics* II 9 of the relationship between form and matter underlies Aristotle's account of the sense organs. 'If the sense organs are to provide the necessary matter for the realization of the forms and ends of the senses, then we can only understand why the sense organs are composed in the way they are from the point of view of the definitions of their forms and ends' (1998, 40). Johansen offers for each faculty of perception a detailed account of how the material features of a sense organ 'can be seen as necessary or useful for the fundamental function of the sense organs, which is to help us perceive'. (1998, 24) For example, in the case of sight, 'we start out by considering sight from the point of view of its highest actuality. This is the end or function of sight. The highest actuality of sight, actual seeing (ὅρασις), is to be changed by color so as to become actually like it. This is what Aristotle calls the second actuality of sight. Sight (ὄψις) itself is an ability, the first actuality, to be so changed. This ability requires transparency, but transparency is realized only in certain sorts of body, water, or air' (1998, 36)

8. This argument also reveals Aristotle's realism about perceptible forms such as colors, odors, tastes, etc., whose identity is used as the criterion for the identification of their respective senses. See also chapter 3. On a different issue, it is important to note that Aristotle's individuation of senses in terms of the special sensibles is not unproblematic, although I will not dwell on this topic here. As an example of this type of problem, here is Johnstone's discussion of the difficulties related to flavor and odor:

> These striking similarities and connections between flavor and odor threaten to create a serious difficulty for Aristotle's theory of smell. This is because if both odor and flavor result from the action of the flavored dry on the moist, it quickly becomes unclear what the ultimate difference between odor and flavor is supposed to be.... The answer to the problem...is that on Aristotle's account taste, unlike smell, involves a mixture of the flavored dry in the moist...In the case of distance senses such as smell by contrast, the sense-object does not travel up to the sense-organ, but rather operates at a distance through a medium.... So how does the flavored dry thing I smell at a distance interact with the moist intervening medium of air or water, if not by mixing with it? The answer...is that it does so by drying it, to some extent and presumably in some highly determinate way. (2012, 166–9)

9. For example in 422a10–11 Aristotle writes: 'The body in which the flavor resides, the object of taste, is in moisture as its matter' (καὶ τὸ σῶμα δὲ ἐν ᾧ ὁ χυμός, τὸ γευστόν, ἐν ὑγρῷ ὡς ὕλη.) (my translation). But in other passages Aristotle talks of the perceptible quality itself as the object of sense (e.g., in DA 424b5–6): 'If the object of smell is smell, then smell must produce, if anything, smelling'.

10. Aristotle assumes it is a causal interaction; but does not give arguments for it. See the discussion of alternative interpretations of the resulting alteration of the sense organ in the appendix to this chapter.

11. This and the above quotation from the De Anima will be discussed in chapter 4.

12. Is the fact that this description of the principle lends itself to a general physical interpretation evidence for a literalist reading of Aristotle's theory of perception (see Appendix)? I submit it isn't; as we see from the Appendix even if the sense organ does not suffer a literal physical change in perceiving, nevertheless it is subject to a 'disturbance' (an activation of its perceptual power), to which the principle above applies.

13. The emphasis in the texts I quoted is on *simultaneous* perception of multiple perceptible qualities; but the one-to-one correspondence principle raises difficulties more generally for complex perceptual content and all the perceptual activities that presuppose it, of which simultaneous perception is only one among many, as I will elucidate in chapter 4, in particular in section 4.1.

14. See e.g. DA 418a3–6: 'The sentient subject is potentially such as the object of sense is actually. During the process of being acted upon [by the object of sense] it is unlike it, but by the end of the process it has been made like the object and is like it'. See also DA 431b28ff, and DA 429a13–18: 'If thinking is like perceiving, it should consist in being acted upon by what is thought about or in something else of this kind. So it must be impassive, and receptive of the form, and potentially of the same type but not identical with it, and related to the objects of thought as the faculty of sense is to sensible objects'. The meaning of 'becoming like' in this context is discussed in the chapter's Appendix. Some of the assumptions of Aristotle's theory of perception here mentioned will be further discussed in relation to the Mixed Contents Model in chapter 6.

15. For the infallibility of special perception see also DA 3.6.430a26–b3 and 3.8.432a11–12 cf. with Cat 2.1a16–19 and 4.2a4–10 and De Int 10.19b11–12. See also chapter 3.

16. An argument can be offered on Aristotle's behalf for the *infallibility* of the special senses with respect to the identification of which particular sensible (e.g. red or crimson) one is perceiving, grounded in the metaphysics of Aristotle's account of causation. Briefly, the perception of the special sensibles is the process that also actualizes them; for example, the color of an object is actualized

in being perceived—the actualized color is not the perceptual experience of the agent, but it is correlative to it and dependent on it—in the way that what is taught is correlative to and depends for its realization on what the student learns, but is not the learning (see *Physics* III 3). See chapters 1 and 3; and my 'It's a Colorful World', *American Philosophical Quarterly*, 2006, pp. 71–80.

17. Does Aristotle's account of causal powers work for all the five senses? He illustrates his key point in *DA* III 2 with the example of hearing, which he probably chooses because there happens to be a specific word in Greek for making a sound that is actually heard (ψόφησις, sounding); but there is no such specific word in the case of color or flavor (as he notes at 426a13–15). There are good textual reasons to believe that Aristotle thought that his causal model developed in *Physics* III 3 and *DA* III 2 applied to all perceptual properties and the corresponding perceptual faculties. He says so explicitly: 'The same account applies also to the other perceptual experiences and perceptibles' (*DA* III 2, 426a8–9). It is far from obvious that the account can be generalized, as certain solutions that can be employed in the case of colors and sounds do not automatically transfer, for instance, to odors. This problem has not been discussed in the Aristotelian literature.

18. *Cat.* 7b36–8a12: 'For the destruction of the perceptible carries perception to destruction, but perception does not carry the perceptible to destruction. For perceptions are to do with body and in body (περὶ σῶμα καὶ ἐν σώματί), and if the perceptible is destroyed, body too is destroyed (since body is itself a perceptible), and if there is not body, perception too is destroyed... But perception does not carry the perceptible. For if animal is destroyed perception is destroyed, but there will be something perceptible, such as body, hot, sweet, bitter and all the other perceptibles. Moreover, perception comes into existence at the same time as what is capable of perceiving—an animal and perception come into existence at the same time—but the perceptible exists even before perception exists; fire and water and so on, of which an animal is itself made up, exist even before there exists an animal at all, or perception. Hence the perceptible would seem to be prior to perception. '

19. See also *DA* 3.2.426a30–b3, 3.4 429a31–b3 and 3.13.435b7–9. Additional textual evidence that perceptible qualities exist whether they are perceived or not is to be found at *DA* II 12, 424b6–8; *DA* III 2, 425b27 ff; *Metaphysics* IX 3, 1047a5; *Meteor.* 4.8, 385a4.

20. Additional justification for the view that perceptible properties can exists without a perceiver comes from the empirical observation that, for example, a harsh sound can destroy the faculty: 'This enables us to explain why excesses in objects of sense destroy the organs of sense; if the movement set up by an object is too strong for the organ, the form which is its sensory power is disturbed; it is precisely as concord and tone are destroyed by too violently twanging the strings of a lyre.' (*DA* 2.12 424a28–32)

21. *DA* 417b20–21: τὰ ποιητικὰ τῆς ἐνεργείας ἔξωθεν, τὸ ὁρατὸν καὶ τὸ ἀκουστόν, ὁμοίως δὲ καὶ τὰ λοιπὰ τῶν αἰσθητῶν.

22. Aristotle proceeds to investigate the rationale of the question thus:

> Since if it were not so, [if its sensible qualities were not divisible, *pari passu* with body], we might conceive a body existing but having no color, or weight, or any such quality; accordingly not perceptible at all. For these qualities are the objects of sense-perception. On this supposition, every perceptible object should be regarded as composed not of perceptibles [but of imperceptibles]. Yet it must [be really composed of perceptibles], since assuredly it does not consist of mathematical [entities, and therefore purely abstract and non-sensible entities]. Again, by what faculty should we discern and cognize these [hypothetical real things without sensible qualities]? Is it by Reason? But they are not objects of Reason; nor does reason apprehend objects in space, except when it acts in conjunction with sense-perception. At the same time, if this be the case [that there are magnitudes, physically real, but without sensible quality], it seems to tell in favor of the atomistic hypothesis. (445b11–18, my emphasis, translation slightly modified)

23. Commentators take this connection to be evident; see e.g., Osborne 1983, 403, footnote 11.

24. See chapter 3.

25. The multiple 'ties' are grounded on ontologically interdependent monadic properties—they are not bridges between them (as explained in chapter 1). Aristotle says: 'of the things perceptible in themselves, the special objects are properly called perceptible and it is *to them that in the nature of things the structure of each several sense is adapted'* (*DA* 418a23–5, my emphasis).

26. At the same time, ἅμα, *DA* line 425b31.

27. Alternative interpretations of this claim, which has been the object of much controversy in the secondary literature, are discussed in the Appendix.

28. See the distinction between belonging-to and being-in that Aristotle draws in *Physics* III 3, discussed in chapter 1; and also the following relevant passages:

> If it is true that the movement (i.e., the acting, and the being acted upon) is to be found in that which is acted upon, both the sound and the hearing so far as it is actual must be found *in that which has the faculty of hearing*; for it is in the passive factor that the actuality of the active or motive factor is realized; that is why that which causes movement can be at rest (*DA* 426a2–6, my emphasis).

For as the acted-and-being-acted-upon is to be found in the passive, not in the active factor, so also the actuality of the sensible object and that of the sensitive subject are both realized in the latter (*DA* 426a9–11).

29. This principle, to which Aristotle is committed by his account of power actualization, is less 'innocent' than it might seem. From this it follows that every causal interaction, with its specificity and idiosyncratic contextuality, determines the conditions of actualization of a power. These are the conditions that define the power's end, and hence the nature of a power (i.e., what the power is). Yet, it is impossible, epistemologically, to have a classification system that individuates powers so finely. I therefore adopt the practice, in explaining Aristotle's system, of grouping together families of actualizations which can be actualized in many different ways depending on the actualization context, and treating each family as a single power.

30. See Marmodoro (2006, 73–4).

31. Silverman's supporting arguments are as follows:

A proper sensible...is not defined in terms of its respective sense... The 'being' of the sensibles is thus somehow prior to and independent of the 'being' of the sense(s), though the sensible are nonetheless related essentially (καθ' αὑτό) to the senses (415a14–22, 418a25, Cat 7, esp. 7b23–8a12, Met V 15) (1989, 271)...[To preserve the position above] Instead of defining the essence of red, for instance, in terms of its second actuality, being seen, he treats the second actuality as the realization of what in the *Posterior Analytics* and *Metaphysics* he calls a necessary accident: a property belonging to a subject in virtue of its essence but not found in the account of that essence... (1989, 272–3)

32. I will come back to this issue in chapter 3.

33. Other views such as Silverman (1989) and Modrak (1987) have been discussed earlier.

34. *Physics* 202b19–20.

35. For my interpretation of Aristotle's views on this problem, see chapter 5.

36. See also the following relevant quotations:

Because a higher-order content type is involved, consciousness is still intentional and hence relational. But in so far as only one token is involved, it must be a *reflexive* relation: in addition to being directed upon an external object, such as an azure sky, the token activity will be directed upon itself. Such awareness is *immediate*. It is unmediated by any further token activity, let alone a representation of itself; nor is there is any transition between the perception and the awareness of it, and hence no inference or causal relation between them. The relation is more intimate: both aspects are *essential* to any token perception. (2002, 778)

The intimacy of this relation is glossed by Caston as: 'The higher-order state and the lower-order state are not 'distinct existences'. (2002, 781)

And yet there remains a kind of *indirectness* about it. We are not aware of the act itself in the same way that we are aware of its primary object. Thus, while we can be said to *perceive* that we see, it will *not* be *exactly like* perceiving an object. (2002, 787)

37. I here follow Caston's way of articulating the difference between the two views (2004, 246).

38. Shields characterizes the position in these terms. See http://plato.stanford.edu/entries/aristotle-psychology/suppl3.html; accessed on February 20, 2014.

39. A less refined purely materialist literalist reading is already in Slakey (1961). Other defenders of a literalist reading are Thorp (1980, 583) and Everson (1997).

40. The examples are from Scaltsas 1996, 25.

41. The view is further developed in Burnyeat (1995), and supported, for example, by Johansen (1997). Broadie (1993,145) says she is 'sympathetic' with the view. Many others have also entered the debate since then.

42. See also: 'The reception of sensible forms is to be understood in terms of becoming aware of colors, sounds, smells, and other sensible qualities, not as a literal physiological change of quality in the organ'. (1992, 21–2)

43. See also Caston (2004, 247): 'In perception, the matter of our sense organs comes to *share the same proportions* that the perceptible quality exhibits. But the organ can realize this proportion in different contraries, and so *without necessarily replicating the perceptible quality within ourselves*' (my emphasis).

Chapter 3

Aristotle's Subtle
Perceptual Realism

INTRODUCTION

What is it that we perceive? Aristotle takes perceptible qualities to be real intrinsic properties of the objects they belong to; like all properties for Aristotle, they are causal powers. This conception of perceptible properties as real causal powers commits Aristotle to a very interesting type of perceptual realism, which will be investigated in the present chapter. This chapter will also highlight the heuristic value of Aristotle's use of his power ontology in his theory of perception. The investigation of the metaphysical status of perceptible qualities leads Aristotle to the innovative view that they are multi-track *and* multi-stage powers; and this adds further sophistication to his power ontology. What we perceive are powers *in their second actuality*. But the second actuality of a power, although different from its first actuality, is simply another state of the very same power. Finally, it might be thought that the role of the medium in perception undermines a realist view of Aristotle's theory of perception, because the medium interrupts the continuity of the causal chain from the perceptible qualities of objects to the perceptual experience of the perceiver. This chapter will show why this is not the case.

3.1 PERCEPTIBLE QUALITIES IN SECOND ACTUALITY

Recall Aristotle's general definition of powers in the *Metaphysics*: a power is first and foremost the capacity to *bring about change*:

All potentialities that conform to the same type are starting points of some kind, and are called potentialities in reference to one primary kind, which is a starting point of change in another thing or in the thing itself qua other. (*Met.* 1046a9–11)[1]

ὅσαι δὲ πρὸς τὸ αὐτὸ εἶδος, πᾶσαι ἀρχαί τινές εἰσι, καὶ πρὸς πρώτην μίαν λέγονται, ἥ ἐστιν ἀρχὴ μεταβολῆς ἐν ἄλλῳ ἢ ἢ ἄλλο.

The change that a power (or its bearer) is able to bring about or suffer is what defines the nature of the power itself. So, if perceptible properties are causal powers, what changes do they cause, and if they bring about more than one change, which one defines their nature? Are they powers that essentially make the world colorful, noisy, tasty, etc., or are they powers that essentially *make us perceive the world* as colorful, noisy, tasty, etc.? Or are they powers that essentially cause *both* kinds of change? On either of the two former options, Aristotle would be committed to thinking of powers as *single-track* with essentially one type of manifestation[2]; on the latter, as *multi-track* powers.[3] Multi-track powers are so defined:

'Multi-track' dispositions... correspond to more than one pair of stimulus condition and manifestation (see Ryle 1963, p. 114; Bird 2005a, p. 367; Bird 2007, pp. 21–24; Ellis & Lierse 1994, p. 29). The thought is that exactly the same conventional dispositions may be picked out by multiple characterizations in terms of stimulus condition and manifestation. (Choi 2012)[4]

Take for example the perceptible quality 'red': if it were a multi-track power, it would, for example, be identified by the stimulus 'light' and the manifestation 'appearing red' (in absence of perceivers), *as well as* by the stimulus 'being seen' and the manifestation 'looking red to the perceiver'. By contrast, single track-powers are picked out uniquely by a stimulus and a manifestation-type; that is, two different types of manifestations such as 'appearing red' and 'looking red to someone' would identify two different properties. In what follows I will argue that perceptible qualities for Aristotle are *not* single-track powers, contrary to what other scholars have suggested. Rather, Aristotle holds a unique position and thinks of perceptible qualities as *multi-track and multi-stage* powers, where a power that is numerically one has different possible types of manifestation and different stages of activation, the second and fullest stage depending on the first. Because of the dependency of the second activation on the first, the two-activations view does not amount simply to a multi-track view.[5] Before presenting my own interpretation, I will review and discuss alternative ones.

3.1.1 *The Single-Track Powers View*

There are two ways of developing the interpretation of perceptible qualities as single-track powers. One might think, as Sarah Broadie (1993) does, that perceptible properties are powers to cause (only) our perception of them; or that they are powers to affect (only) the external medium (for example the surrounding air in the case of color),[6] along the lines of what Alan Silverman (1989) argues for in relation to color.

Broadie (1993) explicitly holds that for Aristotle a perceptible quality such as redness is simply (the basis of) a power to produce perception; and it is responsible for nothing other than our perceptual experience of it (1993:145ff). She calls this 'Aristotle's Principle

of the Restricted Efficacy of the Sensibilia', meaning that perceptible qualities (with the exception of the tangible ones) are causes
'of only a single type of effect: the perception of them by animals'
(1993, 146).[7] Broadie finds textual evidence for the principle in the
later part of *DA* II 12. In reply, Justin Broackes has already argued in
press that '[Aristotle] often talks in fact in terms incompatible with
the principle of Restricted Efficacy. He allows smell to affect other
things: oil and wine take on the scent of what is nearby (*de Insomniis*
2, 460a29). Some smells, in addition to being perceived by us, are
'destructive' (*De sensu* 5, 444b30); many insects are actually 'killed
by the smell of brimstone' (*HA* 4, 8, 20).[8] In addition to the textual evidence being far from compelling (because other passages
point in a different direction), the view that perceptible qualities
are single-track powers would create trouble for the coherency of
Aristotle's theory of perception. In its strictest form, the Restricted
Efficacy principle implies that nothing can mediate perception.[9]
I share Broackes' view that,

> If redness is strictly a power to make people see red, and if that
> power can produce nothing but the definite effect, then there
> will be no room for a story about processes mediating percep-
> tion, either in the medium or in the eye. (1999, 78)

But this would be contrary to what Aristotle holds explicitly (see
section 3.3 of this chapter). I thus conclude with Broackes that
Broadie's version of the single-track powers view is not attractive.
There is however another line of interpretation, to the effect that
Aristotle holds that perceptible qualities are single-track powers.
Silverman (1989) emphasizes that for Aristotle, 'What a color is, its
essence, is the capacity to cause a certain movement in the actually
transparent' (1989, 279). While there is some textual evidence that
might be taken to support this reading, the difficulty for Silverman

is how to explain the generation of perceptual experience in a way that is consistent with Aristotle's general theory of perception. Silverman writes:

> It is a necessary accident of red, given what red is, that it be potentially visible (i.e., that it be able to be seen, and, when that potentiality is realized, that it be seen). (1989, 280)[10]
>
> Colors, in virtue of being able to cause movements in the actually transparent, have the necessary property of being visible, not of being seen. The sensible form as taken on in sensation is, therefore, the realization of a necessary accident of the essence of color. What is novel is that the relationship of first to second actuality is understood as the relationship of essence to necessary or essential accident. (1989, 280)

Thus, on Silverman's interpretation of Aristotle, color, when in full actuality, is *visible*, not seen. But if so, on this view there is no real connection between the nature of things and the perceptible qualities we bring into existence when perceiving them. This weakens Aristotle's perceptual realism significantly, and allows a degree of Protagorean relativism into the relation of the perceptible to the content of the perceptual experience. On Silverman's account, perceptual qualities come into existence by being perceived—but this is the view Aristotle criticizes the Megarians for in *Metaphysics* IX 3, where he also adds that 'the upholders of this view will have to maintain the doctrine of Protagoras' (1047a6–7). In conclusion, Silverman describes an *external* relation of the perceptible quality (in second actuality) to the faculty of perception, which does not determine how the perceptible quality becomes such as it is. Silverman cannot therefore justify his claim that the relation he introduces between the perceptible quality and the faculty of perception (namely that of being a necessary accident) 'allows the sensible to become such as the sensible actually is' (1989, 279). By contrast, as we saw in chapter 2, for Aristotle the relation between the actualized perceptible quality and what is seen is more intimate than that of being a necessary accident; it is *constitutional*.[11] In conclusion, the single-track powers interpretation of Aristotle's perceptible qualities is prey to difficulties, whether it is developed in the way Broadie or Silverman did. In the next section, I will argue for an alternative.

3.1.2 *The Multi-Track and Multi-Stage Powers View*

Aristotle clearly takes the perception of perceptible qualities as the ultimate and fullest activation of these powers. In discussing the views of his predecessors he says that the actuality of a perceptible is its being perceived:

> But the earlier philosophers of nature did not state the matter well, thinking that without sight there is nothing white or black, nor flavor without tasting. For in one way they were right but in another wrong; for since the perception and the perceptible are so spoken of in two ways, as potential and as actual, the statement holds of the latter, but it does not hold of the former. (*DA* 426a20–25, my translation)
>
> ἀλλ᾽ οἱ πρότερον φυσιολόγοι τοῦτο οὐ καλῶς ἔλεγον, οὐθὲν οἰόμενοι οὔτε λευκὸν οὔτε μέλαν εἶναι ἄνευ ὄψεως, οὐδὲ χυμὸν ἄνευ γεύσεως. τῇ μὲν γὰρ ἔλεγον ὀρθῶς, τῇ δ᾽ οὐκ ὀρθῶς· διχῶς γὰρ λεγομένης τῆς αἰσθήσεως καὶ τοῦ αἰσθητοῦ, τῶν μὲν κατὰ δύναμιν τῶν δὲ κατ᾽ ἐνέργειαν, ἐπὶ τούτων μὲν συμβαίνει τὸ λεχθέν, ἐπὶ δὲ τῶν ἑτέρων οὐ συμβαίνει.

This is in line with his explanation of the temporal coincidence of producing a sound and being heard:

It is possible to have the capacity to hear and not to hear, and that which can produce sounds is not always doing so. But when that which can hear is hearing and that which can produce *sound* is producing it, then hearing in actuality and *sounding* in actuality come to be at the same time, and one might call the one hearing and the other sounding. (*DA* 425b28–426a1, my translation and emphasis)

ἔστι γὰρ ἀκοὴν ἔχοντα μὴ ἀκούειν, καὶ τὸ ἔχον ψόφον οὐκ ἀεὶ ψοφεῖ, ὅταν δ' ἐνεργῇ τὸ δυνάμενον ἀκούειν καὶ ψοφῇ τὸ δυνάμενον ψοφεῖν, τότε ἡ κατ' ἐνέργειαν ἀκοὴ ἅμα γίνεται καὶ ὁ κατ' ἐνέργειαν ψόφος, ὧν εἴπειεν ἄν τις τὸ μὲν εἶναι ἄκουσιν τὸ δὲ ψόφησιν.

In the relevant *De Anima* passages Aristotle does not spell out the difference between sound and sounding explicitly in terms of first and second actuality,[12] but this distinction is illuminating in this context. As we saw in chapter 1, there are three states a subject may be in with respect to a power it already possesses. In the case of the capacity to make a sound, a subject may have this capacity without exercising it; it may make an audible sound, in absence of anyone hearing (first actuality); or it may be sounding (second actuality) while—and only while—being heard. Thus, sounding is an object's capacity to produce sound, in second actuality. While an object's capacity to produce sound can be activated independently of anyone perceiving it,[13] an object's sounding depends on the activation of the corresponding perceptual power in the perceiver. When something strikes the surrounding air (and the air is not dispersed), that object activates its capacity to produce sound, but in first actuality only:

What is required for the production of sound is an impact of two solids against one another and against the air. The latter condition is satisfied when the air impinged upon does not retreat before the blow (i.e., is not dissipated by it). That is why it must be struck with a sudden sharp blow, if it is to sound. (*DA* 419b19–22)

δεῖ στερεῶν πληγὴν γενέσθαι πρὸς ἄλληλα καὶ πρὸς τὸν ἀέρα. τοῦτο δὲ γίνεται ὅταν ὑπομένῃ πληγεὶς ὁ ἀὴρ καὶ μὴ διαχυθῇ. διὸ ἐὰν ταχέως καὶ σφοδρῶς πληγῇ, ψοφεῖ·

The air itself is soundless (ἄψοφον) because it is easily dispersed. But whenever it is prevented from dispersing, the movement in it is a sound (*DA* 420a7–9, my translation)

αὐτὸς μὲν δὴ ἄψοφον ὁ ἀὴρ διὰ τὸ εὔθρυπτον· ὅταν δὲ κωλυθῇ θρύπτεσθαι, ἡ τούτου κίνησις ψόφος.

Analogously, something may have the capacity to look, for example, red, but be without light; it may have the capacity to look red in appropriate light conditions but there may be no perceiver present (first actuality); or it may look red to a perceiver (second actuality). Light is sufficient to bring an object's color-in-potentiality into actuality. Aristotle says: 'In a way light makes colors which are potential into actual colors' (*DA* 430a16–17, my translation). But color in the light is color in first actuality only. In conclusion, perceptible qualities may be activated into their first actuality in the absence of any perceiver, if the conditions in the environment are appropriate; but they are activated into their second actuality only when the corresponding perceptual capacity of a perceiver is co-activated. Perceptual qualities in first actuality (e.g., visible blue) are powerful in that they can affect the relevant external medium;[14] when they come to be in second actuality, they affect the perceiver's sense organ.[15]

Thus, on the interpretation I want to motivate, a perceptible quality (e.g. the color of an object) has different *stages* of activation, depending on what is available in its environment. What characterizes a *further* actuality as opposed to a new *first* actuality, according to Aristotle's distinction, is whether the actuality of the power *changes* the subject it belongs to or not. For instance, if a surface is painted green, it is subject to a change in color; if, after having been painted green, the surface is illuminated by bright clear light, its appearance is altered somewhat— the way in which it looks green is different—but its color has not changed. Similarly, being seen is a second actuality of the color of the green surface, not a change. As we saw in chapter 2 already, for Aristotle perceptible qualities fully actualize their nature by interacting with the agent's perceptual powers, 'attaining' thereby what only the agent's perceptual system can actualize—in the case of color, their *colorfulness*, in the case of sound, its *sounding*, etc. The color *we see*, or generally the qualities we perceive, 'reveal' what these qualities can be, and are, when perceived. The interaction between object and perceiver affords all the necessary conditions for the object's attainment of the full activation of its perceptible properties. It is in this state of full activation of its relevant properties that the object possesses (e.g., the color we see it as having). Thus the objects' perceptible qualities in second actuality are just ways the perceptible qualities are activated, and *not* different properties of the object. Colors depend on perceivers to achieve their colorfulness, but it is *their* colorfulness that is actualized, and not only the phenomenal properties of the perceiver's experience. (I want therefore to stress that Aristotle's account is *not* committed to *powers of powers*, namely, *second order powers* that are realized in different circumstances. Rather, objects possess powers, each of which can have a variety of actualizations because of their dependency for actualization on the conditions of the environment.)

3.2 OBJECTIVITY OF CONTENT AND SUBJECTIVITY OF EXPERIENCE

3.2.1 Aristotle's Subtle Perceptual Realism

As we saw in the preceding section, perceptible qualities can be in different states of activation. They are activated when, in appropriate physical conditions (e.g., color in the light), they *manifest* themselves, even in the absence of any perceiver. Yet, there is a further level of engagement, between object and perceiver, which enables the perceptible to attain a fuller activation. This furthest level of activation of perceptible powers gives a dimension of uniqueness and sophistication to Aristotle's perceptual realism. Perception brings out an aspect of the powerfulness of, for example, color that is dormant when the color is in the light but unperceived.[16]

The interdependence between an object's perceptible power and the perceptual power of a perceiver for their mutual activation raises the question of the *objectivity* of perception. If the perceiver's experience, which depends on the sense organ, 'influences' the activation of the perceptible, then variations in the sense organ or differences between the respective states of diverse perceivers will result in qualitative variations in the activations of the perceptible. If the perceptual faculty of the perceiver is not functioning well, say because the perceiver is ill, then the activation of the perceived quality will be qualitatively different than it is with the healthy perceiver. For example, Aristotle explains that 'the same wine might seem, if... one's body changed, at one time sweet and at another time not sweet' (*Met.* 1010b19–26). Each perceiver perceives the same perceptible quality (i.e., causally interacts with the same power in the world), but what they perceive (the activations of that power) may be different. But if so, which one of the multiple possible contents of perception is veridical? What is it for the content of perceptual experience to be veridical? The answer is complex, but it will bring out the metaphysical originality of Aristotle's position.

As we saw in chapter 2, the interaction and activation of the two powers, of the perceptible and the perceiver, results (i.e., constitutes) in the *appearance* of the perceptible *and* the corresponding *experience* of the perceiver [e.g., a sounding (appearance) and a hearing (experience)], which last during the interaction of the ringing bell and the ear; see pp.102–6]. This is why Aristotle says that their interaction is *two in being*:

> When that which can hear is hearing and that which can produce sound is producing it, then *hearing in actuality and sounding in actuality come to be at the same time,* and one might call the one hearing and the other sounding. (*DA* 425b29–426a1, my translation and emphasis).
>
> ὅταν δ᾽ ἐνεργῇ τὸ δυνάμενον ἀκούειν καὶ ψοφῇ τὸ δυνάμενον ψοφεῖν, τότε ἡ κατ᾽ ἐνέργειαν ἀκοὴ ἅμα γίνεται καὶ ὁ κατ᾽ ἐνέργειαν ψόφος, ὧν εἴπειεν ἄν τις τὸ μὲν εἶναι ἄκουσιν τὸ δὲ ψόφησιν.

Aristotle also tells us that the perceptible quality makes the sense organ be like the perceptible is in actuality.[17] We saw that this cannot mean that the sense organ becomes qualified in the way that the perceptible object is qualified. So what does it mean? My reading of this Aristotelian position is that the perceptible always makes the sense organ like it, because this is what the perceptible does when it interacts with the sense organ. But the degree of similarity that results between them is not always the same. The degree of similarity differs according to the state of the perceptible and of the organ. We can think, for example, of things making a mirror 'like' they are; this is what things do when they interact with mirrors. But the degree of similarity between a thing and its mirror reflection depends on the state of the thing and the mirror. The highest degree of similarity is when the conditions are optimal—ample lighting; no dust, dirt, or rust on the mirror; no fog in the air, etc. What is important for understanding Aristotle's position on the objectivity of perception is that although the perceptible always makes the sense organ like it, only some of these interactions are objective, when the perceptible and the organ are in an appropriate condition. By that I mean that when the wine seems bitter to the sick taster, in this case too the wine's perceptible qualities make the sense organ of the taster *like* the wine; but due to the abnormal condition of the sense organ of taste of the sick agent, the taste is not veridical: the wine seems bitter to the agent. Think of this case by analogy to a mirror that is not clear or clean and thus reflects a somewhat distorted image of the reflected thing. By contrast, the healthy taster perceives the sweetness of the wine, just as a clear mirror reflects the image of the thing correctly. Although the form always makes the sense organ like it, it is veridically like it only when the perceptible, the environment, and the sense organ are in normal conditions. Perception is trustworthy then when it takes places in 'standard' or 'normal' conditions. Aristotle does not describe explicitly what he takes 'standard conditions' to be; but we can infer what he thinks they are by looking at the cases in which he thinks that what appears to the perceiver is *not* trustworthy, because the circumstances in which perception takes places are not standard. To begin with, the perceptible must be appropriate for the sense. He notes that in the case of flavor, taste is the appropriate sense for discernment and not sight:

> And again, among sensations themselves the sensation of a foreign object and that of the appropriate object, or that of a kindred object and that of the object of the sense in question, are not equally authoritative, but in the case of color sight, not

taste, has the authority, and in the case of flavor taste, not sight. (*Met.* 1010b15–18, translation slightly modified)

ἔτι δὲ ἐπ' αὐτῶν τῶν αἰσθήσεων οὐχ ὁμοίως κυρία ἡ τοῦ ἀλλοτρίου καὶ ἰδίου ἢ τοῦ πλησίον καὶ τοῦ αὑτῆς, ἀλλὰ περὶ μὲν χρώματος ὄψις, οὐ γεῦσις, περὶ δὲ χυμοῦ γεῦσις, οὐκ ὄψις.

Furthermore Aristotle considers cases where distance plays a role in the way we perceive magnitude, on the one hand, and colors on the other. On the perceiver's side as it were, he considers how things appear to observers who are healthy, as opposed to those who are sick, or cases of how heavy things appear to people who are strong, or to those who are weak; additionally he raises the issue of how things appear in dreams to the sleeping, and how to the waking. In the *Metaphysics* he writes:

Regarding the nature of truth, we must maintain that not everything which appears is true; firstly, because even if sensation—at least of the object peculiar to the sense in question—is not false, still appearance is not the same as sensation. Again, it is fair to express surprise at our opponents' raising the question whether magnitudes are as great, and colors are of such a nature, as they appear to people at a distance, or as they appear to those close at hand, and whether they are such as they appear to the healthy or to the sick, and whether those things are heavy which appear so to the weak or those which appear so to the strong, and those things true which appear to the sleeping or to the waking. (*Met.* 1010b1–10)

περὶ δὲ τῆς ἀληθείας, ὡς οὐ πᾶν τὸ φαινόμενον ἀληθές, πρῶτον μὲν ὅτι οὐδ' <εἰ> ἡ αἴσθησις <μὴ> ψευδὴς τοῦ γε ἰδίου ἐστίν, ἀλλ' ἡ φαντασία οὐ ταὐτὸν τῇ αἰσθήσει. εἶτ' ἄξιον θαυμάσαι εἰ τοῦτ' ἀποροῦσι, πότερον τηλικαῦτά ἐστι τὰ μεγέθη καὶ τὰ χρώματα τοιαῦτα οἷα τοῖς ἄπωθεν φαίνεται ἢ οἷα τοῖς ἐγγύθεν, καὶ πότερον οἷα τοῖς ὑγιαίνουσιν ἢ οἷα τοῖς κάμνουσιν, καὶ βαρύτερα πότερον ἃ τοῖς ἀσθενοῦσιν ἢ ἃ τοῖς ἰσχύουσιν, καὶ ἀληθῆ πότερον ἃ τοῖς καθεύδουσιν ἢ ἃ τοῖς ἐγρηγορόσιν.

Aristotle is explicit that the experience itself each perceiver has of a perceptible is a subjective mental event for each perceiver; its content is objective, in so far as it is qualitatively the same as the perceptible for all normal perceivers in standard conditions, stemming from the same object. Aristotle discusses these questions of the objective and the subjective aspects of perception in the *De Sensu*:

In perceiving the object which first set up the motion (e.g., a bell, or frankincense, or fire) all perceive an object numerically one and the same; while, of course, in the special object perceived they perceive an object numerically different for each, though specifically the same for all... these things [the perceptual content] are not bodies, but an affection or process of some kind... though on the other hand, they each imply a body (*De Sensu* 6, 446b21–26)

ἡ τοῦ μὲν κινήσαντος πρώτου, οἷον τῆς κώδωνος ἢ λιβανωτοῦ ἢ πυρός, τοῦ αὐτοῦ καὶ ἑνὸς ἀριθμῷ αἰσθάνονται πάντες, τοῦ δὲ δὴ ἰδίου ἑτέρου ἀριθμῷ, εἴδει δὲ τοῦ αὐτοῦ... ἔστι δ' οὔτε σώματα ταῦτα, ἀλλὰ πάθος καὶ κίνησίς τις... οὔτ' ἄνευ σώματος.

We thus have evidence that Aristotle is careful in distinguishing the subjectivity of experience from the perceptual content's qualitative and referential objectivity (in standard conditions). A question we need to investigate in relation to Aristotle's perceptual realism is whether his view that perception always requires the presence of an appropriate medium in any way undermines his stance that we perceive what is really there, in the world. Aristotle holds that perception cannot take place by direct contact between the objects of perception and the sense organs; he writes for example that 'If one places something that has color upon the eye itself, it will not be seen' (*DA* 419a12–13, my translation); he says, 'we perceive all things surely through a medium' (*DA* 423b7, my translation). This view is somewhat surprising at this stage in our investigation of Aristotle's theory of perception. If, necessarily, our perceptions of the world are always mediated by something in between the objects of perception and the sense organs, what is it that we actually perceive? Is it the object's perceptible qualities, or whatever it is that stands in between them and us and facilitates our perception? If Aristotle is committed to the former view, why does he introduce a medium of perception? And how does he avoid that the medium makes trouble for his realist theory of perception? The following section addresses these questions.

Aristotle's subtle realism in perception, as described so far, is in line with his more general reliabilist theory of truth. There is no privileged access to reality that confers truth on perceptual content; there are only reliable observations by a well-placed and well-functioning perceiver, whose experiences are veridical in the same sense in which unobjectionable received opinions in society (*endoxa*) are true. The difference between veridical and nonveridical perception for Aristotle is not a difference between having access and not having access to reality; rather, it is a difference between 'appropriate' and 'inappropriate' conditions of interaction with reality. Even in the case of hallucinations, it is the inappropriate stimulation of the sense organ by external perceptibles that gives rise to the hallucinatory experience. To understand Aristotle's position, let us look at an example of causal interaction from *Physics* III 3 (see chapter 1): a teacher can teach a lesson to a whole class. Let us assume that the whole class learns the lesson correctly. Even so, what they have learned is not identical between them, due to their individual intellectual differences and the particular way each student listened to the lesson. What each of them learned is a result of the teacher's lesson making their cognitive state like it. Each individual teacher-learner interaction determined the content of its own specific knowledge transmission. All transmissions count as veridical teaching, but each instance of learning is (ever so) slightly different, and consequently each instance of teaching is slightly different, as well, even if resulting from the same lecture. In that sense, there are (even ever so slight) differences in our perceptions of the color of the rose we are looking at, and so also (even ever so slight) differences in the full activation of the color of the rose we each engender in the world.

3.2.2 Aristotle and McDowell

To explicate Aristotle's unique position further, we may very briefly compare his view with that of the contemporary philosopher John McDowell, who has developed a realist but subjectivist view of colors[18] very much in line with what I call Aristotle's subtle realism. For McDowell, *being in the world* and *being objective* are two notions that can be teased apart (1998, 129); perceptible qualities are in the world and yet they are subjective, in the following sense:

> An object's being such as to look red is independent of its actually looking red to anyone on any particular occasion; so notwithstanding the *conceptual connection* between being red and being experienced as red, an experience of something as red can count as a case of being presented with a property that is there anyway—independently of the experience itself. (1998, 134, my emphasis)

I have already argued, in discussing *De Anima* III 2 (in chapter 2), why I take Aristotle to argue for the dependence of an object's looking, for example, red when it is being perceived as red: the perceptible itself is fully realized in the perceiver, for as long as it is being perceived. So on my account, Aristotle diverges from McDowell, in that McDowell holds that things look red independently of being perceived as red; while on Aristotle's subtle realism, being perceived as red is a necessary condition for looking red. In other words, the redness of the color in full actuality is not 'there anyway', but it comes about when the color interacts with the perceiver. On the other hand, there is an aspect of McDowell's position that brings the two accounts very close to one another. He writes:

> Secondary qualities are qualities not adequately *conceived* except in terms of certain subjective states, and thus subjective themselves in a sense that that characterization defines. (1998,136, my emphasis)

The dependence of the perceptible's full activation on the perceiver, on my account of Aristotle's subtle realism, does not make the color's resulting appearance *private*. But the conditions of the full activation from which it results are typically a *unique* interaction.

3.3 THE ROLE OF THE MEDIUM IN PERCEPTION

We know that, in developing his account of perception, Aristotle is building his explanatory theory within an ontology that is not corpuscularian. His theory of perception does not include anything like physical carriers of information (rays or particles) from the objects in the world to the sense organs of the perceiver. Rather, Aristotle accounts for perception by means of the activation of causal powers in the perceiver and in the object of perception; and the activation of causal powers is for him a qualitative change in the status of the relevant powers. On the other hand, Aristotle is also very much driven by his empirical observation of the perceptual process.[19] A clear indication of this is his derivation of the need for a medium in perception, which appears to be based on empirical considerations. He argues that without a medium there cannot be perception, thus:

> For seeing takes place when that which can perceive is affected by something. Now it is impossible for it to be affected by the actual color which is seen; it remains for it to be affected by what is intervening, so that there must be something intervening..., The same account applies to both sound and smell. For none of these produces sense perception when it touches the sense organ, but the intervening medium is moved by smell and sound, and each of the sense organs by this in turn. And when one puts the sounding or smelling object on the sense organ, it produces no perception. The same applies to touch and taste.[20] (*DA* 419a17–31, my translation)
>
> πάσχοντος γάρ τι τοῦ αἰσθητικοῦ γίνεται τὸ ὁρᾶν· ὑπ' αὐτοῦ μὲν οὖν τοῦ ὁρωμένου χρώματος ἀδύνατον· λείπεται δὴ ὑπὸ τοῦ μεταξύ, ὥστ' ἀναγκαῖόν τι εἶναι μεταξύ...ὁ δ' αὐτὸς λόγος καὶ περὶ ψόφου καὶ ὀσμῆς ἐστιν· οὐθὲν γὰρ αὐτῶν ἁπτόμενον τοῦ αἰσθητηρίου ποιεῖ τὴν αἴσθησιν, ἀλλ' ὑπὸ μὲν ὀσμῆς καὶ ψόφου τὸ μεταξὺ κινεῖται, ὑπὸ δὲ τούτου τῶν αἰσθητηρίων ἑκάτερον· ὅταν δ' ἐπ' αὐτό τις ἐπιθῇ τὸ αἰσθητήριον τὸ ψοφοῦν ἢ τὸ ὄζον, οὐδεμίαν αἴσθησιν ποιήσει. περὶ δὲ ἁφῆς καὶ γεύσεως ἔχει μὲν ὁμοίως.

For Aristotle all modalities of perception require an appropriate medium. Despite the nontrivial physiological differences between the senses, Aristotle is concerned to establish that perception is a single phenomenon differing only in material implementation. This is less obvious to him in the case of touch than it is in the cases of sight, hearing, and smelling, where the respective sense organs—the eye, the ear, the nose—are physically separated from the perceptible qualities they are perceptually engaged with while perception is taking place. In the case of touch this is not evident through observation. Yet, Aristotle is so convinced of the uniformity of the phenomenon of perception that he concludes to the conformity of touch from the analysis of the other senses. He classifies taste with touch in this discussion because of the common role of flesh in these two senses. He argues:

In general, flesh and the tongue are related to the organs of touch and taste, as air and water are to those of sight, hearing, and smell. Hence in neither the one case nor the other can there be any perception of an object if it is placed immediately upon the organ (e.g., if a white object is placed on the surface of the eye). This again shows that what has the power of perceiving the tangible is seated inside. Only so would there be a complete analogy with all the other senses. In their case if you place the object on the organ it is not perceived, here if you place it on the flesh it is perceived; therefore flesh is the medium of touch. (*DA* 423b17–26)

ὅλως δ' ἔοικεν ἡ σὰρξ καὶ ἡ γλῶττα, ὡς ὁ ἀὴρ καὶ τὸ ὕδωρ πρὸς τὴν ὄψιν καὶ τὴν ἀκοὴν καὶ τὴν ὄσφρησιν ἔχουσιν, οὕτως ἔχειν πρὸς τὸ αἰσθητήριον ὥσπερ ἐκείνων ἕκαστον. αὐτοῦ δὲ τοῦ αἰσθητηρίου ἁπτομένου οὔτ' ἐκεῖ οὔτ' ἐνταῦθα γένοιτ' ἂν αἴσθησις, οἷον εἴ τις σῶμά τι λευκὸν ἐπὶ τοῦ ὄμματος θείη τὸ ἔσχατον. ᾗ καὶ δῆλον ὅτι ἐντὸς τὸ τοῦ ἁπτοῦ αἰσθητικόν. οὕτω γὰρ ἂν συμβαίνοι ὅπερ καὶ ἐπὶ τῶν ἄλλων· ἐπιτιθεμένων γὰρ ἐπὶ τὸ αἰσθητήριον οὐκ αἰσθάνεται, ἐπὶ δὲ τὴν σάρκα ἐπιτιθεμένων αἰσθάνεται· ὥστε τὸ μεταξὺ τοῦ ἁπτικοῦ ἡ σάρξ.

We are not aware of the sense organ of touch. We are aware of the fact that we perceive the tangible and the flavorful upon contact between the sensible item and flesh (for touch) and the tongue (for taste). This could have signaled a difference between the operation of these two senses and that of the other three. Aristotle could have concluded that in the case of touch and taste (as opposed to sight, hearing, and smelling) there is no medium required; that flesh is the sense organ of touch and the tongue is the sense organ of taste. In that case direct contact between the sensible and flesh or the tongue would explain the generation of perceptual experiences of touch and taste. Yet, this is not the route that Aristotle chooses. The assumed uniformity of the power of perception includes, for Aristotle, a common structure of the phenomenon spanning the five senses' modalities. Hence, Aristotle concludes that flesh and the tongue must be the media, not sense organs, for the respective senses, *by analogy* with the other senses that have a medium between the sensible and the sense organ.[21]

Recall that in chapter 1, we saw how contact facilitates the activation of causal powers. If Aristotle holds a causal powers theory of perception, is he now contradicting himself when saying that perception could not take place if the object of perception and the sense organ were in direct contact? A clarification will help dispel the impression of contradiction. As we will see in this section, Aristotle's theory of the medium and of its role in perception brings out the explanatory strength and richness of his theory of powers. I mean that, whereas the predominant model of causation Aristotle inherited from his predecessors was roughly 'like causes like', by framing his own theory in terms of the *activation* of powers, Aristotle allowed himself two alternative courses for the activation of causal powers: mere activation of a power, or activation-*cum*-change of a power. The theory of the perceptual medium takes this distinction from Aristotle's power ontology to a higher level of complexity and sophistication. We can outline it as follows. The color of an object causally engages the actually transparent air (i.e., the medium) *without changing it.* The air in turn causally engages the sense organ of sight, the eye, *without changing it,* but giving rise to the perceptual experience of the object's color. So the perceiver perceives the *color* itself, because her experience of it is the result of a chain of activations of causal powers, without change, started by the color itself (similarly with all the other senses). But the account is not yet complete: by positing that there is always a medium in perception, Aristotle is thereby also introducing an additional type of causal engagement, over and above change and activation of powers.[22] In the *De Anima* Aristotle writes:

> Its being color at all means precisely its having in it the power to set in movement what is actually transparent, and the actuality of what is transparent is just light. (*DA* 419a9–10)
> τοῦτο γὰρ ἦν αὐτῷ τὸ χρώματι εἶναι, τὸ κινητικῷ εἶναι τοῦ κατ' ἐνέργειαν διαφανοῦς, ἡ δ' ἐντελέχεια τοῦ διαφανοῦς φῶς ἐστιν.

A little further on Aristotle explains: 'Color sets in movement what is transparent (e.g. the air) and that, extending continuously from the object of the organ, sets the latter in movement.' (*DA* 419a13–15). Thus, in perception even in the presence of the medium the chain of causation is not interrupted by the addition of any further links; the color affects the medium in its activated state of transparency directly. This is Aristotle's point below, which I will elucidate in a moment:

> Color is continuous with the light and the light with the sight. And the same is true of hearing and smelling; for the primary mover in respect to the moved is the air. Similarly, in the case of tasting, the flavor is together with the sense of taste. And it is just the same in the case of things that are inanimate and

incapable of sense-perception. Thus, there can be nothing between that which undergoes and that which causes alteration. (*Phys.*, 245a5–11)

τῷ μὲν γὰρ συνεχὴς ὁ ἀήρ, τῷ δ᾽ ἀέρι τὸ σῶμα. πάλιν δὲ τὸ μὲν χρῶμα τῷ φωτί, τὸ δὲ φῶς τῇ ὄψει. τὸν αὐτὸν δὲ τρόπον καὶ ἡ ἀκοὴ καὶ ἡ ὄσφρησις· πρῶτον γὰρ κινοῦν πρὸς τὸ κινούμενον ὁ ἀήρ. καὶ ἐπὶ τῆς γεύσεως ὁμοίως· ἅμα γὰρ τῇ γεύσει ὁ χυμός. ὡσαύτως δὲ καὶ ἐπὶ τῶν ἀψύχων καὶ ἀναισθήτων. ὥστ᾽ οὐδὲν ἔσται μεταξὺ τοῦ ἀλλοιουμένου καὶ τοῦ ἀλλοιοῦντος.

Light is the state of transparency of what is potentially transparent (e.g., air or water). In daytime, the air is transparent in actuality, while at night it is only potentially transparent. It is surprising here that color affects the actually transparent but does not change it; so color affects what is already activated. It does so without changing the light's state of transparency, or changing the transparent air into colored air. So, what type of activation is the activation by color of the actively transparent air? The answer can be derived from Aristotle's description of the causal chain of perception in the passage just quoted. Color sets the transparent air in motion, and this in turn sets the sense organ of sight in motion, being in contact with both the colored surface and the sense organ. The role of the medium then is to be a causal 'bridge' between the sensible and the sense organ detecting it, for the transmission of what I call a 'disturbance'. The color 'disturbs' the actively transparent medium, without changing it, and this 'disturbance' is transferred to the sense organ, without changing it, but giving rise to the experience of the perceiver. The 'disturbance' that color generates cannot be merely a causal engagement with, for example, the air, since it cannot take place without light. A 'disturbance' may be either physical dislocation or qualitative engagement without change. For example, the bending of a tree's leaves in the wind, or the reflection of an image on a shiny metal surface are qualitative causal engagements of the leaves or the metal surface, without change (in the relevant Aristotelian sense). Either way, a color engages causally with the actually transparent medium—air or water—and through this medium it engages the sense organ of sight, producing the experience of color.

It is plausible that Aristotle conceives of the way a sensible engages the medium and the sense organ analogously to the way he thinks substances mix, in the *De Generation and Corruptione*. In mixing there is qualitative alteration of the mixants, without change, in the sense that, for example, salt dissolved in water is entirely retrievable. In the same way, whatever happens to the medium and the sense organ during interaction with a perceptible quality, the initial state of the sense organ is recoverable—except in cases of 'violent' perception, about which Aristotle writes:

> Excesses in objects of sense destroy the organs of sense; if the movement set up by an object is too strong for the organ, the form which is its sensory power is disturbed; it is precisely as concord and tone are destroyed by too violently twanging the strings of a lyre. (*DA* 424a29–32)
>
> φανερὸν δ' ἐκ τούτων καὶ διὰ τί ποτε τῶν αἰσθητῶν αἱ ὑπερβολαὶ φθείρουσι τὰ αἰσθητήρια (ἐὰν γὰρ ᾖ ἰσχυροτέρα τοῦ αἰσθητηρίου ἡ κίνησις, λύεται ὁ λόγος—τοῦτο δ' ἦν ἡ αἴσθησις—ὥσπερ καὶ ἡ συμφωνία καὶ ὁ τόνος κρουομένων σφόδρα τῶν χορδῶν)

The way that the perceptible quality is commuted to the sense organ through the medium is, as I mentioned above, peculiar to the additional type of effect such causal powers can bring about— what I called 'disturbance', which is not a change or activation of the engaged power. That is, the power of the medium 'carries' the form of the perceptible to the sense organ without being changed by it. Aristotle states explicitly that the transmission of a perceptible form through a medium is fundamentally different from the embodiment of the form—i.e., from being qualified by that form (for example by becoming thorny or saline, etc. while transmitting these forms). While discussing taste, Aristotle distinguishes transmitting from embodying a perceptible quality in these terms:

> Hence, even if we lived in water we should perceive a sweet object thrown into it; but the perception would not have come to us through a medium but because of the mixture of the object with the moisture, just as in a drink. But color is not seen in this way as the result of admixture, nor through effluences. (*DA* 422a10–15, my translation)
>
> διὸ κἂν εἰ ἐν ὕδατι ἦμεν, ᾐσθανόμεθ᾽ ἂν ἐμβληθέντος τοῦ γλυκέος, οὐκ ἦν δ᾽ ἂν ἡ αἴσθησις ἡμῖν διὰ τοῦ μεταξύ, ἀλλὰ τῷ μιχθῆναι τῷ ὑγρῷ, καθάπερ ἐπὶ τοῦ ποτοῦ. τὸ δὲ χρῶμα οὐχ οὕτως ὁρᾶται τῷ μίγνυσθαι, οὐδὲ ταῖς ἀπορροίαις.

Suppose the sweet object is soluble: the water becomes sweet when mixed with it. In such a case the water is not operating as a perceptual medium, despite the fact that it serves to bring the sweetness to the perceiver, because the water is qualified by the sweetness—it embodies it. By contrast, the medium transfers to the sense organ the 'disturbance' the perceptible form generates in it, without coming to embody that form: 'The intervening medium is moved by smell and sound, and each of the sense organs by this in turn.' (*DA* 419a27–28, my translation). This further explains why the cause of perception *is not* the medium, but the perceptible object whose form is transmitted *through* the medium (by contrast with the sweet water in the example above, which *is* the cause of our perception of sweetness, while the object that made the water sweet is not the cause of our perception). In sum, Aristotle allows that in perception the medium is causally affected (there is κίνησις—see, for example *DA* 419a27–28), but the effect is only the 'commuting' of the form of the perceptible. The perceptible form is neither perceived by the medium, nor does it come to belong to the medium as a subject (in the way it belongs to the object of perception): the medium suffers only what is required to enable the perceptible form to be 'commuted' to the perceiver.

My general line interpretation of the role of the medium thus follows Scaltsas (1996): the way the medium is affected, he argues, is by *encoding* the perceptible quality and thus transmitting it to the sense organ that is causally impacted into generating the perceptual experience. Scaltsas explains his encoding model by analogy with human procreation, thus:

My proposal is that *the perceptible form is transmitted through the medium, being encoded in the movement of the medium, rather than being embodied in the medium*... The model I am guided by in understanding the encoding of form in a medium is found in Aristotle's explanation of human procreation, where the human form is transmitted encoded in the movements in the sperm. In procreation, the human form is transmitted through the sperm, which shapes the menstrual fluid into an embryo. The sperm is not a human being, nor is the human form present in it. Yet, the sperm transmits human form to the menstrual fluids, and thus the embryo is created. My suggestion is that the transmission of a perceptible form to a sense organ through its medium can be understood along the same lines. The sense-medium corresponds to the sperm, and the creation of an embryo to the perception of a form by the sense organ. Just as the sperm is not a human being, but it transmits the form of a human being, thus the medium is not hard or sharp or pink, but it transmits these forms to the sense organ. (1996, 32, my emphasis)

This line of interpretation appears to share some features with an alternative offered by Johansen (1998), but there is an important difference between them. According to Johansen, the medium, when taking on the perceptible quality that is being perceived, undergoes a *phenomenal change* of this sort:

[T]he medium is changed by the sense-object insofar as the sense-object *appears to the perceiver through it.* Unlike the kettle which itself had to become hot to mediate the heat to the water, the medium only became colored insofar as the color appeared through the medium to a perceiver...the medium only took on the color in so far as the color acted on the sense-faculty through the medium. (1998, 137, my emphasis)

According to Johansen's 'phenomenal approach', there is:

no description of the change in the medium apart from referring to the effect that this change has or would have on a perceiver at the end of the causal chain, namely the sense-object's becoming apparent to a perceiver in perception. *The medium changes only insofar as the sense-object becomes apparent to a perceiver through it,* and this too is just how we would describe the change in the perceiver. Both the medium and the perceiver change insofar as the sense-object appears to the perceiver (1998, 124; my emphasis)....

[T]his is not the kind of change in the medium that can support a mechanical explanation, for it is not based on there being any causal sequence that we could recognize as having a mechanical explanation. (1998, 126)

One of the strengths of Johansen's interpretation is that it makes it clear that it is the object of perception, and not the medium, which acts causally on the perceiver to bring about the perceptual experience. On the other hand, his interpretation faces the difficulty that it renders the change undergone by the medium into a Cambridge change. Yet, Aristotle goes into physical details of the pathway of the effect of the sensible form on the medium: 'He who is nearer perceives the odor sooner [than the one farther away], and the sound of a stroke reaches us some time after it has been struck'. (*De Sensu* 446a24–25) Such an observably gradual physical progression of the effect of the sensible form on the medium cannot be explained as mere appearing through the medium.

Finally, the interpretation of the medium I want to motivate might be further explicated by contrast with the one Caston (2002) has developed with reference to *De Anima* II 12. Caston writes:

> At the end of *On the Soul* 2.12, for example, he asks whether perceptible qualities can bring about any changes *other* than perception. A smell, by its very essence, is the sort of thing that brings about smelling (424b3–9). But it also can have an effect on inanimate bodies—not, he stresses, simply in virtue of concomitant properties that its material basis happens to have, but precisely in so far as it is a smell (b10–12). A smell, he concludes, can also make air *smelly*, that is, make the air something that can provoke further incidents of smelling (b14–16)....What, then, is smelling *besides* undergoing a certain change (424b17)? His use of 'besides' (παρά) here sharpens the difficulty. It presupposes that a change is undergone (πάσχειν, b17) when someone smells *just as much* as when the air takes on an odor (παθών τι, b16). Had Aristotle meant to contrast smelling with undergoing a change outright, he would have used 'instead of ' (ἀντί). On the contrary, his worry stems precisely from the fact that

undergoing a certain kind of change is *common* to both cases, that there is a univocal sense in which both can be said to change in this way. Otherwise, the problem evaporates. If perceiving is a special case of undergoing a change (Burnyeat (1992) 1995, p. 25), it can only be because of *what else* is true of the event, and not because it involves a distinct sense of 'undergoing a change.' The difference between these two changes must therefore be explained by some further difference. (2002, 755–6)

I understand the (acutely debated) text in question—that is, *De Anima* 2.12, 424b14–18—as follows. Aristotle states there that smells and sounds affect all bodies. They affect them *qua* bodies, whether they are animate or inanimate. So, a sound may make a tree leaf vibrate if it is loud enough, and for the same reason, may make the whole body of a small bird vibrate too—including its perceptual organs. When bodies that are loosely, if at all formed, are impacted upon by these perceptible qualities, they take them on (i.e., embody them)—for instance, when air is affected by a scent it becomes odorous. Here the contrast is between, for example, a stone under the influence of a scent and air under its influence: the stone does not suffer change because its own form is far too powerful for the scent that is operating on it, while the air does suffer change from the scent operating on it and becomes odorous. But none of this is smelling. Rather, over and above the scent's causal operation on every body around it, which in some cases makes things odorous, smelling is perceiving the scent. Smelling does not result from the ubiquitous causal activity of the scent on every body, but from the transmission of the perceptible form of the scent through the medium to the sense organ of smell. Although Aristotle's text does not facilitate our extracting this claim from it, on my understanding it is possible that the same body may be both affected *qua* body by the perceptible form and 'disturbed' *qua* medium by that form.

In conclusion, this review of different interpretations of Aristotle's views on the medium brings out in which ways the one I offer is original, and more apt to explain how the causal role of the medium in perception fits with Aristotle's more general theory of causation. When he posits that without the medium perception is impossible, Aristotle appears to be driven by empirical considerations. On the other hand, these empirical considerations actually lead him to innovate in metaphysics, by introducing a new type of effect that causal interaction among powers can give rise to, namely 'disturbance'. It would be outside the scope of the present investigation to explore further the metaphysics of this special type of change that the medium undergoes in perception; but its importance in enriching Aristotle's theory of causation should not be underappreciated.

CONCLUDING REMARKS

This chapter contributes to our ongoing investigation of Aristotle's theory of perception an account of the subtle realist stance Aristotle takes regarding what it is that we perceive. We perceive real features of the world via their causal impact on our sense organs. This causal engagement between us and the world gives rise not only to our perceptual experience, but also to the full actualization of the qualities of objects: the world is truly colorful, but only if—and as long as—we are looking at it. Additionally, this chapter highlights in which ways Aristotle's theory of perception is more than a direct application of his general theory of causation in terms of activation of causal powers that we discussed in chapter 1. In accounting for the role of the medium for example (which is introduced on the basis of empirical considerations) Aristotle breaks new ground with respect to how many types of activation causal powers may undergo.

Notes

1. The qualification that change might be brought about in the something else, or in the bearer of the causal power itself *as if it were other* aims at including in the account complex entities which have the capacity to bring about a change in a part or the whole *of themselves* (e.g., an athlete training herself).

2. Silverman (1989) and Broadie (1993) have argued so, but without using the terminology I use.

3. Broackes (1999) lends itself to this reading.

4. For example: 'Being electrically charged, an electron is disposed to experience an electrostatic force F in response to being placed at a distance d away from an electric charge q but it is also disposed to experience an electrostatic force F^* in response to being placed at a distance d^* away from an electric charge q^*. Similarly, it might be plausibly claimed that fragility is a multi-track disposition with many different stimulus conditions: x's being struck, x's being stressed, x's being twisted, x's being shaken, and so on' (from Sungho Choi, 2012 at: http://plato.stanford.edu/entries/dispositions/), accessed February 20, 2014.

5. Intuitively we can think of a multi-track power as having 'parallel' definitions, each doing the same work of picking out the power; while we can think of a multi-stage power as having definitions arranged as a series, where any one of the stages in the series picks out the same power. Aristotle's powers are both multi-track and multi-stage, so that picking out the power by one of its later stages of activation serves as an alternative definitional track of the very same power.

6. The role of the medium in perception will be discussed in section 3.3 of this chapter.

7. See earlier discussion of contact in chapter 1. Broadie allows for a second interpretation of the principle according to which perception may be mediated, but only by processes that occur just 'as and when it is necessary to produce perceptions' (1993, 151).

8. See also *De Caelo* 2.9, 290b33.

9. Broadie allows also for a modified version of the principle: perception may be mediated, but only by processes that occur 'just and when it is necessary to produce perceptions' (1993, 151) Broackes has arguments against this version of the principle as well.

10. Silverman expounds his view in more details thus: 'Special sensation...is an essential (καθ' αὑτό) relation between the sensible and the sense. Since the sense and the sensible cannot be definitionally related, (i.e., the definition of each cannot mention the other—because the being of the sense and sensible are distinct and the sensibles are ontologically prior to and independent of the senses), we need a different καθ' αὑτό relation between

the sense and the sensible, a relation which both allows the sensible to become such as the sensible actually is and simultaneously preserves the distinct essences of both. There is such an alternative way for a property to hold καθ' αὐτό of a subject, namely the way in which necessary (or essential) accidents are related to something. So for instance, in virtue of what man is man has καθ' αὐτό the property of being able to learn grammar' (1989, 279).

11. As we will see in section 3.3 of this chapter, the medium does not interact causally with the activated transparent, lest the perceiver see not the object's color, but the medium. The medium does not serve as a causal link between the transparent medium, activated by, for example, the color and the sense organ, but as a venue for the transmission of the activation of the transparent.

12. See *DA* II.1, 412a10–11, 21–27, cf. II.5 417a22–29, 417b2–16.

13. The first actualization of an object's power to produce sound is also dependent on the actualization of another corresponding power, in appropriate conditions. See chapter 1.

14. See section 3.3 of this chapter.

15. See the earlier argument in chapter 1 to the effect that powers always retain their powerfulness, even when activated.

16. It is not the case however that perception reveals a hidden aspect of color, in the sense in which the far side of the moon is hidden from view and revealed only by travelling to it. For example Aristotle writes in the *De Anima*: 'A smell is just what can be smelt, and if it produces any effect it can only be so as to make something smell it...what can smell can be affected by it only in so far it has in it the power to smell (similarly with the proper objects of all the other senses) (*DA* 424b5–10).

17. 'What can perceive is potentially such as the object of sense is actually' (*DA* II 5, 418a3–4).

18. See, for example, McDowell, 'Secondary Qualities and Values' and 'Aesthetic Value, Objectivity, and the Fabric of the World' in *Mind, Value and Reality* (1998) Harvard University Press.

19. See Johansen, *Aristotle on the Sense Organs*, 1998, and especially his excellent discussion of the medium in chapter 2.

20. Experience tells him that contact of the eye with the object does not generate sight, any more than contact of a smelly object with the nose generates smell.

21. Despite the analogy with the other senses, Aristotle vacillates between flesh being a medium and a sense organ (*PA* 653b24–26).

22. Recall from chapter 1 that the active power gets activated; the passive one gets activated and changed in the causal interaction.

Chapter 4

The Problem of Complex
Perceptual Content

INTRODUCTION

In Aristotle's theory of perception the five senses enable us to
perceive the real colors, sounds, fragrances, etc., that qualify the
worldly objects of our experience. We perceive such qualities *as they
are*, for, in a sense, by perceiving them *we make them* be what they
are. This is Aristotle's distinctive subtle realist view of perception,
which we examined in chapter 3. Our perceptual experience of the
world would be however extremely limited if it relied only on the
operation of the five senses as described thus far. This is because
each sense can perceive only its own special sensibles (sight colors,
for example) and no sense can operate in more than one modality—none of the five senses would allow us to perceive sweet yellow
honey for example: we would see the yellow and taste the sweet,
but in different, unrelated perceptual contents. Generalizing, if
the perceptual input of each sense modality comes in different
contents, all we would perceive would be arrays of disjoint perceptibles. Unless our perceptual faculty somehow can do more, its service to us will be rather poor. Aristotle explicitly acknowledges a
number of perceptual operations that the five senses individually
cannot perform: simultaneous perception of two different special

sensibles at once; secondly, 'incidental' perception of one special sensible by a sense other than its special one; and finally, perception of the so-called common sensibles (movement, shape, etc.) which do not fall under the remit of any of the special senses. Yet, all these operations are integral to the way we experience the world and its *objects*. The difficulty for Aristotle lies in the fact that all these perceptual operations require *complex perceptual content* (i.e. content comprising multimodal input). How *can* the perceiver acquire such input? The question exercises Aristotle. His solution is to posit the so-called 'common sense', in addition to the five special ones. The common sense does not have its own sense organ or special sensibles; yet, it performs its own operations, operations that the five senses cannot perform—in sum, the common sense enables to perceiver to have complex perceptual content. How does Aristotle account for this? This and the following chapters motivate a metaphysically 'robust' interpretation of the common sense: the common sense is the perceptual *system* as a whole, comprising the five senses but *empowered with extra perceptual capacities*, which enable the perceiver to handle complex perceptual content. How the five senses compose the common one is for Aristotle an exercising question, which will be addressed in chapters 6 and 7; the present chapter examines what motivates Aristotle to posit in the first place that there is a common sense in addition to the five special ones.

4.1 THE COMMON SENSE AND THE PERCEPTION OF COMPLEX PERCEPTUAL CONTENT

Aristotle's theory of perception is built around a few central, well-known assumptions, which have been presented in the earlier chapters of this book. As we saw in chapter 2, for Aristotle each type of perceptible quality identifies a different sense: a special sense, with its own sense organ (sight for color, hearing for sound, etc.). Each perceptible quality can generate a causal change within the sense through which it is perceived. The perceptible quality's impact on the sense gives rise to the perceptual content of the perceiver's experience. Aristotle takes it for granted that perceptual awareness occurs as perceptual content is generated by the causal activation of a sense by a perceptible quality.[1] For Aristotle there is a one-to-one correspondence among the object's perceptible quality, the activation/alteration of the sense organ, and the content of the perceptual experience arising from it (e.g., a correspondence between this desk's color, the modification of my sense organ of sight stimulated by this instance of color, and the content of my experience of the color). In chapter 2 I introduced two key representative statements by Aristotle as evidence for the one-to-one correspondence principle, from the *De Anima* and *Sense and Sensibilia* respectively, where we read that,

It is impossible that what is one and the same [i.e., a sense] should be moved at one and the same time with contrary movements in so far as it is undivided, and in an undivided moment of time. For if what is sweet be the quality perceived, it moves the sense ... in this determinate way, while what is bitter moves it in a contrary way, and what is white in a different way (*DA* 426b29–427a1, translation slightly modified) ...,

ἀλλὰ μὴν ἀδύνατον ἅμα τὰς ἐναντίας κινήσεις κινεῖσθαι τὸ αὐτὸ ᾗ ἀδιαίρετον, καὶ ἐν ἀδιαιρέτῳ χρόνῳ. εἰ γὰρ γλυκύ, ὡδὶ κινεῖ τὴν αἴσθησιν ἢ τὴν νόησιν, τὸ δὲ πικρὸν ἐναντίως, καὶ τὸ λευκὸν ἑτέρως.

In one and the same faculty the perception actualized at any single moment is necessarily one, only one stimulation or exertion of a single faculty being possible at a single instant. (*SS* 447b17–19)

ἀλλὰ κατὰ μίαν δύναμιν καὶ ἄτομον χρόνον μίαν ἀνάγκη
εἶναι τὴν ἐνέργειαν· μιᾶς γὰρ ἡ εἰσάπαξ μία χρῆσις καὶ κίνησις,
μία δὲ ἡ δύναμις.

On the basis of this one-to-one correspondence principle, each
sense can only allow the perceiver a single, simple (that is, unimodal) perceptual content at one time. The quotations from *Sense
and Sensibilia* and the *De Anima* well illustrate the (*prima facie*, as
we will see) impossibility arising in the case of one sense perceiving at once multiple special sensibles of the same type (e.g., taste
perceiving sweet and bitter at once); but the same difficulty arises
if hypothetically one sense were to perceive at once multiple special
sensibles of different types. The *De Anima* passage has is fact already
prepared us with an example to see that the difficulty generated by
the one-to-one correspondence principle is not restricted to the
perception of special sensibles of the same type, such as sweet and
bitter, but extends to the case of a sense perceiving multiple special
sensibles of different types, such as sweet and white. This point will
be important in driving Aristotle' investigation, as we will see in the
chapters to follow: (anticipating somewhat the results of the forthcoming discussion) Aristotle does posit that there is a sense, the so
called 'common sense', that enables the perceiver to perform perceptual operations involving multiple special sensibles of different
types at once. Is the common sense too *qua* sense governed by the
one-to-one correspondence principle?[2] Yes, it is. We find a generic
formulation of the difficulty which well applies both to the special
senses (perceiving multiple special sensibles of the same type at
once) and to the common sense (perceiving multiple special sensibles of different types at once) in the *Sense and Sensibilia* where
Aristotle states conclusively: 'Hence, it is not possible to perceive
two distinct objects simultaneously with one and the same sense'
(*SS* 447b20–21). How, then, can there be *simultaneous perception* of

multiple (types of) perceptible qualities in one perceptual content? If a sense (whether it is a special one or the common one) was *not divided* into many sensing-parts—namely parts each of which can, on its own, perceive a quality—then it could perceive only one quality at an instant since it cannot be activated multiply. In this case, the difficulty would be to account for how simultaneous perception (and thus more generally complex perceptual content) is possible at all. If, on the other hand, the sense (whether it is a special one or the common one) *was divided* into many sensing-parts, this would facilitate simultaneous perception. But how could there be in this case a *single content* of awareness—enjoyed by a single perceiving subject?[3]

It is here important to note that the above quotations from the *De Anima* and the *Sense and Sensibilia* emphasize the (*prima facie*) impossibility of *simultaneous* perception of multiple special sensibles by a single sense. But as already mentioned in chapter 2, the problem of simultaneous perception of multiple perceptible qualities (of the same or of different types) in a single perceptual content is an aspect of the more general challenge Aristotle's theory of perception has to address, that is, how we become aware of *complex perceptual content*.[4] Without the ability to perceive complex perceptual content, we would not be able to perceive *objects*, but only disjoint instances of different qualities in separate perceptual contents: sounds, colors, textures—never entities qualified in such and such a way. If all we could perceive were disjoint arrays of properties, the senses would do a rather poor service to us. This is why the challenge to account for how the perceiver can acquire via the senses complex perceptual content is so pressing for Aristotle. Complex perceptual content is involved in a variety of operations, which Aristotle explicitly identifies:

> *Simultaneous perception* (within one sense modality—e.g., seeing the blueness of the sky and the whiteness of the clouds—and

also across sense modalities—e.g., seeing the blueness of the
sea and hearing the sound of the waves; see e.g. *DA* 426b17–19);
Perceptual discrimination (within one sense modality—e.g.,
telling yellow from green; and also across sense modalities—
e.g., telling whiteness from sweetness; see e.g. *DA* 426b10–14);
Cross-modal binding (e.g., perceiving a sweet white item,
such as when drinking milk; see e.g. *DA* 425a30-425b3);

Additionally, objects have perceptible qualities that are not
exhausted by the five types that fall under the remit of the special
senses: objects are unified clusters of properties, they move, they
are continuous in space and time, etc.; perception of these features
of the world also requires a theory of perception that includes more
than the operation of the five special senses in isolation from each
other. Thus we can add to the three listed operations where complex
perceptual content is involved the following one too:

Perception of common sensibles which are *multimodally composed perceptible qualities* (e.g., feeling and seeing the *shape* of
a tree, or the *movement* of a drop of rain on one's hand; see, for
example, *DA* 425a15–16).

All these types of experiences ultimately enable us to perceive
objects, but require the possibility of acquiring complex perceptual content. Before moving forward to investigate how Aristotle
explains complex perceptual content, it is important to emphasize his commitment to the view that we *perceive* modally complex
objects. An alternative position available to Aristotle, and indeed
endorsed by Plato, would have been to argue that we grasp modally
complex objects of perception by involving a higher cognitive faculty than the senses. This is Plato's stance in the *Theaetetus*, where
he draws a distinction between our perception of basic sensible

qualities, and the *cognitive* process of grasping 'common' features (such as sameness and difference), which Plato assimilates to thinking.[5] In contrast to Plato, Aristotle holds that we *perceive* objects and their qualitative differences, similarities, continuity, and behavior; for him we do not 'assemble' objects together by means of a higher faculty of the soul. Aristotle's general motivation for this view is to explain the complex cognitive abilities of animals without appealing to the capacities of the intellective part of the soul, because this is unique to humans and not common to all animals.[6]

How then can the perceiver be aware of complex perceptual content for Aristotle? The general direction he pursues is that perception of complex perceptual content requires *extra powers* over and above the ones that the special senses have and activate when engaged in the perception of their special sensibles. The special senses are endowed with these additional powers *when acting together as one*, that is when acting as integrated parts of a perceptual system. The perceptual system as a whole, which is endowed with these extra powers, is what Aristotle calls the *common sense* (αἴσθησιν κοινήν). The perceptual operations that allow the perceiver awareness of complex perceptual content consist in the activation of such extra powers by the external objects. We can classify the powers into three groups according to the operations they enable to perceiver to accomplish:

- Powers relevant to perceptual discrimination within one modality, and activated when we discriminate (e.g., white from blue; or cold from wet); they operate on complex content of one type;

- Powers relevant to awareness of modally complex content, that is involving more than one type of modality (e.g., when we perceive sweet and white sugar);

- Powers that enable the perceiver's awareness of multimodal content common to more than one sense (e.g., movement).

These are the powers relevant to the perception of the common sensibles, as we will see shortly.[7]

In what follows I will argue that there are essential perceptual operations that only the common sense can perform, because it allows the perceiver to have complex perceptual content, without which perception of objects would be impossible on Aristotle's theory. I will defend a metaphysically 'robust' interpretation of the common sense: it is an entity in its own right, individuated by the perceptual functions it can uniquely perform. On the other hand, it is not an additional sense. It is rather the way the special senses operate when engaged all together in perception. The question for Aristotle therefore becomes that of explaining how the special senses achieve the required degree of unity that allows them to perform their integrated operations. On the one hand, Aristotle thinks there is empirical evidence that we perform perceptual operations that involve unified complex perceptual content, and this indicates that there must be a unified common sense. On the other, he derives (metaphysically) the unity of its perceptual content from the unity of the common sense. In the remaining part of this chapter I will introduce the cases of complex perceptual content Aristotle investigates and I will show where and how the common sense is essential to such perceptions. In the subsequent chapters I will address the metaphysical questions regarding the constitution of the common sense that are left unaddressed in the secondary literature, and I will motivate a new account of Aristotle's position.

4.2 SIMULTANEOUS PERCEPTION

There are a number of cases of complex perceptual content to be distinguished. Complex perceptual content obtains for example when two modally different perceptible qualities are perceived by two different special senses *at the same time*, thus becoming present to the perceiver's awareness at once (e.g., when I taste bitter coffee while looking at the blue sea). The two experiences are in some ways unified, because they happen at the same time. This is of course a weak sense of unity, as it is derived from the external conditions in which the perceptions take place. Yet it gives rise to a set of questions that, as we shall see, will drive Aristotle further in his investigation of the metaphysics of perception. Aristotle's own example is of a visible quality and a gustatory quality perceived at the same time through different senses, vision and taste respectively:

> [In the case of our] perception of what is sweet by vision... [W]e have a sense for each of the two qualities [e.g. white and sweet], in virtue of which, when they happen to meet in one sensible object [e.g. milk], *we are aware of both contemporaneously.* (DA 425a22–24, my emphasis)
>
> οὕτω γὰρ ἔσται ὥσπερ νῦν τῇ ὄψει τὸ γλυκὺ αἰσθανόμεθα...ἀμφοῖν ἔχοντες τυγχάνομεν αἴσθησιν, ἢ ὅταν συμπέσωσιν ἅμα γνωρίζομεν.

Aristotle gives other examples too, in which the perceptible qualities perceived simultaneously belong to one and the same object; also, examples of qualities which one perceptually discerns and which may well belong to different objects. Aristotle also makes a statement that suggests he might have been aware of the possibility that there is simultaneous perception of qualities which are not perceived in the same perceptual content:

> For, assuredly,... it is not by taste, or sight, *or both together* that one discerns that sweet things are different from white things. (DS 455a17–19 my emphasis)

οὐ γὰρ... κρίνει δὴ... ὅτι ἕτερα τὰ γλυκέα τῶν λευκῶν οὔτε
γεύσει οὔτε ὄψει οὔτε ἀμφοῖν

This seems to suggest that Aristotle envisages the possibility that
one is aware of sweet and white by taste and sight sensing together,
but not discerning these sensibles in a single perceptual content—
this would be simultaneous perception that is not in a single content.

Since the perceiver can have simultaneous perceptions, we can
assume that for Aristotle the perceiver thereby has *simultaneous
awareness* of the perceptions.[8] But how is it that perceptual awareness is activated in more than one sense at once—rather than, for
example, being activated serially in each sense in turn? And what is
the outcome of perceptual awareness being activated in more than
one sense at once? What does the perceiver experience? The answer
to these questions is to be found in the metaphysics of the common
sense, which will be investigated in the chapters to follow.

4.3 INCIDENTAL PERCEPTION

Aristotle acknowledges that perceptible qualities falling within the
remit of one special sense may be perceived through another special
sense too. Importantly, Aristotle considers this a case of *indirect* or
incidental (κατὰ συμβεβηκός) perception.[9] He describes incidental
perception thus:

> The senses perceive each other's special objects inciden-
> tally... this incidental perception takes place whenever sense
> is directed at one and the same moment to two disparate quali-
> ties in one and the same object (e.g. to the bitterness and the
> yellowness of bile). (*DA* 425a30–b2)

τὰ δ᾽ ἀλλήλων ἴδια κατὰ συμβεβηκὸς αἰσθάνονται αἱ
αἰσθήσεις…ὅταν ἅμα γένηται ἡ αἴσθησις ἐπὶ τοῦ αὐτοῦ, οἷον χολῆς
ὅτι πικρὰ καὶ ξανθή (οὐ γὰρ δὴ ἑτέρας γε τὸ εἰπεῖν ὅτι ἄμφω ἕν)·

Aristotle's example is perception of what is sweet by sight:

[In the case of our] perception of what is sweet by vision … [w]e
have a sense for each of the two qualities [e.g., white and sweet],
in virtue of which, when they happen to meet *in one sensible
object* [e.g., milk], we are aware of both *contemporaneously*. (*DA*
425a22-24, my emphasis)

οὕτω γὰρ ἔσται ὥσπερ νῦν τῇ ὄψει τὸ γλυκὺ
αἰσθανόμεθα…ἀμφοῖν ἔχοντες τυγχάνομεν αἴσθησιν, ᾗ ὅταν
συμπέσωσιν ἅμα γνωρίζομεν.

Incidental perception of the sweet by vision happens when the white
and the sweet are perceived through vision *at the same time*. Thus, generalizing, incidental perception requires simultaneous perception of
modally different qualities. It has a second requirement as well: that
the perceptible qualities pertaining to different modalities *belong to
the same object*—e.g., white and sweet to milk.[10] The sweetness perceived by sight is the sweetness of the milk, whose whiteness is seen at
the same time. Thus in perceiving the white, sight thereby perceives
incidentally what is sweet.[11] This raises the question of whether the
perceiver needs be aware that the white and the sweet are two qualities of the same object. It seems that to be aware that she is perceiving incidentally (e.g., the sweet through sight), the perceiver must be
aware that the two perceptible qualities belong to the same object. So,
how does the perceiver become aware of this? Aristotle writes:

The senses perceive each other's special objects incidentally;
not because the percipient sense is this or that special sense,

but because *all form a unity*: this incidental perception takes place whenever *sense* is directed at one and the same moment to two disparate qualities in one and the same object (e.g. to the bitterness and the yellowness of bile); *the assertion of the identity of both cannot be the act of either of the senses.* (*DA* 425a30–b2; my emphasis)

τὰ δ' ἀλλήλων ἴδια κατὰ συμβεβηκὸς αἰσθάνονται αἱ αἰσθήσεις, οὐχ ᾗ αὐταί, ἀλλ' ᾗ μία, ὅταν ἅμα γένηται ἡ αἴσθησις ἐπὶ τοῦ αὐτοῦ, οἷον χολῆς ὅτι πικρὰ καὶ ξανθή (οὐ γὰρ δὴ ἑτέρας γε τὸ εἰπεῖν ὅτι ἄμφω ἕν).

It is not any one of the special senses that can discern that the two perceptible qualities belong to the same object, because no special sense has access to more than one type of perceptible quality of any object. Which sense, then, is Aristotle referring to in this passage (l. 425b1)? It must be different from both sight and taste, and, generalizing, from any one of the special senses. Hence, some further mechanism is required to give the perceiver the information that the two perceptible qualities belong to the same object (ὅτι ἄμφω ἕν, 425b2–3), that for example the bitter is the yellow. In the passage under discussion Aristotle says that it is the sense that is constituted of the special senses operating *qua* one that detects the oneness of the yellow and the bitter. This is crucial, because the coincidence of the yellow with the bitter is not perceptually accessible to the special senses, but *is* accessible to the sense they constitute together. Hence, the sense the special senses constitute, the *common sense*, can detect *more* than they can individually, even if it is constituted by them and relies *totally* on the input they provide. If the common sense can perform more functions than the special senses, it follows that it has more powers than the senses individually have. But how do the senses, all of them acting *qua one*, perceive the oneness of an object, if none of the special senses through which the world is perceived can?[12]

4.4 PERCEPTION OF THE COMMON SENSIBLES

In addition to the special sensibles, Aristotle acknowledges a further set of objects of perception that he calls the *common sensibles*. (The meaning of 'common' in this context will be explicated shortly). They are introduced in book II of the *De Anima* thus: 'Common sensibles are movement, rest, number, figure, magnitude' (418a17–18).[13] With respect to the perception of the common sensibles, Aristotle holds that while they aren't special sensibles of any of the five senses—'these are not special to any one sense', (418a18–19)—there is no special sense dedicated to the common sensibles either. He writes that 'it is clearly impossible that there should be a special sense for any one of the common sensibles (e.g. movement)' (*DA* 425a20–21; see also 425a14). So, how are the common sensibles perceived? They too require the operation of the common sense, as I will argue in this section.

The special senses must have access to the common sensibles, otherwise the common sensibles would not be perceived at all, as they lack their own special sense. Aristotle first makes a reductive move, by saying that the perception of all the common sensibles is achieved by the perception of the special sensibles, the perception of movement, and the perception of continuity:

For, all these [common sensibles] we perceive [1] by movement (e.g. magnitude by movement) and therefore also figure (for figure is a species of magnitude), what is at rest by the absence of movement; number is perceived [2a] by the negation of continuity, and [2b] by the special sensibles; for each sense perceives one class of sensible objects. (*DA* 425a16–20)

ταῦτα γὰρ πάντα [κινήσει] αἰσθανόμεθα, οἷον μέγεθος κινήσει (ὥστε καὶ σχῆμα· μέγεθος γάρ τι τὸ σχῆμα), τὸ δ' ἠρεμοῦν τῷ μὴ κινεῖσθαι, ὁ δ' ἀριθμὸς τῇ ἀποφάσει τοῦ συνεχοῦς, καὶ τοῖς ἰδίοις (ἐκάστη γὰρ ἓν αἰσθάνεται αἴσθησις)·

We then want to know: how is movement perceived? And how is continuity? As to movement, Aristotle writes: 'There are certain kinds of movement which are perceptible both by touch and by sight' (*DA* 418a19–20).[14] This claim might be read in different ways. Is Aristotle saying, by means of the example of movement, that each common sensible is perceptible by *each one* of the special senses? Or is he claiming that each common sensible is perceptible by *more than one* special sense? Or that a common sensible is perceptible by *all the senses operating together* (i.e., doing something in common)? Or that each common sensible is perceptible by *more than one special sense operating together with others*? Aristotle's claim that certain kinds of movement are perceptible by touch and by sight (for example, the movement of a drop of rain on one's hand can be perceived by sight and touch) makes the second reading, that each common sensible is perceptible by more than one special sense, more plausible than the other three. That not all movements are perceptible by sight also follows from experience that would have been evident to Aristotle (for example, the movement of the wind cannot be seen directly, even if one can see its effects—e.g., seeing the shuffling of the leaves). Additionally the proposed reading is the one that fits the Greek text best.

So, for Aristotle the common sensibles are such that they are *somehow* perceptible by more than one sense. He however appears to vacillate between saying that the special senses perceive, with no qualifications, the common sensibles (in Book II of the *De Anima*), and that the special senses perceive them *only incidentally* (in Book III of the *De Anima*). If shape is detected through sight and through touch, do we perceive visible shape and tactile shape as different sensibles? If not, how is it then possible to perceive visible-tactile-shape, since none of the relevant senses can cross over into the domain of the other senses so as to perceive the whole multimodal sensible? (The reason why no sense can 'cross over' the domain of another sense is the principle, discussed in chapter 2, that for Aristotle there is one sense for each type of sensible quality; for the type of quality individuates the sense). At *DA* 418a19–20 Aristotle says that in the case of movement, both touch and sight perceive it (unqualifiedly). Is this inconsistent with his general claim here below that the special senses perceive the common sensibles *incidentally*?

> There cannot be a special sense-organ for the common sensibles either (i.e., the objects which we perceive incidentally through this or that special sense—e.g., movement, rest, figure, magnitude, number, unity). (*DA* 425a14–16)
> ἀλλὰ μὴν οὐδὲ τῶν κοινῶν οἷόν τ' εἶναι αἰσθητήριόν τι ἴδιον, ὧν ἑκάστῃ αἰσθήσει αἰσθανόμεθα κατὰ συμβεβηκός, οἷον κινήσεως, στάσεως, σχήματος, μεγέθους, ἀριθμοῦ·

Before addressing the question of whether Aristotle's statements are consistent or not, we need to investigate how we ought to understand the incidental perception of a common sensible. Recall that a special sense perceives its own special sensible and incidentally other types of sensible, which might happen to be com-present in the same object of perception and which can be perceived by another special sense. For example, sight perceives the sweet quality of milk incidentally, by perceiving the milk's white color. If Aristotle wanted to explain the incidental perception of a common sensible on the same model as the incidental perception of a special sensible, he would have to say that sight, for example, incidentally perceives movement by perceiving a color that is compresent with the movement, which movement sight does not perceive directly, but which is perceived by another sense. Yet this other sense, which is supposed to perceive movement directly (by analogy with what happens in the case of incidental perception of the special sensibles) could not be a special sense, since if this were the case, sight too, *qua* special sense, ought to be able to perceive some common sensible directly, and not only incidentally. If this other sense cannot be a special sense, what sense would there be that perceives the common sensibles directly? The answer for Aristotle is that no special sense can perceive movement, the single sensible that is common to a moving-color and a moving-tickle (e.g., when a drop of milk trickles down our hand). The reason is that each sense can perceive its own type of sensible and not sensibles of the other senses. We are then back to the question: how are we to understand the way in which special senses incidentally perceive the common sensibles if not along the model of the way each special sense incidentally perceives the objects of the other senses? In what follows, I will argue that the special senses perceive the common sensibles incidentally, but not according to the white-sweet model of incidental perception, where both qualities belong to the same object.

I submit that each special sense neither fails to perceive a common sensible, nor succeeds. Rather, each special sense has only a *partial grasp* of the common sensibles; a special sense does not have the capacity to fully discern and identify a common sensible. As we will see shortly, a full grasp of the common sensibles is possible only in the context of all the perceptions of the common sensibles supplied by the special senses acting as one. Support for this interpretation is to be found in an interesting thought experiment Aristotle performs regarding the number of our senses: he wonders,

It might be asked why we have more senses than one. Is it to prevent a failure to apprehend the common sensibles (e.g., movement, magnitude, and number) which follow on the special sensibles? (*DA* 425b4–6, translation modified)

ζητήσειε δ' ἄν τις τίνος ἕνεκα πλείους ἔχομεν αἰσθήσεις,
ἀλλ' οὐ μίαν μόνην. ἢ ὅπως ἧττον λανθάνῃ τὰ ἀκολουθοῦντα καὶ
κοινά, οἷον κίνησις καὶ μέγεθος καὶ ἀριθμός;

From the quotation above we learn that none of the common sensi-
biles is tactile, or visual, or acoustic, etc. Rather, the common sensibles are qualities that 'follow on' or 'accompany' (ἀκολουθοῦντα,
l. 425b5) the special sensibles of the special senses (e.g., movement
accompanies color). They 'accompany' the special sensibles in two
ways. Firstly, the common sensibles are *co-instantiated* with the special sensibles (for example, colored items move, and are continuous,
and have a shape, size, and are one or more in number; and correspondingly with soft items, with sweet ones, etc.). Secondly, the
common sensibles are *perceived with* the special sensibles (e.g., we
perceive movement by perceiving a colored item that is moving).
The greater the *variety* of types of special sensible the common
sensibles are observed to accompany, the more fully we can discern what each common sensible is, and what it is not. (Crucially,
as I will explain in what follows, it is not that with a special sense
in isolation we perceive, for example, *partial* movement; rather we
perceive movement but with *limited* information about it.)

Aristotle conceives of what I call the White World thought
experiment to further explain the nature of our perception of the
common sensibles, and the sense in which they 'accompany' the
special sensibles. The experiment goes as follows:

Had we no sense but sight, and that sense no object but white,
they [*sc.* the common sensibles] would have tended to escape
our notice and everything would have merged for us into an
indistinguishable identity because of the concomitance of
color and magnitude.[15] (*DA* 425b6–9)

εἰ γὰρ ἦν ἡ ὄψις μόνη, καὶ αὕτη λευκοῦ, ἐλάνθανεν ἂν μᾶλλον
κἂν ἐδόκει ταὐτὸν εἶναι πάντα διὰ τὸ ἀκολουθεῖν ἀλλήλοις ἅμα
χρῶμα καὶ μέγεθος.

In the White World the common sensibles would accompany the
special sensibles (white objects would have movement, magnitude,
number, etc., just as they do in our world), but they would escape our
notice, and all we would perceive by our single sense would be white.
Additionally, all we would perceive would appear to us to be one,
because we would have no perceptual access to differentiating features
so as to distinguish between things. By contrast, in our world, Aristotle
argues, we can detect movement, because we can, for example, perceive differently colored items moving against their background colored items, and hence we can differentiate color from movement, etc.;
and the same for the other sense modalities. Aristotle writes:

> As it is, the fact that the common sensibles [e.g., movement] are
> given [embedded] in the objects of more than one sense [e.g.,
> in colored and hard items] reveals their distinction from each
> and all of the special sensibles. (DA 425b9–11)
> νῦν δ᾽ ἐπεὶ καὶ ἐν ἑτέρῳ αἰσθητῷ τὰ κοινὰ ὑπάρχει, δῆλον
> ποιεῖ ὅτι ἄλλο τι ἕκαστον αὐτῶν.

In sum, Aristotle's position is that when we for example see a *colored* item that is moving, we also feel by touch a *moving* item.
Each special sense takes note of the common sensible, in this case
movement; but the special senses are unable, with the information
available to each, to *fully discern* the common sensibles. Sight for
example can tell moving colors from colors at rest, but it cannot tell
that the movement of a color is *the same sensible as* the movement of
a tangible item, and it is unable to recognize movement when it is
not following on color.[16]

In conclusion, when the special senses perceive the common sensibles, each special sense has only a *partial epistemic hold* on each of the common sensibles. It follows that a special sense *neither perceives nor fails to perceive* the common sensibles. This case is not the same as the case of incidental perception of a special sensible by a special sense, where, for example, sight fails to see the sweet, which it perceives incidentally when it is co-instantiated with the white. In the present case sight does see movement in seeing a moving colored thing. After all, if the special senses did not register movement or any of the other common sensibles at all, then the common sensibles would be missed altogether by the perceiver, since there is no other vehicle of perceptual input for them than through the special senses. The special senses do perceive the common sensibles, but they discern them partially, and with varying degrees of accuracy. The full grasp of the common sensibles is a 'common perception' resulting from the working together of the special senses. To recapitulate the overall argument of this section so far: we have seen that the individual special senses are *partly* aware of the common sensibles, which are *fully* perceived[17] only when the special senses operate *as one* (and thus have additional perceptual powers). The special senses perceive the common sensibles *only incidentally* because each special sense does not discern the common sensibles as such. On the other hand, since the special senses are individually partly aware of the common sensibles, Aristotle reasonably says that the special senses can perceive the common sensibles.

The next question to address is this: how do the special senses operate as one when perceiving the common sensibles? Aristotle takes the view that, 'In the case of the common sensibles we already have a common perception [αἴσθησιν κοινήν], which is not incidental' (*DA* 425a27–28). The expression αἴσθησις κοινή at 425a27 refers to the perception of the common sensibles achieved through the special senses *acting as one*—i.e., as the common sense. But we still do not have a clear understanding of what it is for the special senses to perceive, not *qua* themselves, but *qua* one. One of the interpretative conclusions established so far is that the senses *qua* one have access to *all* the perceptual input that each of the special senses receives. This in itself makes it possible for the overall perceptual system, or common sense, to achieve cognitive tasks that are not possible for the individual special senses. I gave Aristotle's reasons why the common sense must be endowed with extra perceptual powers over and above the ones the special senses have. In what follows I will argue that the perception of the common sensibles results from the *operation* of the common sense on the perceptual content made available by the special senses. This makes Aristotle's account of the perception of the common sensibles very different from his account of the perception of the special sensibles. This result is however to be expected, in view of the fact that the common sense has no sense organ of its own, but relies for its perceptual contents on the input from the individual special senses. My proposed understanding of the workings of the perceptual system finds support in the description of the perceptual process Aristotle gives here:

> The air modifies the pupil in this or that way and the pupil transmits the modification to some third thing (and similarly in hearing), while *the ultimate point of arrival is one, a single mean, with different manners of being.* (DA 431a17–20, my emphasis)
>
> ὥσπερ δὲ ὁ ἀὴρ τὴν κόρην τοιανδὶ ἐποίησεν, αὕτη δ' ἕτερον, καὶ ἡ ἀκοὴ ὡσαύτως, τὸ δὲ ἔσχατον ἕν, καὶ μία <ἡ> μεσότης, τὸ δ' εἶναι αὐτῇ πλείω.

No common sensible is perceived through this or that special sense organ. Rather, a common sensible's causal impact on the perceiver is articulated in the alterations of the different sense organs that perceive the special sensibles that a common sensible accompanies. For example, movement will impact on the perceiver by generation of a visual perception of the color of the rolling ball, and a tangible perception of the hardness of the rolling ball, etc. These 'compartmentalized' alterations of the special senses by a common sensible come together in the common sense itself, complementing each other. It is only in the context of all the input available to the common sense that the common sensibles are properly discerned for what they are, and distinguished from their concurrent special sensibles. Thus, it is only the common sense that can discern the common sensibles *as such*, by dissociating the common sensible (e.g., movement) from all other perceptible qualities of what is moving. The common sense, and it alone, perceives movement as a single sensible. The movement the subject perceives through the common sense *via* different sense modalities is one because *it is one and the same sensible* that one perceives through two or more special senses (for instance in the case of the movement of a drop of rain on one's hand which one perceives with sight and touch). This is different from the case we have seen above of two sensibles which are one because they coincide in a third item (e.g. white and sweet in a lump of sugar), in which case, Aristotle tells us, we perceive 'two disparate qualities *in* one and the same object' (*DA* 425b1, my emphasis).

An important qualification is needed here. In claiming that the common sensibles 'accompany' the special sensibles, Aristotle is not suggesting that the common sensibles appear to the perceiver's awareness as *further* qualities when the special sensibles are perceived. For example, the number of an object is not a further sensible that the object possesses, over and above its other perceptible qualities; nor are size and shape sensibles like color or scent; nor is the object's being at rest such a sensible either.[18] The common sensibles are *constituted*, rather than *elemental*, qualitative features of objects.[19] In a sense, the common sensibles are *ways in which the special sensibles are clustered together*: ways in which the special sensibles are or behave in their spatiotemporal locations—as being at rest, or moving, or being thus distributed in space, or being continuous, or separate, etc.[20] Therefore perception of the common sensibles makes a crucial contribution towards the perceiver's awareness and identification of *objects*, rather than arrays of disjointed perceptible qualities.

Interpreters have accounted for the capacity of the common sense to detect the oneness of the object of perception in various ways, from which my interpretation departs. For example Catherine Osborne (1988) and Pavel Gregoric (2007)[21] share the view that, in Osborne's words:

> The sense *corresponds in a fundamental way* to the objects to which it is attuned, and while the individual senses are specially adapted to their own class of the proper sense-objects, the sense-faculty as a whole *is like* the total object to which it is attuned, *and it recognizes that object as a unity, in virtue of itself being such a unity* with sensitivity to all the various classes of sensible qualities that the object possesses. (1988, 444, my emphasis)

Osborne's interpretative proposal is that Aristotle posits a (primitive?) likeness (in number?) between the multimodally composed sense and the object of perception, and this is what explains the special sensitivity of the sense to objects *as wholes*, rather than disjointed perceptible qualities. But the principle that the multimodally composed sense recognizes an object as a unity because the sense itself is a unity is not unproblematic; for, by the same reasoning, the sense ought to perceive all co-occurring perceptible qualities as one, since their unity as objects is derived from the unity of the sense itself. In other words, anything that the sense perceives ought be perceived as one because what would make it one is the unity of the perceiving sense. David Charles (2000) on the other hand offers an alternative explanation by appealing to the principle of causal assimilation (becoming alike) between sense and object of perception. He writes:

> Perception would be of this one yellow, bitter object (425b1–3) provided that it was brought about, in appropriate conditions, by this one object. Causal assimilation to one cross-modal moving object explains why perception is of one such object rather than of (e.g.) one visual object and one tactile object (in which case further inference would be required to reach the discrimination of one cross-modal object). (2000, 125)

The difficulty with Charles' account is that the model of causal assimilation with respect to the special senses presupposes that the sense organ (e.g., the eye jelly) becomes *like* the perceptible quality that the sense is perceiving. But in the case of a cross-modal object, to use Charles' terminology, there is no one sense organ that perceives it (*DA* 425a14–16), and which can become like it. So the causal assimilation model cannot transfer from the case of the special sensibles to the case of the multimodal objects of perception. I will argue that our ability to perceive objects is based on our ability to perceive the common sensibles through the common sense, to which we shall come in the following section.

4.5 FROM THE PERCEPTION OF THE COMMON SENSIBLES TO THE PERCEPTION OF OBJECTS

We saw in section 4.4 that when, for example, sight perceives movement incidentally, *qua* special sense it perceives only some information about movement (e.g., its visibility); the movement might also be noisy (e.g., the sight and sound of a fly), but sight does not perceive that. This is similar to the case of a special sense perceiving the proper perceptible of another sense (e.g., sight incidentally perceiving sweet by perceiving white); white is an 'aspect' of the perceived white-sweet object, say milk, as we saw in section 4.3. There is however an important difference between the incidental perception of common sensibles and the incidental perception of a special sensible by a special sense: the visible movement that sight perceives is *the same sensible* as the movement that is also, for example, audible, or tangible; whereas the white that sight perceives is *not the same* sensible as the sweet that taste perceives. In other words, the special senses perceive incidentally the common sensibles by perceiving aspects of these sensibles; while each special sense perceives incidentally a special sensible by perceiving modally different special sensibles that are co-instantiated in the same object. So the relevant unity for the incidental perception of a common sensible is *the unity of the common sensible itself*; whereas the relevant unity for the incidental perception of special sensibles is *the unity of the object* in which these special sensibles are instantiated. This is crucial. It is the key to understanding Aristotle's explanation of how we perceive external objects as objects, as opposed to as clusters of properties: *the common sensibles are multimodal sensibles perceived directly by the common sense.*

The agent perceives a unified object by perceiving the unified common sensibles that qualify it (e.g., its shape, size, number, movement). She perceives *directly* via the common sense the multimodally unified common sensibles that qualify objects in the world. This grounds her recognition of the unity and oneness of the external object itself. Thus for example, I perceive directly via the common sense the shape of the ball I see with my eyes and feel with my hands as *one shape*; and I so can attribute the color and texture of that shape to the ball which

I thereby perceive as a single object. I emphasize that Aristotle does not say, and he need not say, that to perceive the shape of the ball the perceiver needs to first be aware that the color and texture belong to the same object. Rather, the perceiver perceives *directly* via the common sense the ball's shape, as color and texture unified in a certain spatio-temporal location. In the *Metaphysics* Aristotle remarks on the role of perception (as well as of knowledge) thus:

> Knowledge...and perception, we call *the measure of things*...because we know something by them...Evidently, then, being one in the strictest sense, if we define it according to the meaning of the word, is a measure, and especially of quantity and secondly of quality. And some things will be one if they are indivisible in quantity, and others if they are indivisible in quality. (*Met.* 1053a31–b8)
>
> καὶ τὴν ἐπιστήμην δὲ μέτρον τῶν πραγμάτων λέγομεν καὶ τὴν αἴσθησιν...ὅτι γνωρίζομέν τι αὐταῖς...ὅτι μὲν οὖν τὸ ἑνὶ εἶναι μάλιστά ἐστι κατὰ τὸ ὄνομα ἀφορίζοντι μέτρον τι, καὶ κυριώτατα τοῦ ποσοῦ, εἶτα τοῦ ποιοῦ, φανερόν· ἔσται δὲ τοιοῦτον τὸ μὲν ἂν ᾖ ἀδιαίρετον κατὰ τὸ ποσόν, τὸ δὲ ἂν κατὰ τὸ ποιόν.

The common sensibles are not indivisible in the strictest sense, any more than objects are. But the perception of the common sensibles is the measure of the oneness of objects. *The indivisibility of a common sensible 'measures' the oneness of an object.* Thus for Aristotle, the direct perception of the common sensibles grounds our awareness of unified objects (i.e., of their being one). Therefore the common sense is as cognitively primitive a sense as its constituent special senses.

In conclusion, in the interpretation I am proposing the common sense (i.e., the special senses 'not *qua* themselves, but *qua* one') (*DA* 425a31), is unified and has access to much more perceptual input than any of the special senses has. This informationally enriched context allows the perceiver, via the common sense, to be aware of the common sensibles (and hence of *objects*). For this to happen, it must be possible that the perceiver is aware of the input from any one special sense *in the same unified perceptual content* as the input from any other special sense. This is a difficult problem for Aristotle. An account of the composition and operation of the overall perceptual system is required. In different parts of his work Aristotle offers a variety of different metaphysical explanations of the perceptual system as a whole, which will be examined in chapters 6 and 7.

CONCLUDING REMARKS

In this chapter we examined the considerations that lead Aristotle to posit the existence of a common sense over and above the five special ones. There is a variety of perceptual operations that the five senses cannot perform, for they all presuppose unified modally complex perceptual content. These are simultaneous perception of different perceptible qualities at once; incidental perception of a perceptible quality with a sense that is not its special one; perceptual discrimination between different perceptible qualities; cross-modal binding of different qualities in one content; and finally, direct perception of modally complex sensibles (i.e., perceptible qualities that essentially fall under the remit of more than one sense at once, and cannot be perceived by any special sense operating individually). Aristotle is thus driven to enrich his theory of perception with a common sense, whose metaphysics will be examined in chapters 6 and 7.

APPENDIX: VARIETIES OF INCIDENTAL PERCEPTION

Aristotle investigates in his work three cases of incidental perception, which are quite different from each other. This appendix teases them apart, for the fact that Aristotle uses the same wording to refer to these three different cases might generate some confusion in the reader. Aristotle talks about incidental perception when a special sense perceives incidentally the special sensible of another sense. This type of incidental perception requires simultaneity of perception of the two modally different perceptible qualities belonging to the same object. We examined it in section 4.3. In addition, Aristotle reckons that the special senses can perceive incidentally not only the special sensible of another sense, but also the common sensibles (e.g., movement, shape, size). These are perceptible qualities of objects that do not fall under the remit of any of the special senses; but nevertheless the special senses perceive them, incidentally. We discussed this case in section 4.5. Both the first and the second case of incidental perception are relevant to the study of how Aristotle accounts for complex perceptual content and ultimately the perception of objects, as we saw in section 4.6. There is also a third case: Aristotle calls 'incidental' the awareness of a non-perceptible quality (e.g., being Cleon's son) that the agent may gain by perceiving a perceptible quality (e.g., white) *via* a special sense. Aristotle talks about it in the following terms:

> We have a sense for each of the two qualities [white and sweet], in virtue of which when they happen to be in one sensible object we are aware of both simultaneously. If not [i.e., if we were not aware of *both* qualities simultaneously] our perception would always be incidental, as for example in the perception of Cleon's son, where we perceive him not as Cleon's son

but as white, and the white thing which we really perceive happens to be Cleon's son. (*DA* 425a23–27)

τοῦτο δ' ὅτι ἀμφοῖν ἔχοντες τυγχάνομεν αἴσθησιν, ἢ ὅταν συμπέσωσιν ἅμα γνωρίζομεν. εἰ δὲ μή, οὐδαμῶς ἂν ἀλλ' ἢ κατὰ συμβεβηκὸς ἠσθανόμεθα (οἷον τὸν Κλέωνος υἱὸν οὐχ ὅτι Κλέωνος υἱός, ἀλλ' ὅτι λευκός, τούτῳ δὲ συμβέβηκεν υἱῷ Κλέωνος εἶναι)·

In the case here described the perceiver incidentally perceives the son of Cleon by perceiving through sight the white object which is the son of Cleon. What is interesting about this example is that one cannot perceive the property of 'being the son of'; but since one can perceive the white, and the white is Cleon's son, one thereby incidentally perceives by sight the son of Cleon. In this example, it is explicit that sight has access to the otherwise imperceptible property 'being the son of Cleon' in virtue of the fact that what sight perceives, the white, is the son of Cleon. Aristotle makes a similar point elsewhere in the *De Anima*:

> We speak of an incidental object of sense where for example the white object which we see is the son of Diares; here because "being the son of Diares" is incidental to the white, we speak of the son of Diares as being (incidentally) perceived or seen by us. (*DA* 418a20–23)
>
> κατὰ συμβεβηκὸς δὲ λέγεται αἰσθητόν, οἷον εἰ τὸ λευκὸν εἴη Διάρους υἱός· κατὰ συμβεβηκὸς γὰρ τούτου αἰσθάνεται, ὅτι τῷ λευκῷ συμβέβηκε τοῦτο, οὗ αἰσθάνεται.

In conclusion, we saw above that we can perceive the white and sweet simultaneously, where, generalizing, simultaneous perception requires the perception of modally different qualities at the same time. Aristotle is interested in the cases where the simultaneously perceived qualities pertaining to different modalities belong to the same object (e.g., white and sweet to milk). His interest in isolating these cases is that they give rise to incidental perception, which does not arise in the case of mere simultaneous perception of properties that do not belong to the same object. Aristotle then moves to incidental perception of the imperceptible. We can perceive objects with multifarious properties, perceptible or not, which are incidentally perceived by our perceiving the perceptible properties of these objects. He calls all these cases too 'incidental' perception.

Notes

1. My remarks are of course not intended to suggest that for Aristotle there are many centers of perceptual awareness (i.e., as many as the special senses). There is only one center of awareness, the perceptual system as a whole, which gathers perceptual content through the special senses.
2. The one-to-one correspondence principle applies to the special as well as the common sense. The common ground for the application to the principle to both is that *the activity of a single power at an instant is a single type of activity.* The correspondence follows from this. Each sense is a perceptual power, with a distinctive type of activity that defines it.
3. As we will see in the concluding chapter, Aristotle's final solution to these problems is that the common sense is a single perceptual system, which does not have different *perceiving parts,* but different *implementations of one and the same perceptual function.* How are the perceptual powers so composed to achieve such unity? Aristotle's breakthrough is to recognize that the perceptual system is unified, not bottom-up, but top-down. The inclusion of various simultaneous awarenesses into a single complex perceptual content does not result from the co-instantiation of changes (activations) in a single sense organ. (The common sense does not even have a sense organ). It is rather a result of a *functional* unification of the activity of the various special sense organs. The perceptual system is not unified physically but functionally, where the activity of the various sense organs realizes one and the same perceptual function of the subject. Is this solution a deviation from the one-to-one correspondence principle? It is not. The one-to-one correspondence principle still holds. The perceptual system is so bound together physically that the sense organs implement the same perceptual functionality. This is the unity

of the common sense, where hearing, seeing, tasting, etc., are different ways of serving, each and all together, the same perceptual function. These issues are examined in chapters 6 and 7 and in the overall Conclusions.

4. Possibly Aristotle gives emphasis to the problem of accounting for simultaneous perception of multiples special sensibles (of one or different types) in one complex perceptual content, because in a way this makes the challenge even more perspicuous: even if a sense was sensitive to more than one type of sensible quality, and could enable the agent to, for example, see and hear, it would still be challenging to explain how it can be activated simultaneously by two different types of activities at once. See the footnote immediately preceding this one for a brief account of how Aristotle addresses the problem.

5. As P. Gregoric (2007, 3, note 1) reports, this is suggested by the use of διανοεῖν at 185a4, 9, b7; ἀναλογίζεσθαι at 186a11, c3; and συλλογισμός, 186d3. At 187a2–8 Plato even proposes to call the process δοξάζειν. Further, at 184d1–5 Socrates commends the idea of seeing with the soul 'by means of' the eyes, rather than 'with the eyes' (according to the latter view, it would be like several senses were sitting in us as in a wooden horse).

6. Gregoric (2007, 6) notes that '[t]he far-reaching consequences of this premise have been rightly emphasized by Sorabji (1992, 196; 1993, 7–20)'. Sorabji stresses that Aristotle, due to his denial of reasoning and belief to animals, must account for their abilities (for example to connect a scene and a direction) by assigning predicative powers to perception, thence expanding its content 'beyond the rudimentary level to which Plato had reduced it' in *Theaetetus*. Accordingly, 'Aristotle does three things. First, he tidies up the concept of reason (*logos*) in the direction of the *Theaetetus*, by bringing all of *doxa* (belief) under it (*DA* 428a19–24, see below). Secondly, he gives to perceptual content one of the most massive expansions in the history of Greek philosophy. Thirdly, despite expanding the role of perception, he maintains Plato's denial that perception involves belief or is a function of reason' (Sorabji 1992, 196).

7. Additionally, Aristotle attributes to each special sense a wider range of discriminatory powers, even powers that are not associated with specific objects of sense—such as the power of sight to detect light or darkness. See *DA* 425b21. See also *DA* 422a20–31:

> Just as sight apprehends both what is visible and what is invisible (ὥσπερ δὲ καὶ ἡ ὄψις ἐστὶ τοῦ τε ὁρατοῦ καὶ τοῦ ἀοράτου) (for darkness is invisible and yet it is discriminated by sight; so, in a different way, what is over-brilliant), and as hearing apprehends both sound and silence, of which the one is audible and the other inaudible, and also over-loud sound or violent sound as sight does what is bright, etc.

8. There is no evidence in the texts that Aristotle offered an explanation of the perceiver's *simultaneous* awareness; but it is plausible to think that he would have had something to say about this issue, given the sophisticated understanding he shows of perception—see for example *DA* 425b20–22.

9. In what follows I shall use 'indirect' and 'indirectly' as synonyms of 'incidental' and 'incidentally'.

10. The fact that Aristotle specifies that there is incidental perception *only* when white and sweet are com-present in the same object marks the difference with mere simultaneous perception, when one may happen to perceive the white and the sweet in different objects, at the same time.

11. Aristotle's claim that the special senses perceive each other's special sensibles incidentally is a major difficulty for Corcilius' and Gregoric's view that 'it is the perceptual capacity of the soul that receives all kinds of sensible forms without matter. The five special senses are *just names* for its ability to receive five different kinds of sensible forms' (2011, 112, my emphasis)AU: X-ref source in References is dated 2010.. If the five senses are just names of the same ability of the soul to perceive, how can there be incidental perception, which Aristotle unequivocally claims there is? See K. Corcilius K. and P. Gregoric, 'Separability vs. Difference: Parts and Capacities of the Soul in Aristotle', *Oxford Studies in Ancient Philosophy*, 39 (2010).

12. For a discussion of all cases of incidental perception Aristotle considers, see the appendix at the end of this chapter.

13. Ross (1961, 239) refers to the inclusion of other objects as 'common': SS 437a3–17 also mentions roughness and smoothness, and *Mem.* 450a9–10, a lapse of time. Further, Ross traces back the origin of the doctrine to *Theat.* 158a8–186a1, while warning that 'number is the only object found both in Plato's list and Aristotle's and that Plato ascribes awareness of such objects to the soul and not to sensation.

R. Polanski (2007, 256) remarks:

Roughness, smoothness, sharpness, bluntness, and time are offered as common sensibles in *De Sensu* 442b5–7 and *De Memoria* 450a9–10 and 451a16–17). Though Aristotle does not mention direction or place as a common sensible, each of the five senses is cognizant of directionality, and hence he allows that we can be mistaken about where the pale thing or the sounding thing is (see 418a15–16).... Perhaps the reason he does not refer explicitly to other common sensibles is that they can be understood in terms of the five types named.

14. καὶ γὰρ ἁφῇ κίνησίς τίς ἐστιν αἰσθητὴ καὶ ὄψει

15. This is all Aristotle says, but for the desired conclusion to follow, we need to complete his thought experiment by assuming not only that white is the only

color we could see, but that white (of a single hue, saturation, and intensity) is the only color in a world where there is no brightness or shadow, etc.; or assume that all colors are seen by us as white, and that there are no patches of colorlessness in the world, which would allow us to see movement, magnitude, shape, number, etc.

16. Interestingly, Aristotle's White World thought experiment in the *De Anima* is very similar to an argument in Plato's *Theaetetus* concerning the inadequate individuation of an entity. In the *Theaetetus*, Plato argues that one does not have knowledge of a syllable if one can correctly identify the syllable in one context but not in another context:

> When a person at the time of learning writes the name of Theaetetus, and thinks that he ought to write and does write Th and E; but, again, meaning to write the name of Theodorus, thinks that he ought to write and does write T and E — can we suppose that he knows the first syllable of your two names? (*Theaetetus* 207e–208a)

In the case Plato considers, the speller fails to recognize that the syllable 'The' is the same in its two occurrences in two different names. Because of this failure, Plato argues that the speller does not have knowledge of the syllable 'The'. It is not the case that the person has no cognitive contact at all with the syllable 'The'. In fact she spells it correctly in writing the first name, Theaetetus. Rather, the speller has only *partial* knowledge of the syllable, because she identifies it correctly in some occurrences, but fails to identify it in other occurrences. Aristotle's argument in the White World thought experiment is very similar to Plato's, in that in Aristotle's thought experiment the perceiver does see the moving white items, among all the other white items; but she cannot tell the moving items apart from the ones at rest. Thus in the White World, Aristotle says, movement 'would have tended to escape our notice and everything would have merged for us into an indistinguishable identity because of the concomitance of color and magnitude' (*DA* 425b7–9). The case is similar to Plato's syllable case: there the person spells 'The' correctly in writing one name, but in writing the other name she does not recognize it is the same syllable; in the White World thought experiment, she sees the movement, but cannot recognize it is different from size and shape, and hence from rest.

17. That is, full information about them is acquired.

18. This is also why Aristotle says that we perceive magnitude and figure by perceiving movement, and rest by perceiving the absence of movement; while we perceive number by the negation of continuity (*DA* 425a16–19).

19. It is important to bear in mind that on Aristotle's way of thinking, the common sensibles are *not* constructed *by abstraction* from the contributions of

the special senses. Rather, they are perceptually *'revealed'* to the perceiver in the context of all the perceptual input which reaches the common sense.

20. This is why Aristotle says that 'number is perceived by the negation of continuity and *by the special sensibles*' (*DA* 425a19; my emphasis). How is number perceived by perceiving the special sensibles? It is found in the way the special sensibles cluster together.

21. See Gregoric (2007, 138).

Chapter 5

Unity of Subject, Operation, Content, and Time

INTRODUCTION

Aristotle reckons that there are a number of perceptual operations that are essential for a full perceptual grasp of the world and its 'furniture', but cannot be performed by the special senses in isolation—we examined them in chapter 4. They all require the possibility of complex perceptual content, the nature of which is investigated in this chapter. Complex perceptual content cannot be what any of the special senses is aware of, for each sense is defined by its sensitivity to a narrow domain of *special* perceptible qualities (sight to colors, etc.). Thus Aristotle posits a *common sense*, that gathers complex perceptual content and can operate on it, enabling the perceiver to perform perceptual discrimination, cross-modal binding, etc. This chapter examines the constraints Aristotle places on the common sense for the performance of such operations. The common sense is a *sui generis* sense, not only because it does not have its own sense organ, but also because it is individuated differently from the special senses. These are individuated by the type of perceptible quality they are sensitive to; by contrast the common sense is individuated by the type of perceptual *content* it is aware of. Finally, it is clear that the common sense needs to have a unity of its own, in order to satisfy the above requirements and be able to perform the perceptual operations Aristotle ascribes to it. These considerations motivate a 'robust' interpretation of the common sense, whose metaphysics will be investigated in chapters 6 and 7.

5.1 PHYSICAL CONSTRAINTS ON COMPLEX PERCEPTUAL CONTENT

We saw in chapter 4 that simultaneous perception, incidental perception and perception of the so-called common sensibles require the operation of the common sense, as they cannot happen by means of any of the special senses. There are further perceptual operations that point toward the same conclusion, as they presuppose that the perceiver is aware of multiple instances of special sensibles at once, in a single unified perceptual content. These operations are *perceptual discrimination* (within one sense modality, for example telling yellow from green; and also across sense modalities, for example telling whiteness from sweetness); and *cross-modal binding* (e.g., perceiving a sweet white item, such as when drinking milk). On the other hand, as we saw in chapter 2, a key background assumption for Aristotle is that the reception of each perceptible quality generates a causal 'movement' or alteration within the sense through which it is perceived. The perceptible quality's impact on the sense organ gives rise to the perceptual content in the perceiver's experience. There is a one-to-one correspondence between an instance of a perceptible quality, the causal change it brings about in the sense organ, and the perceptual content which results. For example Aristotle claims that,

> In one and the same faculty the perception actualized at any single moment is necessarily one, only one stimulation or exertion

of a single faculty being possible at a single instant... Hence, it is not possible to perceive two distinct objects simultaneously with one and the same sense. (*Sense and Sensibilia* 447b17–19)

    ἀλλὰ κατὰ μίαν δύναμιν καὶ ἄτομον χρόνον μίαν ἀνάγκη εἶναι τὴν ἐνέργειαν· μιᾶς γὰρ ἡ εἰσάπαξ μία χρῆσις καὶ κίνησις... οὐκ ἄρα ἐνδέχεται δυοῖν ἅμα αἰσθάνεσθαι τῇ μιᾷ αἰσθήσει.

The restriction to one stimulation or exertion at each moment in time is driven not by mental, but by *physical* order considerations. The challenge that Aristotle faces in accounting for complex perceptual content is thus that:

> It is impossible that what is one and the same [i.e., a sense] should be moved at one and the same time with contrary movements in so far as it is undivided, and in an undivided moment of time. For if what is sweet be the quality perceived, it moves the sense... in this determinate way, while what is bitter moves it in a contrary way, and what is white in a different way. (*DA* 426b29–427a9)
>
>   ἀλλὰ μὴν ἀδύνατον ἅμα τὰς ἐναντίας κινήσεις κινεῖσθαι τὸ αὐτὸ ᾖ ἀδιαίρετον, καὶ ἐν ἀδιαιρέτῳ χρόνῳ. εἰ γὰρ γλυκύ, ὡδὶ κινεῖ τὴν αἴσθησιν... τὸ δὲ πικρὸν ἐναντίως, καὶ τὸ λευκὸν ἑτέρως.

One and the same physical item cannot suffer contrary changes, or even different (and incompatible) changes. This is relevant to perception because for Aristotle we become aware of a perceptible quality (e.g., of blue) as the sense organ of sight somehow becomes affected by the external quality, resulting in its becoming like it.[1] Aristotle states the problem explicitly:

> It is not possible to be at once white and black, and therefore it must also be impossible for a thing [e.g., a sense organ] to

be affected at one and the same moment by the forms of both.
(*DA* 427a5–9)

οὐχ οἷόν τε ἅμα λευκὸν καὶ μέλαν εἶναι, ὥστ' οὐδὲ τὰ εἴδη
πάσχειν αὐτῶν.

This argument aims at generating an aporetic stance regarding the
possibility of a complex perceptual content in the experience of a
single subject. The physical impossibility of a double-effect on the
sense organ (e.g., by white and black at once) corresponds to the
(supposed) mental impossibility of double-awareness: it is impossible for one to be aware of, for example, white and black at the same
time, since the sense organ of sight cannot be stimulated by both
perceptible qualities at the same time. The number of the mental
appears to follow the number of the physical. Different perceptible
qualities stimulate the relevant sense organ differently, giving rise
to distinct perceptual contents. On the principle that the number
of the mental follows the number of the physical sensibles, for two
perceptible qualities to be perceived in a single content Aristotle
must explain how the different physical alterations they generate
in the sense organ(s) can be unified. Their unification seems *prima
facie* impossible: in the case of multiple perceptible qualities of the
same type because they bring about mutually incompatible alterations in one sense organ; and in the case of multiple perceptible
qualities of different types, because they are physically distributed
in different sense organs. Aristotle needs to think of novel types
of physical oneness, to explain the oneness of complex perceptual
content. At its heart, the difficulty that Aristotle has to resolve here
is not just to combine complexity with unity, which he has successfully achieved in his account of substance in the *Metaphysics*
and elsewhere. It is also to mirror the complexity of the physical
(the alterations of the sense organs) onto the complexity of the
mental (the articulated perceptual content). Assuming that such

unification of modal inputs into complex contents is possible, according to what principles and processes does this unification take place?

5.2 THE UNITY OF SUBJECT, OF OPERATION, AND OF TIME

Aristotle holds that perceptions involving complex content must be performed by a single subject,[2] at one and the same time. There cannot be two time intervals, a now and a later, for the discrimination, for example, of white from sweet to occur; nor can the discrimination be the exercise of two different powers (e.g., the visual-power-activity and the taste-power-activity). He writes:

[D]iscrimination between white and sweet cannot be effected by two agencies which remain separate; both the qualities discriminated must be present to something that is one and single...What says that two things are different must be one; for sweet is different from white. Therefore what asserts this difference must be self-identical, and as what asserts, so also what thinks or perceives. That it is not possible by means of two agencies which remain separate to discriminate two objects which are separate, is therefore obvious...Both the discriminating power and the time of its exercise must be one and undivided. (*DA* 426b17–29, translation slightly modified)

οὔτε δὴ κεχωρισμένοις ἐνδέχεται κρίνειν ὅτι ἕτερον τὸ γλυκὺ τοῦ λευκοῦ, ἀλλὰ δεῖ ἑνί τινι ἄμφω δῆλα εἶναι...δεῖ δὲ τὸ ἓν λέγειν ὅτι ἕτερον· ἕτερον γὰρ τὸ γλυκὺ τοῦ λευκοῦ· λέγει ἄρα τὸ αὐτό· ὥστε ὡς λέγει, οὕτω καὶ νοεῖ καὶ αἰσθάνεται—ὅτι μὲν οὖν οὐχ οἷόν τε κεχωρισμένοις κρίνειν τὰ κεχωρισμένα, δῆλον...ὥστε ἀχώριστον καὶ ἐν ἀχωρίστῳ χρόνῳ.

This passage describes the metaphysical problem that needs to be resolved in order to establish that a perceiver has the power to discriminate between, for example, white and sweet. First, although white and sweet are perceived through sight and taste, and are perceived contemporaneously, the discrimination of the two sensibles cannot be achieved through either of the two senses. On the one hand, since sight has no direct access to the sweet item, and taste no direct access to the white, their parallel simultaneous operation will be that *of two distinct agencies*; white is perceived through one of them, and sweet through the other. The two agencies have two distinct perceptual contents, unrelated to one another, and so discrimination between the two sensibles seems to be impossible. Even if the two perceptual agencies, sight and taste, belong to the same perceiver, it still does not follow that perceptual discrimination can take place by the simultaneous perception of the two sensibles. It is not simply that the same agent must be aware of them. It is that the agent must be aware of them in the same act of awareness in order to discriminate between them. Aristotle's justification of this claim, essential to his account of the perceptual system, is not based on metaphysical arguments, but on common sense reasoning. He writes that 'both the qualities discriminated must be apparent to something that is one and single' (*DA* 426b17–18). That is, a comparison must be based on the possibility of considering all items involved in the same 'viewing' context. This is a principle that we observe in everyday life when evaluating or selecting: the context of comparison must be common, and they must all be viewable and viewed within it. This requirement is related to the unity of time one: there cannot be two time intervals, perceiving white now and sweet later, for the discrimination of white from sweet to occur; the two must be compared in a single 'viewing', a single perceptual awareness. Nor, for the same reason, can the discrimination be the exercise of two different powers, for example the visual-power-activity and the taste-power-activity. The act of awareness of the discrimination must not be divided in any way. Both the agent and the content can be complex, comprising the exercise of more than one power; but the discriminating activity must be numerically one and undivided.

5.3 NO DUPLICATION OF PERCEPTUAL AWARENESS

The unity of subject and unity of operation, in order to achieve unified awareness of visual, auditory, tangible, etc. inputs in a single complex perceptual content, excludes the theoretical possibility that operations such as perceptual discrimination, cross-modal binding, etc. are performed by a cluster of centers of perceptual awareness. Of immediate relevance to the view that there is only one center of awareness in perception is Aristotle's No Double Vision Argument in the *De Anima*.[3] The argument runs as follows:

> Since it is through sense that we are aware that we are seeing or hearing, it must be either by sight that we are aware of seeing, or by some sense other than sight. But the sense that gives us this new sensation must perceive both sight and its object, namely color: so that *either there will be two senses both percipient of the same sensible object,* or the sense must be percipient of itself. Further, even if the sense which perceives sight were different from sight, we must either fall into an infinite regress, or we must somewhere assume a sense which is aware of itself. If so, we ought to do this in the first case. (*DA* 425b12–18, my emphasis)
>
> Ἐπεὶ δ' αἰσθανόμεθα ὅτι ὁρῶμεν καὶ ἀκούομεν, ἀνάγκη ἢ τῇ ὄψει αἰσθάνεσθαι ὅτι ὁρᾷ, ἢ ἑτέρᾳ. ἀλλ' ἡ αὐτὴ ἔσται τῆς ὄψεως

καὶ τοῦ ὑποκειμένου χρώματος, ὥστε ἢ δύο τοῦ αὐτοῦ ἔσονται
ἢ αὐτὴ αὑτῆς. ἔτι δ' εἰ καὶ ἑτέρα εἴη ἡ τῆς ὄψεως αἴσθησις, ἢ εἰς
ἄπειρον εἰσιν ἢ αὐτή τις ἔσται αὑτῆς· ὥστ' ἐπὶ τῆς πρώτης τοῦτο
ποιητέον.

In relation to our investigation into what accounts for the unity
of the perceptual system, this argument gives only Aristotle's
initial position. It does not tell us *how* a sense could be aware of
itself. Its conclusion is that if one wants to account for perceptual self-awareness, by exercising ontological parsimony and
not multiplying senses, one may just as well attribute the power
of self-awareness to the special senses themselves. (I shall give
my interpretation of how Aristotle explains how self-awareness
is achieved in chapter 7). For the moment I want to highlight an
important principle that the No Double Vision Argument mentions: that there cannot be two senses both percipient of the same
sensible at the same time (*DA* 425b14–17). This principle has gen-
erality of application. It regulates not only the perception of the
special sensible, but also cases of nonstandard perception such as
perceptual self-awareness and perception of darkness (see below),
and perceptual discrimination of different sensibles at one time.
It is a fundamental principle for the very structure of the perceptual faculty, functioning as a norm of ontological economy. In the
present context it points toward each of the special senses having
the capacity of self-awareness—rather than there being a dedicated meta-sense of self-awareness following on each of the special
senses to facilitate awareness of that sense's operation. The significance of the principle for Aristotle becomes even clearer once we
come to investigate the difficulties that Aristotle himself identifies for his own theory, as arising from that principle. Yet, even
when encountering such difficulties, Aristotle does not abandon
or revise the principle; rather he tries to address the difficulties and

mitigate their impact. Here is what he writes, immediately following the quotation above:

> This [i.e., the principle that a sense will be aware of its own operation] presents a difficulty: if to perceive by sight is just to see, and what is seen is color (or the colored), then if we are to see that which sees, that which sees originally must be colored. It is clear therefore that 'to perceive by sight' has more than one meaning; for even when we are not seeing, it is by sight that we discriminate darkness from light, though not in the same way as we distinguish one color from another. That is why even when the sensible objects are gone the sensings and imaginings continue to exist in the sense-organs. (*DA* 425b18–26)
>
> ἔχει δ' ἀπορίαν· εἰ γὰρ τὸ τῇ ὄψει αἰσθάνεσθαί ἐστιν ὁρᾶν, ὁρᾶται δὲ χρῶμα ἢ τὸ ἔχον, εἰ ὄψεταί τις τὸ ὁρῶν, καὶ χρῶμα ἕξει τὸ ὁρῶν πρῶτον. φανερὸν τοίνυν ὅτι οὐχ ἓν τὸ τῇ ὄψει αἰσθάνεσθαι· καὶ γὰρ ὅταν μὴ ὁρῶμεν, τῇ ὄψει κρίνομεν καὶ τὸ σκότος καὶ τὸ φῶς, ἀλλ' οὐχ ὡσαύτως. ἔτι δὲ καὶ τὸ ὁρῶν ἔστιν ὡς κεχρωμάτισται· τὸ γὰρ αἰσθητήριον δεκτικὸν τοῦ αἰσθητοῦ ἄνευ τῆς ὕλης ἕκαστον· διὸ καὶ ἀπελθόντων τῶν αἰσθητῶν ἔνεισιν αἰσθήσεις καὶ φαντασίαι ἐν τοῖς αἰσθητηρίοις.

On the hypothesis that each special sense is endowed with the additional capacity to be aware of its own operation, the difficulty that follows is that if each sense is defined by the special objects that can be perceived through it, then each sense must be the same in kind as its own special objects. So, for sight to be aware of its own operation, that it is seeing the colored, sight itself must be colored. This is the difficulty that seems to arise. Immediately Aristotle responds with the solution that each sense can do more than perceive its own special sensibles. Thus, sight can also tell that it is dark, where darkness, here assumed to be lack of light, is not a color. This does not indicate that there is a different capacity or power other than sight, which can perform these functions, but only that sight's range of objects is wider than color. Interestingly, having just explained how the difficulty might be addressed, Aristotle then goes back on his proposed solution by indicating that maybe it is not needed. He makes the point that the senses are indeed in possession of the special sensibles they can each detect:

> Further, in a sense even that which sees is colored; for in each case the sense-organ is capable of receiving the sensible object without its matter. (*DA* 425b23–24)
>
> ἔτι δὲ καὶ τὸ ὁρῶν ἔστιν ὡς κεχρωμάτισται· τὸ γὰρ αἰσθητήριον δεκτικὸν τοῦ αἰσθητοῦ ἄνευ τῆς ὕλης ἕκαστον.

The point Aristotle makes and the position he thus proposes are clearly not motivated by how the senses appear to be (our nose is not itself smelly, our ears not noisy, etc.). It rather follows from Aristotle's account of the operation of the senses. If a sense receives, through its medium, the perceptible qualities that are its special sensibles, and if this is what the sense is able to detect, the sense ought be able to detect itself as somehow having those perceptible qualities when it has received them. There are difficulties with this move, which must be why Aristotle does not revoke the solution he has just offered of each sense having a wide scope of operation, and why he does not pursue the implications of the new position of each sense possessing its special sensible. One of its implications is that there should be a vantage point of observation for the sense to observe itself in operation. But it is not at all obvious how the sense organ can function, so to speak, reflexively. Secondly, Aristotle has clearly explained that on his account the sense organ does *not* receive and take on perceptible qualities in the way that the object perceived possesses such qualities.[4] I take Aristotle's point at lines 425b23–24 to be only speculative.

In conclusion what the No Double Vision argument contributes to the investigation of Aristotle's account of the metaphysics of the common sense is that there is *only one* act of perceptual awareness through which a *single subject* gathers multimodal perceptual input and is thereby aware of it.

5.4 A 'ROBUST' INTERPRETATION OF THE COMMON SENSE

In the preceding sections we established the requirements that need to be satisfied so that a perceiver can acquire complex perceptual content. But *how* does she acquire it? Aristotle writes:

> Each sense is relative to its particular group of sensible qualities.... [But] since we also discriminate white from sweet, and indeed each sensible quality from every other, *with what* do we perceive that they are different? It must be by *sense*; for what is before us is sensible. (*DA*, 426b8–15; my emphasis)[5]
>
> ἑκάστη μὲν οὖν αἴσθησις τοῦ ὑποκειμένου αἰσθητοῦ ἐστίν...ἐπεὶ δὲ καὶ τὸ λευκὸν καὶ τὸ γλυκὺ καὶ ἕκαστον τῶν αἰσθητῶν πρὸς ἕκαστον κρίνομεν, τινὶ καὶ αἰσθανόμεθα ὅτι διαφέρει. ἀνάγκη δὴ αἰσθήσει· αἰσθητὰ γάρ ἐστιν.

Since it is through sense that one can discriminate white from sweet (and generally perform operations involving complex perceptual content), the question is: through *which* sense? It cannot be a special sense, but on the given criterion for sense individuation, there seem to be no other senses than the special ones. Although white and sweet are perceived through sight and taste, and are perceived simultaneously, the discrimination of the two sensibles cannot be achieved through either of the two senses. It cannot be through sight since sight is sensitive to colors but not flavors, and correspondingly for taste. Since sight has no direct access to the sweet, nor taste to the white, there can only be parallel simultaneous operation; white is perceived through one of them, and sweet through the other. The two faculties have two distinct perceptual contents, unrelated to one another, and so the discrimination between the two sensibles seems *prima facie* impossible. Even if the two perceptual faculties, sight and taste, belong to the same perceiver, it still does not follow that perceptual discrimination can take place through the simultaneous perception of the two sensibles. How could any one of the five senses, each of which is dedicated to a modally different type of perceptible quality, deliver a single modally complex content? This is another of the domains of perception (in addition to those investigated in chapter 4) that cannot be explained through the operation of the individual special senses, but which the common sense (i.e., the senses acting as one) is called upon to facilitate. The common sense is the sense that can gather modally complex perceptual content, and use it, for example, for perceptual discrimination.

On the basis of these considerations (which I will further develop especially in chapter 6) I propose a 'robust' interpretation of the common sense, as unified and empowered with its own perceptual abilities and functionality. I thus make a departure from the view taken, for example, by Pavel Gregoric (2007), who offered one of the most recent comprehensive studies of the topic. Gregoric examines all the occurrences of the expression 'common sense' in Aristotle's works, and classifies them into three uses:

i) an adjectival use which applies to one or more individual senses, indicating that they are *shared by animals of different species* (*HA* I 3, 489a17; *Met.* I 1, 981b14);

ii) an adjectival use which applies to all the individual senses, and indicates their shared sensitivity to a type of feature in the world which Aristotle calls *common perceptible*—e.g., shape, movement, number, etc. (*DA* III 1,425a27);

iii) a noun-use, referring to *the common sense* (*PA* IV 10 686; *DM* 450a10; *DA* III 431b5).

On the basis of his very scholarly survey of the texts, Gregoric argues that not all the perceptual functions Aristotle is traditionally taken to assign to the common sense are in fact performed by it. When Aristotle says that those functions involve 'common sense', he uses the expression sometimes as a noun but sometimes as an adjectival qualification for the individual senses. Gregoric makes two main original interpretative points. Firstly, he holds that perception of the so-called 'common sensibles' (movement, shape, number, etc.) and cross-modal perception should not be taken to be functions performed by the common sense—even if this is what commentators have traditionally thought. Gregoric argues that in the relevant contexts Aristotle uses the expression 'common sense' only adjectivally. But he reaches his conclusion on merely textual and linguistic grounds, without pausing to examine the philosophical view he is thereby attributing to Aristotle. Gregoric thus attributes to Aristotle the view that perception of the common sensibles does not require anything over and above the individual senses; it happens in virtue of the appropriate sensitivity that the individual senses share (that is common to them). But *how* does it happen? What is it that the individual senses share ontologically that endows them with a common function? What does the required shared sensitivity consist in? Is it moving colors or moving colored objects that sight sees, and is this—can it be—the same as the sensitivity to hearing moving sounds or moving sounding objects? (I argue that is in virtue of *extra powers* that the senses operating as one have that they can perceive the common sensibles—and not in virtue of a shared sensitivity). As for cross-modal perception, Gregoric appears to have even less of an explanation to offer on behalf of Aristotle; he writes that:

> Even if we suppose for the sake of argument that cross-modal perception is performed by the common sense, I do not think we should consider it a function of the common sense. Rather, it seems to be a coincidence of having a perceptual capacity of the soul which is a unity with some internal complexity. (2007, 201)

As to the other perceptual functions at issue, Gregoric shares the traditional view according to which for Aristotle the common sense is responsible for simultaneous perception, perceptual discrimination, activation and deactivation of all the senses in waking and sleep, and perceptual awareness (which Gregoric understands as monitoring of the activity and inactivity of the senses). On the other hand, the second main original interpretative conclusion Gregoric offers is that, of the aforementioned perceptual functions, some pertain to the *perceptual* capacity of the soul, and others, which require the involvement of imagination, to the *sensory* capacity of the soul. Gregoric warns us against two interpretative mistakes that he takes all commentators to have made so far. The first is to assign both types of perceptual functions (whether they involve imagination or not) to a single capacity of the soul. The second mistake traditionally made, he tells us, is to take the single capacity of the soul that supposedly performs both types of functions to be the perceptual capacity of the soul, which is what *we* (mistakenly, for him) designate with the Aristotelian notion of the common sense. What Aristotle designates with the noun-use of the expression 'common sense' is rather, according to Gregoric, the sensory capacity of the soul. The sensory capacity of the soul is its nonrational cognitive power and it comprises the perceptual and the imaginative capacities. Gregoric comments thus on the results of his textual analyses:

> We should not suppose that various functions which go beyond the individual senses taken separately are achieved all by the same thing (2007, 205)...This is a conclusion whose importance for our subject can hardly be exaggerated (2007, 204)...This should come as a great relief to interpreters of Aristotle's notion of the common sense, because the diversity of its functions has presented them with an acute problem... Fortunately, we do not need to saddle Aristotle with such a problem (2007, 205)...In that way we save Aristotle from an incoherent notion of the common sense. (2007, 206)

A methodological issue first: Identifying what functions the common sense performs in order to understand what the common sense is, is certainly a move in the right direction, in keeping with Aristotle's own philosophical methodology. But it is disappointing that in describing at great length the functions of the common sense, Gregoric does not derive from the texts he analyzes, nor give us an understanding of, what is required in the makeup of the common sense for it to perform these functions. There is an air of irony in the 'fortunate' (his words) overall conclusion Gregoric considers the main achievement of his investigation. For, after the reader has gone through many pages of meticulous scholarship that are supposed to clear the ground from confusion and misinterpretations of Aristotle's texts, here is what there is to learn: On Gregoric's view, Aristotle's account for two out of four functions of the common sense, simultaneous perception and perceptual discrimination, is ultimately 'not satisfactory' (207), 'disappointing' (208), and 'not promising' with respect to what it can do to explain cross-modal binding (208). Furthermore, two other functions, namely perception of the common sensibles and cross-modal perception, are not accounted for at all, as seen above.

Gregoric's interpretation of Aristotle's account of the meta-physical constitution of the common sense may be put in a nut-shell thus: the common sense is a single thing, although complex. Ontologically, it is a single *unified whole* (2007, 213, et al.) Its complexity is only 'in notion': its parts are only 'conceptual, or logical parts' (2007, 25). I shall label the metaphysical account Gregoric offers for the common sense '*presumed holism*'. It is presumed rather than explained, for it offers no answers to the following crucial questions: what is it that is unified at the ontological level if the parts are only conceptual? Is the common sense unified or atomically one? (Atoms have properties that can be conceptually but not ontologically distinguished in the atom. Is hearing related to seeing, and both to imagination, as weight is related to size in an atom? Would we want to attribute such a position to Aristotle? What textual evidence would justify it?) Either way, how does this oneness perform the very diverse functions that the common sense performs? The *presumed holism* model is not derived from the texts or from the functional requirements (unity and complexity) the common sense has to meet. Rather, it is drawn by analogy to the structure of the soul, which Gregoric merely assumes. Likewise, the structural analogy between the soul and its own lower-level capacities is just assumed. In Gregoric's own words:

I submit that the unity of the perceptual capacity of the soul is achieved in the same way in which the unity of the soul is achieved... The soul is a single thing divided only conceptu-ally, in the sense that we can analyze it into different parts or aspects according to the most salient activities of living beings...however in reality there is only one soul...which is what ensures integration and cooperation of various parts or aspects of the soul... Likewise, only at a lower level, the perceptual capacity of the soul is one single thing divided only conceptually, in the sense that we can analyze it into different senses according to different kinds of the special perceptibles... However, *there is really one single perceptual capacity of the soul, which ensures that it can operate not only as this or that individual sense, but also as one.* (2007, 39, my emphasis)

The soul allows only for a conceptual division, and *such a division guarantees both the unity* of the soul and the unity of the living body. Now the same sort of division can be applied at a lower level, that is, on the capacities of the soul themselves.... The perceptual part of the soul... turns out to be itself conceptually divisible into capacities of a lower order, namely the individual senses... *The perceptual capacity of the soul is not an aggregate of the individual senses, but a unified whole'* (2007, 27, my emphasis).

The above quotations illustrate Gregoric's position, but also bring out its inadequacies. What accounts for the unity of the common sense? Claiming only conceptual division of the soul guarantees nothing about its unity, and does not tells us anything about its oneness (*pace* Gregoric, 2007, 29); it rather demands explanation of the unity presumption. Positing that the soul's perceptual capacity is one single thing (2007, 39) and not an aggregate (of what?) (2007, 27) is not a solution, because an account of its internal constitutional complexity is still missing. Remarking that 'Aristotle's framework operates with a series of related but distinct notions' (2007, 205) does not further our understanding of the common sense's unity.

Johansen argues along the same 'deflationary' line as Pavel Gregoric (2007). The stance is clear: 'the common sense [responsible for multisensory perceptual content] does not point to a capacity over and above the individual sense, even one that is somehow constituted by the individual senses' (2012, 178). But how then is multisensory perceptual content acquired? Johansen answers: common perception 'points to an ability that each of the senses have' (in this sense, their 'common' power), by analogy with 'the ability that each of the players [of a football team] has to control the ball, on top of the different specialized abilities that might be characteristic of the goal keeper, the striker, or the defender as such' (2012, 179). But a football player's ability to control the ball is in fact *more basic* than the capacity for striking, defending, goalkeeping, etc. If we follow the analogy through, multisensory perception and its corresponding capacity ought to be the most basic perceptual activity of each sense, more basic than the specialized perceptual activity and ability of each sense. But neither Aristotle, nor Johansen I take it, would agree to this. The problem I find with Johansen's explanation of the role of the common power of each sense through the analogy of the ability of the players to control the ball is that the player's ability is not an extra ability each player has, but the generic classification of each player's ability *qua* striker, defender, and such. But the common perceptual power each sense has is not the genus of that sense's perceptual ability. Assuming that it is leads to the results mentioned a few lines previously.

There is a further difficulty with the more general stance Johansen takes on the common power of each sense. He takes it that each of the senses can perceive the common sensibles like number, shape, movement, etc., through the common power it has (2012, 179). But the common sensibles are perceptually complex sensibles. That is, for Aristotle, shape is tactile and visual; it is not that an object has tactile shape and also visual shape; rather, the shape of the object is one and the same, and it can be perceived through more than one sense. If, as Johansen believes, for Aristotle each sense is capable of perceiving the common sensibles through its common power, then sight ought to be able to perceive a sensible that is tactile, namely shape. But sight cannot do this, because it is limited to perceiving through its sense organ, which is not sensitive to tactile sensibles. In general, the common power of each sense cannot be sensitive to multisensory sensibles, because it depends on the specific sense organ of the respective sense. Rather, Aristotle's introduction of the common power is to facilitate a cooperation between the senses, giving rise to a perceptual faculty whose abilities transcend those of each sense.

The deflationary approach to the status of the common sense appears equally problematic when Johansen comes to giving an account of the perceptual discrimination of, for example, yellow from bitter. He writes that 'Aristotle says that the individual senses perceive that the yellow is the same as the bitter by virtue of being one, rather than themselves.... He is not saying that another capacity than the individual senses perceive the incidental perceptibles, but that the individual senses perceive as one rather than as individuals' (2012, 183). Johansen further explains the senses perceiving as one should be understood as follows: 'To return to our football analogy, the senses are now considered not like the individual players who have the same skill but as players who have a skill by virtue of playing together, like the skill of winning matches. This is not a separate capacity but a capacity the capacities have by virtue of working together' (2012, 183). But how do they get this capacity merely from their togetherness? The oneness of the senses working together must be explained metaphysically for it to have explanatory force in multisensory perception. Consider the following scenario: a monolingual French woman and a monolingual English woman are each reading a document in their own language. Is there a way in which they could cooperate to tell whether the contents of the two documents are the same or different, without requiring an extra capacity other than their own capacities to understand their respective texts? How can the analogy of the 'players who have a skill by virtue of playing together' help us understand how the two women can discern sameness or difference in their texts, if they do not understand each other's language? How can the analogy help us understand how senses with different types of sense organs work together to perceive multisensory contents?

I take it that incidental perception is the key to Johansen's interpretation of Aristotle. Although he does not explain this explicitly, I take it that Johansen sees incidental perception as corresponding to the ability of the players to pass the ball to each other. According to Johansen, Aristotle's account of incidental perception is his way of enriching the perceiver's perceptual range; Johansen writes: 'Accidental perception allows perception to be even richer in content than does common perception. We can see that the white is sweet by accidental perception, though sight as such does not inform us of sweetness, and we can see that this is the son of Diares, though no special sense as such is primed to grasp this kind of information' (180). But is this what Aristotle says? Following Johansen's translation, 'one perceives this [the son of Diares] accidentally because this [the son of Diares] which is perceived belongs to white, and that is why nothing suffers by the perceptible as such [as son of Diares]' (418a20–4) (2012, 181). So Aristotle says that we perceive the son of Diares by perceiving the white. He does not say that we perceive '*that* this is the son of Diares' (my emphasis). We couldn't perceive it, because no sense organ is sensitive to 'being the son of Diares'. Nor does sight 'see *that* the white is sweet' (180, my emphasis); it could not, but can only see the sweet, because the white happens to be sweet. The link is ontological, not perceptual; external, not part of the perceptual content. More generally, for Aristotle, incidental perception on its own cannot allow for multimodal perception, for the reason that each sense, by itself, can be aware of only contents of a single sensory modality. Suppose that the French and the English women read the same text, each in her own language translation. We could say that the Frenchwoman understood the text the Englishwoman was reading, but not that she understood that she was reading the same text as the Englishwoman.

I presented in chapter 4 Aristotle's arguments for why the special senses are inadequate to perceive the common sensibles, and thus objects, unless they are unified in a perceptual system endowed with extra perceptual abilities. I won't repeat the arguments here; by way of contrast with mine, I have here highlighted the line Johansen and Gregoric take, which I submit leaves the senses simply bereft of the capacity to have complex perceptual content.

5.5 A NEW INDIVIDUATION PRINCIPLE FOR THE COMMON SENSE

The common sense is the sense through which we gain awareness of multimodally complex contents (which include the common sensibles). It is clear that it is a *sui generis* sense. In this section I shall call attention to some of its unique features *qua* sense. In the *De Sensu* Aristotle writes,

> If then, as is the fact, the soul with one part perceives sweet, with another, white, either that which results from these is some one part, or else there is no such one resultant. But there must be such a one, inasmuch as the general faculty of sense-perception is one. What one object, then, does that one faculty perceive? For assuredly no one object arises by composition of these. We must conclude, therefore, that there is, as has been stated before, some one faculty in the soul with

which the latter perceives all its percepts, though it perceives each different genus of sensibles through a different organ. (*SS* 449a5–10)

εἰ δὲ δὴ ἄλλῳ μὲν γλυκέος ἄλλῳ δὲ λευκοῦ αἰσθάνεται ἡ ψυχὴ μέρει, ἤτοι τὸ ἐκ τούτων ἕν τί ἐστιν ἢ οὐχ ἕν. ἀλλ' ἀνάγκη ἕν· ἐν γάρ τι τὸ αἰσθητικόν ἐστι μέρος. τίνος οὖν ἐκεῖνο ἑνός; οὐδὲν γὰρ ἐκ τούτων ἕν. ἀνάγκη ἄρα ἕν τι εἶναι τῆς ψυχῆς ᾧ ἅπαντα αἰσθάνεται, καθάπερ εἴρηται πρότερον, ἄλλο δὲ γένος δι' ἄλλου.

This text gives evidence of the introduction of a new criterion for the individuation of a sense. In the case of the special senses, we saw in chapter 2 that it is their special sensibles (color, sound, flavor, etc.) that individuate the senses (see e.g. *DA* 418a24–25). The nature of the common sense, on the other hand, is not determined by its sensitivity to any special type of sensible. So Aristotle introduces for the common sense a new, *intensional criterion* of individuation: the common sense is individuated by the type of perceptual content it is aware of, rather than by the types of sensible object.

We have already seen that the common sense does not have a special sense organ for the common sensibles (e.g., in *DA* 425a14–16). Additionally, in his account of self-awareness, Aristotle takes the position that there cannot be 'two senses both percipient of the same sensible' (*DA* 425b14–17). So it cannot be that, for example, a blue item is perceived through both sight and through the common sense, separately, when one is aware that one is seeing blue. And how could the common sense perceive on its own, as it were, since the common sense does not have a sense organ? It has to rely on the sense organs of the special senses, through which only the special sensibles can be perceived. So how does the common sense become aware of blue, and of any other special perceptible form? The claims Aristotle makes e.g. in *DA* 427a2–5 and *SS* 449a5–10 that the common sense is all the special senses operating as one, points towards a constitutional explanation of why what is perceived through the special senses is also perceived through the common sense. The common sense in other words is constituted by the special senses. This is what we will investigate in the forthcoming chapters.

CONCLUDING REMARKS

We examined in chapters 4 and 5 a number of perceptual operations that presuppose the possibility of complex perceptual content. For two perceptible qualities to be perceived in a single perceptual content, Aristotle needs to explain how different (contrary or at any rate mutually incompatible) physical movements can be *physically com-present*, and in fact somehow unified. Additionally, for any operation involving complex perceptual content the agent, the time of the operation, and the operation itself need to be one. A final constraint on the account of complex perceptual contents concerns the *way* that the common sense accesses the perceptual input of the special senses. It does not have its own sense organ. All these are physical constraints that will play a role in Aristotle's thinking about the metaphysics of the common sense, as we shall see in chapters 6 and 7. Also, Aristotle introduces a *different individuation principle* for the common sense from the one he used previously for the special senses: not from the uniqueness of the object of sense (as in the case of the special senses), nor from the uniqueness of the sense organ (as the common sense does not have an organ), but *from the oneness of the complex perceptual content to the oneness of the perceiving sense*—in this case the common sense.

Notes

1. For the meaning of 'becoming like' the object of perception, see the appendix of chapter 2.
2. Here the unity of the subject does not refer to the unity of consciousness of a person, but to the unity of awareness in perception. Thus, the question driving the investigation is not how yesterday's thought is related to today's feelings, so as to belong to the same subject; rather, it is how the subject can tell, for example, that the toothache she feels is different from the headache she is also experiencing.
3. The argument has been much discussed in the secondary literature. Since there are excellent analyses of it already in press, here I will only briefly comment on how the argument is relevant to our present investigation. The reader might want to pursue the topic by studying, for example, Victor Caston 'Aristotle on Consciousness', *Mind*, 111: 751–815 (2002); and Thomas Johansen 'In Defense of the Inner Sense: Aristotle on Perceiving that One Perceives', *Proceeding of the Boston Area Colloquium in Ancient Philosophy* 21: 235–76 (2005).
4. See chapter 2.
5. The terminology Aristotle uses in the passage should not mislead us. For Aristotle, it is not the senses that perceive, but the agent—the soul—*through the senses*. Hence, looking for a sense that can have a complex perceptual content, as in discerning white from sweet, he is looking for the subject that *perceives* these sensibles in a single perceptual experience.

Chapter 6

Mixing the Many and Partitioning the One

INTRODUCTION

Aristotle's solution to the problem of how we perceive complex perceptual content is to posit the so-called 'common sense' as the only center of perceptual awareness,[1] operating on the inputs received from all the special senses. The metaphysics of the common sense is an exercise in 'complexity in unity' for Aristotle, for which he tries to develop a variety of models. What Aristotle is looking for is a way to understand how the perceptual system operates *as a unified whole*, with enhanced perceptual abilities, despite the multiplicity of the special senses involved. Ultimately Aristotle's position, as we will see in the following chapters, is that the common sense is not an additional, sixth sense; rather, it is the perceptual system as constituted by the five special senses, but not metaphysically reducible to them. It is not reducible to them because it has additional perceptual powers that the special senses do not have.[2] These additional powers enable the common sense to perform those operations involving complex perceptual content that the individual senses in isolation, as it were, could not perform. The constitutive relation between common and special senses facilitates Aristotle's general stance that awareness through the special senses is thereby—transparently—awareness through the common sense. As we saw in chapter 5, there is no inter-nal homunculus or additional inner faculty of awareness observing the perceptual contents produced by the special senses and bringing about awareness of them. There is only one act of awareness when we, for example, see white and discern it from sweet.

The questions this chapter and the forthcoming one will inves-tigate are these: what does Aristotle mean when saying that the special senses 'form a unity' which is the common sense? How does this unification of the senses into one perceptual system explain not only perception of the common sensibles, but also the gen-eration of complex perceptual content? In examining Aristotle's answers to such questions, my approach will be problem-oriented; thus I will draw from different works of Aristotle's, without follow-ing the chronological order in which they are thought to be writ-ten.[3] I will distinguish six different models Aristotle investigates, as possible candidates for the required account of the unity and com-plexity of the common sense. I will first present two models that explore the explanatory value of intuitions that appear to Aristotle relevant to the problem under consideration. In discussing these first two models, Aristotle does not present himself explicitly as exploring common sense views or appealing to common sense intuitions; on the other hand, it seems very plausible that he would proceed in this way with his philosophical inquiry about the com-mon sense, following his usual practice, even when such *endoxa* or intuitions might ultimately be non-starters from his own philo-sophical point of view. The first two models appear to be driven by the idea that physical unity (of the object of perception in the first model, or of the common sense in the second model) will deliver unity at the mental level of the experience. I shall call them the Mixed Contents Model and the Multiple Sensors Model, respec-tively; they are both presented in the *De Sensu*. Ultimately however neither the Mixed Contents Model nor the Multiple Sensors one can deliver a philosophically adequate solution to the problem of the structure and operation of the common sense. Thus in the *De Anima* Aristotle explores a more abstract approach to the question of how what is one can be many too, resulting in two new models. I call the first the Ratio Model: it pursues the idea that qualitatively different things are many in being but somehow unified by the very qualitative difference that divides them. Aristotle draws on the idea that a ratio has a single value, which runs through an equation of such ratios as the common single identity shared by all the ratios in the equation, unifying the equation into one notwithstanding its multiple complexity. The model offers a very abstract way of thinking of the unity of the perceptual system and of complex perceptual content; but ultimately no metaphysical account of it. Thus elsewhere in the *De Anima* Aristotle makes a fresh start, driven this time by explicitly metaphysical considerations. One might think, reasons Aristotle, that the difficulty in accounting for unity and complexity of the common sense and its complex perceptual content stems from the fact that they are supposedly somehow like a surface that is all over black and white at once.[4] In the case of complex perceptual content, the same perceptual input is both, for example, visual and tactile; the same sense (the common sense) is both, for example, sight and touch. But this is clearly impossible— it seems. Or is it not? Aristotle establishes the viability of giving a metaphysical account of the common sense by breaking new ground in metaphysics, by arguing for the *relative identity* of the five senses, that are many in being and one in number, by analogy with the case of a single point that is the limits of many semi-lines. Yet, the Relative Identity Model, which I will examine in chapter 7, does not capture an essential feature of the common sense, namely that it is endowed with additional powers of its own that enable it to perform operations on the perceptual inputs gathered via the special senses. Ultimately therefore none of the four models introduced thus far provides by itself the full requisite account of the metaphysics of the common sense. This motivates Aristotle to pursue the investigation further, with two new models, which I shall examine in chapter 7. These will be the Substance Model and the Common Power Model. A number of insights deriving from the Relative Identity Model, the Substance Model, and the Common Power Model will contribute to Aristotle's final account of the common sense, as I shall argue in my overall conclusions. For presentation purposes, I divide the models in two groups; the first three (the Mixed Content, Multiple Sensors and Ratio Models) are investigated in this chapter; the other three, which contribute more substantially to Aristotle's final account (the Relative Identity, Substance, and Common Power Models), are examined in the next chapter.

6.1 THE MIXED CONTENTS MODEL

Aristotle's investigation of the problem of complex perceptual content in the *De Sensu* begins with an observation from everyday experience: two different causes 'mixed' together have a joint causal impact and bring about a single effect. For example cold and hot water mixed together in a single stream would fill a swimming pool of lukewarm water. So in perception, two different perceptible qualities, if somehow mixed before being perceived, when impacting causally on the same organ at the same time would bring about a single content of experience. This is what I call the Mixed Contents Model. Aristotle's starting point in thinking about this model is his oft-reiterated commitment that,

> [T]he perception actualized at any single moment is necessarily one.... Hence it is not possible to perceive the possibility of

perceiving two distinct objects simultaneously with one and the same sense. (SS 447b17–21)

ἀλλὰ κατὰ μίαν δύναμιν καὶ ἄτομον χρόνον μίαν ἀνάγκη εἶναι τὴν ἐνέργειαν.... οὐκ ἄρα ἐνδέχεται δυοῖν ἅμα αἰσθάνεσθαι τῇ μιᾷ αἰσθήσει.

Why does Aristotle think this? He does not offer any argument in the present context, but, as we know from the way his theory was set up (see chapter 2), his reason must be that it is *physically* impossible for the sense organ to be affected by two different perceptible qualities at the same time if the qualities are not mixed. Recall how Aristotle conceives of the alteration of the sense organ by the action of the perceptible quality of an external object: on the *literalist* and the *disturbance* interpretations of what sort of alteration this is, it is evident that the sense organ cannot be changed in two different ways at the same time.[5] Therefore it seems plausible to think that the cause of perception must be one if the effect is one, namely if there is one perceptual content. But if the objects of perception are two different perceptible qualities, how can they be a single cause? Aristotle suggests that they can act as a single cause *if* they are mixed:

It is impossible to perceive two objects simultaneously in the same sensory act *unless they have been mixed, for their amalgamation involves their becoming one*, and the sensory act related to one object is itself one.... Hence, when things are mixed we of necessity perceive them simultaneously: for we perceive them by a perception actually one. (SS 447b9–21, my emphasis)

τῇ μιᾷ δὲ ἅμα δυοῖν οὐκ ἔστιν αἰσθάνεσθαι ἂν μὴ μειχθῇ (τὸ γὰρ μεῖγμα ἓν βούλεται εἶναι, τοῦ δ' ἑνὸς μία αἴσθησις, ἡ δὲ μία ἅμα αὐτῇ), ὥστ' ἐξ ἀνάγκης τῶν μεμειγμένων ἅμα αἰσθάνεται, ὅτι μιᾷ αἰσθήσει κατ' ἐνέργειαν αἰσθάνεται.... μιᾶς

γὰρ ἡ εἰσάπαξ μία χρῆσις καὶ κίνησις, μία δὲ ἡ δύναμις. οὐκ ἄρα
ἐνδέχεται δυοῖν ἅμα αἰσθάνεσθαι τῇ μιᾷ αἰσθήσει.

Thus, Aristotle seeks an account of the unity of the external object
of perception, to ground in that the unity of the perceptual experience of it. Would thinking of complex content in terms of a 'mixture' of perceptual qualities be a solution for the problem of complex
perceptual content? Aristotle takes this possibility seriously, and
there are reasons why he does so. To understand why he thought
that the Mixed Contents Model might address the question of
how we perceive complex perceptual content, we need to look at
Aristotle's theory of mixing.[6] According to this theory, as set out in
Generation and Corruption, when two items mix, they 'survive' mixing; Aristotle makes the point thus:

> Since some things that are, are potential, and some actual, it is
> possible for things after they have been mixed in some way *to be*
> *and not to be*. Some other thing [the mixture] which comes to
> be from them is actually, while each of the things which were,
> before they were mixed, still is, but potentially, and has not
> been destroyed. (GC 327b23–25)
>
> Ἐπεὶ δ' ἐστὶ τὰ μὲν δυνάμει τὰ δ' ἐνεργείᾳ τῶν ὄντων,
> ἐνδέχεται τὰ μιχθέντα εἶναί πως καὶ μὴ εἶναι, ἐνεργείᾳ μὲν
> ἑτέρου ὄντος τοῦ γεγονότος ἐξ αὐτῶν, δυνάμει δ' ἔτι ἑκατέρου
> ἅπερ ἦσαν πρὶν μιχθῆναι, καὶ οὐκ ἀπολωλότα·

It is the 'survival' of the mixed items, albeit in potentiality, that
makes mixing relevant and possibly explanatorily valuable in
relation to the problem of the complex perceptual content. If for
Aristotle each of the original items survives in their mixture, then
each of the (hypothetically) mixed perceptible qualities may be
thought to survive in the perceptual content they would jointly

bring about when mixed. If so, then the mixed perceptual content would include the two mixed perceptible qualities without 'destroying' them, thus allowing for perceptual operations such as discrimination, cross-modal-binding etc.

Even if this seems a promising start, Aristotle does not finally conclude that the Mixed Contents Model will provide the answer to the problem of how it is that we perceive complex perceptual content. He does not explain his views explicitly in the *De Sensu*, but, once again, we can derive them from his theory of mixing. He holds that when two items are mixed, their qualities affect each other and come to be the same, as they operate on each other, *equalizing their differences* midway between the two original forms. So, hot wine and cold honey become lukewarm honey-wine when mixed, and the resulting mixture is uniform. Aristotle writes that,

> when the two are more or less equal in strength, then each changes from its own nature in the direction of the dominant one, though it does not become the other but something in between and common to both. (*GC* 328a28–31)
>
> Ὅταν δὲ ταῖς δυνάμεσιν ἰσάζῃ πως, τότε μεταβάλλει μὲν ἑκάτερον εἰς τὸ κρατοῦν ἐκ τῆς αὑτοῦ φύσεως, οὐ γίνεται δὲ θάτερον, ἀλλὰ μεταξὺ καὶ κοινόν.

In the same way, say the sweet and bitter in a cocktail, or the low and high pitch sounds of a piano would mix into a single perceptible quality, *intermediate* between the two extremes, bittersweet in taste, or medium pitch in sound. Thus mixing perceptible qualities results in a single (qualitatively intermediate) quality causally impacting on the sense organ, which gives rise to the perception of one *qualitatively simple* taste or sound, intermediate between the two original ones. The two original perceptible qualities in each case are in a way perceived, because they survive in potentiality in the mixed content, but they are perceived as one, as a perceptual content *without articulation* and qualitative complexity. On the other hand, it is precisely this articulation that is required for complex perceptual content. In conclusion, the Mixed Contents model will not provide a way of understanding, for example, perceptual discrimination, such as between bitter and sweet, red and blue, sweet and white, etc.; for this, there needs to be qualitative complexity in the content of experience. Mixed sensation does not produce complex perceptual content, because the perceptual stimuli are mixed, so their effect on the sense organ is as one homogeneous stimulus.

6.2 THE MULTIPLE SENSORS MODEL

Elsewhere in the *De Sensu* Aristotle explores a different way of addressing the problem of complex perceptual content and the unity of the common sense. What this and the previous model have in common is the implicit assumption that unity at the physical level would guarantee unity at the mental level. While the previous model investigates whether the different perceptible qualities the subject perceives (e.g., in discriminating white from blue) might be in some way unified, as a mixed stimulus impacting on the sense, the present model investigates whether the sense itself might be partitioned into many while also remaining one. I call this the Multiple Sensors Model. The relevant text, *SS* 448b18–449a5, is difficult to interpret, because the arguments are dense, and occasionally the text lends itself to ambiguities. Nevertheless it is an important text to consider because of the originality of Aristotle's suggestions, and because it gives us insights into how Aristotle conceived of the problem of complex perception. This leads to a further way of exploring the question, driving Aristotle's investigation towards a final resolution. Aristotle asks,

Whether it is possible or impossible to perceive several objects simultaneously; by 'simultaneously' I mean perceiving the several objects in a time one and indivisible relatively to one another. (SS 448b18–20)

πότερον ἐνδέχεται ἅμα πλειόνων αἰσθάνεσθαι ἢ οὐκ ἐνδέχεται. τὸ δ' ἅμα λέγω ἐν ἑνὶ καὶ ἀτόμῳ χρόνῳ πρὸς ἄλληλα.

He proceeds to explore the following possibility:

First, then, is it possible in this way, that one perceives different things simultaneously but *with different parts of the soul*, and in such an indivisible way as *all being continuous*? (SS 448b20–21, my translation and emphasis)[7]

πρῶτον μὲν οὖν ἆρ' ὧδ' ἐνδέχεται, ἅμα μέν, ἑτέρῳ δὲ τῆς ψυχῆς αἰσθάνεσθαι, κἂν [οὐ τῷ ἀτόμῳ] οὕτως ἀτόμῳ ὡς παντὶ ὄντι συνεχεῖ;

In addressing this question, Aristotle begins by narrowing the scope of the investigation to the case of a single sense, and takes sight as his example. The starting hypothesis is that, '[w]e assume it [*sc.* sight] to perceive one color with one part and another with another' (SS 448b23–24).[8] Aristotle's statement might be taken to mean that sight has different parts (i.e., sense organs), all sensitive to colors, but which might happen to perceive different instances of color at a particular time. Alternatively, it might be taken to mean that sight has different parts (i.e., sub-sense-organs) each *dedicated* to the perception of a particular color. The latter reading would allow sight to discriminate between, for example, red and black: the two perceptual qualities would impact on different sense organs of sight, and yet be in one and the same visual content (without mixing). I take this to be the intended meaning of Aristotle's statement, because otherwise it would require a very complex physical account to explain why this part of the sense organ of sight sees only the green of leaves of the tree and this part only the white of the tree's bark. Such an account is not provided anywhere by Aristotle; in fact it is far from clear that it would be available within Aristotle's physics. In addition, difficulties would follow if the principle were applied to cases where a multiplicity of stimuli is not physically distributed in the world (e.g., flavors in a drink). In such cases there could not be isomorphism between the distribution of qualities in the object and their causal impact on different parts of the sense organ, because there would not be distribution of properties in the first place.

Even if we take the Multiple Sensors Model to suggest that sight has different parts (i.e., sense organs), all equally sensitive to colors, but which might happen to perceive different instances of color at a particular time, the model is not free from difficulties. Aristotle himself offers an objection: on this hypothesis, he thinks, the sense faculty 'will have several parts *the same in kind*. For what it perceives is the same in genus' (*SS* 448b24–5; my emphasis). The difficulty, in other words, is that the partitioning of the sense organ will achieve only an unnecessary duplication of the sense, rather than unification of its content; each part will still function like the sense itself, each with its own content. The goal however was to show how the perceiver sees different colors together, in a single complex content. The Multiple Sensors Model only shows how one could see different colors through different sense organs of sight, but even if the different colors were perceived at the same time by these different senses, they would *not* be in a single perceptual content. This conclusion is not stated explicitly in the text, but it can be inferred from the next step Aristotle takes in the argument. He considers the suggestion that the different parts of sight might be operating in the way that two eyes operate, *as one* sense organ:

> As there are two eyes, there may be in the soul something analogous; that equally from these parts some one organ is formed,

and hence their [i.e., the parts in the soul that function like the eyes] actualization in perception is one; but[9] if this is so in the soul, then, in so far as what is formed of both [perceiving parts of the soul] is one [sense organ], the perceiving subject also will be one. (SS 448b26–29, with minor alterations of the translation)

ὡς ὄμματα δύο, φαίη τις οὐδὲν κωλύειν οὕτω καὶ ἐν τῇ ψυχῇ, [ὅτι] ἴσως ἐκ μὲν τούτων ἔν τι γίγνεται καὶ μία ἡ ἐνέργεια αὐτῶν· ἐκεῖ δέ, εἰ μὲν ἓν τὸ ἐξ ἀμφοῖν, ἐκεῖνο τὸ αἰσθανόμενον ἔστα

This suggestion is meant to address the problem I just highlighted arising from partitioning each sense faculty. Aristotle notes that two eyes function *collaboratively*, not separately, thus without duplicating the sense. Each of the eyes is supposed to be a different part of the sense of sight,[10] but the two eyes operate as a single organ; and their actualization in perception (i.e., seeing) is one. This move allows for some progress in the right explanatory direction, but yet another difficulty arises with the two eyes suggestion (which again, Aristotle himself does not make explicit). Although their shared actualization entails a single perceptual content, the result is no improvement on the philosophical problem under consideration. This is because the two eyes make up one sense organ and have the same perceptual content; but this does not account for *how* they could perceive different perceptible qualities in one and the same content. Nothing in the two eyes example indicates that they provide a mechanism for the perception of different colors in the same content. That this must be Aristotle's ultimate stance regarding the Multiple Sensors Model is supported by the choice he makes for his next step in the argument, namely the denial that the parts of the sense operate like the eyes, as one organ. He writes: 'if the two parts of soul remain separate, the analogy with the eyes will fail' (εἰ δὲ χωρίς, οὐχ ὁμοίως ἔξει) (SS 448b28–29). Here Aristotle returns to the idea he started with, that the parts of a sense operate as different senses (of the same type), perceiving different qualities. But in this case the analogy of the two eyes will not apply, since the two eyes do not function like separate senses, and so the problem of how the different parts of each sense perceive their different perceptible qualities in the same perceptual content remains.

Showing the two eyes analogy to be ultimately unhelpful toward resolving the problem of how the different parts of a sense can operate as different senses prepares the ground for Aristotle's next objection to the suggestion of the separateness of the parts of a sense. So, Aristotle continues, if the parts of a sense which perceive different perceptible qualities operate separately, rather than function like the eyes as one sense, then,

> Each of the senses will be many, as if we should say that they were each a set of diverse sciences; for neither will an activity exist without its proper power, nor without activity will there be a sensation. (SS 448b30–449a2, modified translation)
> αἰσθήσεις αἱ αὐταὶ πλείους ἔσονται, ὥσπερ εἴ τις ἐπιστήμας διαφόρους φαίη· οὔτε γὰρ ἡ ἐνέργεια ἄνευ τῆς κατ᾽ αὐτὴν ἔσται δυνάμεως, οὔτ᾽ ἄνευ ταύτης αἴσθησις ἔσται

The reason each sense will be many is that the activity of perceiving requires a corresponding power (as we have seen in the earlier chapters). Hence, each part of the soul that perceives a different color will exercise its own power, have its own perceptual activity, and be a separate sense, even if of the same genus as the other parts of the sense.[11] The coda that immediately follows (SS 449a2–5), which completes this line of argument, is puzzling to commentators, as well as to translators—although the language itself is not. Aristotle writes:

> But if the soul does perceive in one and the same individual time sensibles of the same sense, thus a fortiori it perceives sensibles of different senses. For it is more conceivable that it

should perceive a plurality of the former together in this way than a plurality of heterogeneous objects. (SS 449a2–5, with minor alterations of the translation)

εἰ δὲ τούτων ἐν ἑνὶ καὶ ἀτόμῳ αἰσθάνεται, δῆλον ὅτι καὶ τῶν ἄλλων·

μᾶλλον γὰρ ἐνεδέχετο τούτων ἅμα πλειόνων ἢ τῶν τῷ γένει ἑτέρων

As it stands, the text appears to state that if multiple instances of special sensibles (of one modality) are perceived in one and the same perceptual content, then evidently special sensibles of different modalities are perceived in the same perceptual content too, because it is more likely that sensibles of the same special sense are perceived together than sensibles differing in genus. The because clause (at l. 449a3) seems unproblematic: different senses have different types of sense organ, which makes it more difficult for their special sensibles to be perceived together. The initial clauses on the other hand are surprising; first, because they seem to assume that special sensibles of the same sense are indeed perceived together in one content, which has not been granted[12]; second, because even if this were granted, it would not show that special sensibles of different senses are perceived together as well, let alone evidently so. Indeed, how would the different parts of each sense, which, says Aristotle, differ between them like different sciences, perceive their special sensibles *together* when, as Aristotle said in the previous sentence, each part has its own perceptual power and its own type of perception corresponding to the exercise of that power (SS 449a1–2)? It must be this way of reasoning that led Alexander of Aphrodisias to emend the text by adding the negation 'not' in the first clause of the quotation, so that it reads:

But if the soul does *not* perceive in one and the same individual time sensibles of the same sense, *a fortiori* it is not thus that it perceives sensibles of different senses. For it is more conceivable that it should perceive a plurality of the former together in this way than a plurality of heterogeneous objects. (SS 449a2–5, with minor alterations of the translation)

εἰ δὲ τούτων ἐν ἑνὶ καὶ ἀτόμῳ <μὴ> αἰσθάνεται, δῆλον ὅτι καὶ τῶν ἄλλων·

μᾶλλον γὰρ ἐνεδέχετο τούτων ἅμα πλειόνων ἢ τῶν τῷ γένει ἑτέρων

To see how Alexander's emendation solves the difficulty we need to assume that the different parts of a sense, which are like different sciences, differ from each other only in species. If so, the passage tells us that it is more likely that perceptible qualities differing only in species (i.e., falling under the remit of one sense) will be perceived together, than that perceptible qualities differing in genus (i.e., falling within the remit of different senses) will be perceived together.[13] Yet, even if the amended text reads better, there is no improvement in the philosophical import of the overall argument.

In conclusion, the Multiple Sensors Model does not provide an explanation of the metaphysics of the common sense. If the sensors are, for example, two eyes functioning as one sense organ, then there is no explanation of how they perceive different colors at the same time; and if they function as organs of different types, then there is no explanation of how the perceived qualities are perceived in the same perceptual content. The difficulty comes from the one-to-one correspondence principle between sensible and perceptual content (see chapter 2), which the Multiple Sensors Model does not challenge. In fact the one-to-one correspondence principle is reinforced in this context by the association of type of sensation to type of perceptual activity that has its own type of perceptual power (see SS 449a1–2). The articulation of each sense into many parts only *replicates the problem*, because the parts are shown to be merely sub-senses, with no extra connectivity between them.[14]

6.3 THE RATIO MODEL

In the *De Anima*, Aristotle explores a new approach to the question of which metaphysics might deliver the required unity and complexity at the same time for the common sense. The starting point is the following thought: things are said to be analogous when they are equal in some respect; they are not equal one-to-one, as to what each is, but they are equal between pairs of them with respect to some difference in what each is (e.g., as 1 is to 3 so 4 is to 12). I call the model Aristotle develops from this idea the Ratio Model. It is a very unusual but sophisticated and original model for entities that are many-in-one. Its ingenuity is a measure of the degree to which the metaphysical composition of the common sense exercised Aristotle.

Consider a ratio that is the same across many analogical relations, as for example between 536/1072, and 77/154, etc., namely, 1/2. In the example, every fraction has its own constitution, involving different numbers than the other fractions. Each of these fractions is thus a different fraction, with different properties. But each of these *many* fractions is also *one* with the other fractions in the equation, because all of them stand for *the same ratio*. Thus, Aristotle reasons, suppose a perceiver discerns white from sweet on a variety of occasions. Each time she is aware of a perceptual content that is numerically different from the other times. But these perceptual contents have something in common, namely they all represent the same difference between perceptible qualities (e.g., between white and sweet). This difference can be thought of as a ratio—a specific relation of dissimilarity between two ways of being, white and sweet. Then, on this model when a perceiver discriminates between white and sweet on the different occasions of their perceptual discrimination, her complex perceptual content on each occasion will represent the same ratio of ways of being. More generally, complex perceptual contents representing the difference between visual and flavorful items are all instances of just this ratio, of the visual to the flavorful. By extension, the senses of vision and taste can be thought of as being related to each other by the same ratio, since the nature of each sense is determined by the perceptible quality it is sensitive to.[15] Aristotle describes the Ratio Model thus:

> The ultimate point of arrival [i.e., the common sense] is one, a single mean, with different manners of being. With what part of itself the soul discriminates sweet from hot I have explained before and must now describe again as follows: That with which it does so [i.e., the common sense] is a sort of unity, but in the way a *boundary* is; and these things [sc. sweet and hot] being one *by analogy* and *numerically*, are each to each as those [sc. the corresponding perceptual modifications, or perceptual contents, or senses—or even white and black] are to one another (for what difference does it make whether we raise the problem of discrimination between disparates or between contraries—e.g., white and black?). Let then C [sc. perceptual content of white] be to D [sc. perceptual content of black] as A, white is to B, black: it follows *alternando* that C: A:: D: B. If then C and A belong to one [sc. type of sensible], the case will be the same with them as with D and B; D and B are the same and one, with different modes of being; so too will the former ones. The same reasoning holds if A be sweet and B white. (*DA* 431a19–b1, my emphasis)
>
> τὸ δὲ ἔσχατον ἕν, καὶ μία <ἡ> μεσότης, τὸ δ᾽ εἶναι αὐτῇ πλείω...—τίνι δ᾽ ἐπικρίνει τί διαφέρει γλυκὺ καὶ θερμόν,

εἴρηται μὲν καὶ πρότερον, λεκτέον δὲ καὶ ὧδε. ἔστι γὰρ ἕν τι, οὕτω δὲ ὡς ὁ ὅρος, καὶ ταῦτα, ἓν τῷ ἀνάλογον καὶ τῷ ἀριθμῷ ὄντα, ἔχει <ἑκάτερον> πρὸς ἑκάτερον ὡς ἐκεῖνα πρὸς ἄλληλα· τί γὰρ διαφέρει τὸ ἀπορεῖν πῶς τὰ μὴ ὁμογενῆ κρίνει ἢ τὰ ἐναντία, οἷον λευκὸν καὶ μέλαν; ἔστω δὴ ὡς τὸ Α τὸ λευκὸν πρὸς τὸ Β τὸ μέλαν, τὸ Γ πρὸς τὸ Δ [ὡς ἐκεῖνα πρὸς ἄλληλα]· ὥστε καὶ ἐναλλάξ. εἰ δὴ τὰ ΓΑ ἑνὶ εἴη ὑπάρχοντα, οὕτως ἕξει, ὥσπερ καὶ τὰ ΔΒ, τὸ αὐτὸ μὲν καὶ ἕν, τὸ δ᾽ εἶναι οὐ τὸ αὐτό—κἀκεῖνα ὁμοίως. ὁ δ᾽ αὐτὸς λόγος καὶ εἰ τὸ μὲν Α τὸ γλυκὺ εἴη, τὸ δὲ Β τὸ λευκόν.

The text is brief and elliptical; it lends itself to many alternative interpretations. I will not give a detailed discussion of the alternatives here, nor of what advantages or difficulties each version of the argument has, as this has already been done in the literature.[16] Rather, I will advance a new reading that makes a contribution towards understanding how Aristotle addresses the question that he set out within the passage quoted. This is the question of the nature of the perceiving *subject*, specifically the common sense that perceives complex perceptual contents.

The goal is to show that despite the distinctness of the special senses and of what each is sensitive to, it is possible for the perceiver to have awareness of, for example, sweet and white in the complex perceptual content, via the operation of a single unified multi-modal sense, the common sense. So what is at issue is the unity and, yes, complexity of the common sense. The main claims Aristotle advances with the Ratio Model are the following: First, the common sense is a unified sense. Second, the common sense is a unified sense *despite* being constituted of a multiplicity of different senses— in the way a boundary is a unity, despite the multiple regions that individuate it. Third, perceptible qualities such as sweet and white are related to each other analogously to the way their respective perceptions are, and as their respective sense modalities are related in the common sense. I take Aristotle's point to be that the two perceptible qualities can thus be related (and be in the same perceptual content) even if they are not special sensibles of the same sense. The justification for this point is that if what relates the two qualities is their being qualitatively different from each other, there can be qualitative difference both between qualities of different species (e.g., two colors) and qualities of different genera (e.g., a color and a sound). Two qualities of the same genus are on the same qualitative spectrum, and, as such, there can be a borderline between them (between hot and cold; sweet and sour, etc.). On the other hand, two qualities that belong to different genera are not on the same qualitative spectrum. But the principle generalizes. Genera belong themselves to higher genera. The differences between genera within the same higher genus allows for a qualitative division between them; and in that sense, for a qualitative boundary or at least ratio between them. Any qualitative difference can be viewed as a qualitative division that sets a boundary between two items.[17]

The most important conceptual difficulty with the Ratio Model is that of understanding in which sense an analogy is unified. Aristotle says that the common sense is unified as a *mean* and as a *boundary*; and that complex perceptual content is unified like an *analogy*; and it is *analogous* to the common sense. I shall start by providing an account of the unity of a ratio, and then extend it to explain also the unity of an analogy between ways of being. It is easier to understand the unity of a numerical ratio because it corresponds to a single value—e.g., the ratio of 1 to 2, i.e. ½, is 0.5. But we need not grasp 0.5 in order to see the unity of ½, since the ratio is determinate even when it is relationally expressed as the ratio of 1 to 2. The *relational expression* of a ratio is appropriate for analogies between ways of being, since the latter cannot be expressed as a single value of a common unit and without a common unit there is no numerical analogy. What the qualitative analogies stand for is a single qualitative form expressed by the analogy. Examples of qualitative analogies are the following: as the central processing unit is to the computer, so the brain is to the human being; or, as a sophism is to reasoning, so a counterfeit note is to money. In the present case, as the sweet is to the white, so the content of the perception of the sweet is to the content of the perception of the white, and the sense of taste is to the sense of sight.

The simplest way to think about the analogy of a mean or a boundary in this context is to think of a fraction, defined by the relation of two numbers; so is a boundary defined by the relation of two regions, and similarly for a mean, or an analogy. A fraction is unified and one in various ways. First, a fraction is the *unification* of two numbers into a ratio; namely, it is one as a complex structured entity. Second, a fraction is *numerically one* as a value, namely, it is one as a simple entity. Third an analogy between two fractions is itself a *unification* of the two fractions into an equation, which is a complex structured entity (e.g., $186/372 = \frac{1}{2}$). But the equality of the fractions is a kind of shared identity, which is simple and *numerically one*. What Aristotle expresses through the Ratio Model, in my interpretation, is that a ratio has a single value, which runs through an equation of such ratios as *the common single identity shared by all the ratios* in the equation, unifying the equation into one, notwithstanding its multiple complexity.[18] Correspondingly, as color is to sight so sound is to hearing, and the tangible is to touch, and scent is to smell, and taste is to the sense of taste. The single identity that unifies the common sense (by being the common value—i.e., the common form of the ratios, throughout its structure and constitution) is the ratio between the modalities of the senses and the modalities of their contents respectively. Each ratio is equal to the other ratios, but different from them in being, just as the fractions in an equation are equal to one another but different in being. The equal value (i.e. the common form) unifies the common sense, and the diversity of being of the ratios of modalities articulates the common sense into its senses.[19]

In conclusion, Aristotle intends the oneness of the analogy to reflect the oneness and unity of the common sense, from which the unity of complex perceptual contents is derived. It is important to note that whereas in the case of the special senses it is the causal impact of the special sensible on the sense organ that determines the structure of the perceptual content—one causal alteration to one content, of white or sweet, etc.—in the case of complex content it is the structure of the common sense (which has no sense organ of its own) that determines the complex content of the experience comprising, for example, white and sweet.[20]

It is a measure of the difficulty that Aristotle finds in accounting for the oneness of a subject perceiving complex contents that he devises explanations of the common sense as abstract as the Ratio Model. The model offers too abstract a conception of a unity to give a satisfactory account of the way, for example, two different perceptible qualities modify the same sense at the same time. On the other hand, the model is helpful because it illustrates a further domain of what we may call the *oneness-of-division*. There are various ways in which this theme could be explored—boundaries, limits, ratios, etc.—and Aristotle explores most of them.

CONCLUDING REMARKS

In this chapter I examined three metaphysical models Aristotle develops to account for the unity and complexity of the common sense and of complex perceptual content. The Mixed Contents Model attempts to solve the problem of complex perceptual content by somehow unifying the different perceptible qualities that impact on a sense organ. They become one by mixing, and yet survive in potentiality in the mixture. Nevertheless, we saw that the type of presence in a mixture that Aristotle's theory of mixing allows for is not what is required for the operations of the common sense. The Multiple Sensors Model shifts the focus of the inquiry on to the common sense itself, from whose partition the complexity of its perceptual content is supposedly to be derived. The Multiple Sensors Model explores whether different types of perceptible quality can be perceived by different parts of a sense organ, each part operating as a separate sense (even if generically of the same type), so that the sense as a whole would perceive a complex perceptual content through its parts. Ultimately this model too was found wanting, because it did not provide a way of combining the perceptual contents gathered by the different parts of the sense into one single but complex content. Finally the Ratio Model offers a way of thinking of the common sense as one and many by analogy with the ratio that unifies many different pairs of different numbers. The drawback of this model is that it does not provide any metaphysics for the common sense and its operation, but only an abstract way of conceptualizing its unity and complexity. None of these three models is by itself apt to account for the metaphysics of the common sense, but each helps the investigation to move forward.

Notes

1. Even if Aristotle talks, for explanatory purposes, of how the common sense achieves perceptual awareness of the external objects, it is clear that for Aristotle the seat of perceptual awareness is ultimately the perceiver, and not the senses.
2. See the classification of perceptual powers given in chapter 4.
3. Debates about the chronological order of Aristotle's writings were popular among scholars up to the end of the 1960s as an (often abused) device to explain apparent doctrinal discrepancies in Aristotle's thought (a useful brief survey concerning psychological writings can be seen in Preus 1968, 175).

According to Ross' view (inspired by Nuyens'), *De Anima*'s hylomorphist conception represents the last stage of Aristotle's psychological theory, and its characteristic holism is incompatible with the instrumentalist dualism supposedly entailed by the attribution of primary functions to a precisely localized part of the body, the heart (Ross 1955, 5–7, 16; cf. Block 1961, 51). The latter view, in Ross' opinion, is found not only in *De Somno* but also in *De Sensu* and *De Memoria* (Ross 1955, 16–7; cf. Block 1961, 52, 54–6). A criticism of this view is offered by Block (1961, 50–61), who argues for the opposite views and considers *Parva Naturalia* the latest stage of development in Aristotle's theory, incompatible with the *De Anima* (Block 1961, 62–77, esp. 67–68). Contemporary scholarship appears to incline towards a 'unitarian' and compatibilist stance (see for example Polanski, 2007, 25–6) even when endorsing the view that the theses contained in *De Sensu* constitute a further elaboration of the views presented in the *De Anima* (cf. Johansen 2006, 163–64).

4. This is on account of Aristotle's stipulations on how perception works in the case of the special senses (see chapter 2) which suffer a physical disturbance when taking on each perceptible.

5. On the literalist view, nothing can be colored in two ways at the same time in the same part. On the disturbance view, Aristotle takes each sense organ to have a physiology that allows it to be a mean, and receive stimuli that do not physically change the organ so that it embodies the perceived quality but nevertheless cause a 'disturbance' in the organ. On the spiritualist view presumably there would be no problem if there were two different spiritual changes in the same organ at the same time. The three interpretations are discussed in chapter 2.

6. See the very helpful discussion of the metaphysics of mixture in Scaltsas 2009.

7. This is the closest Aristotle ever gets to explicitly describing what for us is the *perceptual field*. At this point in the reasoning he has not focused on a single sense (as he immediately will with sight as an example); so it is not just the visual field he has in mind but more broadly *the continuum of percepts* as they come in through seeing, hearing, tasting, smelling, and feeling. In Greek, Aristotle's way of expressing this point is: οὕτως ἀτόμῳ ὡς παντὶ ὄντι συνεχεῖ. This sentence has been interpreted differently by translators rendering it either as about the time of perception being continuous (J.I. Beare, in Barnes 1984) or the sensing parts of the soul being continuous (Hett 1957). The first proposed reading is difficult to understand as it suggests that the perceptions happen with different parts of the soul—different sense organs—which are continuous: 'is it possible to perceive...with a different part of the soul,...one indivisible in the sense of being all continuous'. What would it mean for the sense organ of sight to be continuous with the sense organ of taste? The second suggestion clashes with the claim in this sentence that the perceptions are simultaneous, where 'simultaneous' is explained by Aristotle in the previous

sentence as occurring at 'a time one and indivisible' (SS 448b19); it would also not be obvious why Aristotle would be interested in explaining perception of different sensibles over a period of time, which is what continuous time would entail, when he has not yet explained perception of different sensibles at one time. In suggesting this interpretation I depart from D. Frede (1992, 283), who thinks that 'it is doubtful that for Aristotle we can have something like a "panoramic" view of a whole situation, for he does not seem to include anything like a "field of vision" in his explanations'.

8. εἰ ἔσται ἄλλῳ αἰσθανομένη ἄλλου καὶ ἄλλου χρώματος

9. I take this to be where the objection to the two eyes analogy begins. If it is not read in this way, then the analogy of the eyes would not face any objections, and would need to be treated as a positive contribution towards an account of complex content. But then we would not be able to explain why the very next sentence introduces an objection against the suggestion of the parts of a sense with the word ἔτι, which signifies an additional objection.

10. Although Aristotle mentions the parts of the soul, it must be that he is still operating on the initial hypothesis of the parts of a single sense, here sight (SS 448b22–23). It is these parts he began discussing at SS 448b24.

11. In this argument Aristotle associates difference in species between the different parts of a sense with difference in sense; whereas in the argument at SS 448b24–25 as we saw he associates difference in genus with difference in sense. This shows that there is a grey area in the criteria for individuating a sense, once we divide a sense into parts.

12. Unless one took the two eyes analogy as the resolution of the complex perceptual content problem for sensibles of one modality, which we had no reason to assume above.

13. The text says τῶν τῷ γένει ἐτέρων, which is not clearly reflected in the translation as 'heterogeneous', but would be better rendered as 'different in genus', as Hett does in the "Loeb" edition ('for it would be more possible for it to perceive several of these simultaneously than things different in genus').

14. For this reason, Aristotle proceeds to a different model in the middle of this discussion in the De Sensu, the Substance Model (discussed in chapter 7).

15. See DA 418a24–25: the 'special objects of the several senses constitute the objects of sense in the strictest sense of the term and it is to them that in the nature of things the structure of each several sense is adapted'.

16. There are also alternative ways of filling out the text, inserted here below within square brackets:

With what part of itself the soul discriminates sweet from hot I have explained before and must now describe again as follows: That with which it does so is a sort of unity, but in the way a boundary is; and these things [sc. the sensibles, sweet and hot] being one by analogy [sc. as a ratio is a relationally unified whole] and numerically [*sc.* in the way that a sense experience is numerically one], are each to each as those [*sc.* the sensible forms, sweet and hot] are to one another (for what difference does it make whether we raise the problem of discrimination between disparates [such as sweet and hot] or between contraries—e.g., white and black?). Let then C [sensible white? sight?] be to D [sensible black? sight?] as A, white [sensible form? sensible?] is to B, black [sensible form? sensible?]: it follows *alternando* that C: A:: D: B. If then C and A belong to one [genus? subject?], the case will be the same with them as with D and B; D and B are the same and one [in genus], with different modes of being [sensible form versus sensible? sensible versus sense]; so too will the former ones [C and A]. The same reasoning holds if A be sweet and B white. (*DA* 431a20–b1)

Gregoric (2007, 158) provides a brief survey of the traditional readings of this passage.

17. I am in disagreement on this point with Charlton (1981, 107); and also with Gregoric (2007, 156), who bases his own interpretation on Charlton's point that there cannot be a boundary between white and sweet.

18. The equation is complex vertically, as it were, because of the complexity of beings in each ratio; and horizontally, because of the complexity of beings of each ratio in the equation.

19. Contrast this with the interpretation in Gregoric (2007, 159–60):

Let us assume that sweet and hot are one in analogy in the sense that they are co-specific perceptibles... [T]he perceptions of sweet and hot are one in analogy in the sense that they are acts of the same *intensity*... they actualize the corresponding senses with equal *intensity*. (My emphasis)

Gregoric himself admits that his reading is not 'foolproof' ('I wish to stress that the interpretation of the *DA* III.7 passage I have offered is neither foolproof nor the only one possible', Gregoric 2007: 161) but there is no textual evidence to begin with that Aristotle is making use of the concept of intensity in this context.

20. This point will be further discussed in chapter 6, section 6.4.

Chapter 7

One *and* Many Perceptual Faculties

INTRODUCTION

In his theory of perception, Aristotle is committed to a *unified* common sense with *unified* complex perceptual content. In chapter 6 we saw that he approaches the question of how to account metaphysically for the unity of the common sense and of its perceptual content in two ways: starting from the many (many inputs, in the Mixed Contents Models; many analogous items, in the Ratio Model) and trying to unify them into one; and starting from the one (one faculty, in the Multiple Sensors Model) and partitioning it into many. This latter approach guides Aristotle in developing a further model in the *De Anima*, in which the common sense is one and many by analogy with the way in which a point can be many limits at once, in relation to different semi-lines. This latter model is a metaphysical breakthrough as it introduces the idea of *relative identity*. I thus call it the Relative Identity Model. While the Mixed Contents, the Multiple Sensors, and the Ratio Models help in advancing Aristotle's inquiry into the metaphysics of the common sense, none of them ultimately contributes the final solution. By contrast the Relative Identity Model does, as I will argue in the overall conclusions. But by itself, even this model is not fully adequate to account for the metaphysics of the common sense. The reason is that it does not account for the *operations* of the common sense on the perceptual inputs it gathers via the special sensibles. The Relative Identity Model explains successfully how one thing can be many at once—how it can instantiate many beings. Thus the common sense can be at once the faculty of vision, of touch, of smell, etc. But this is not all Aristotle needs to account for. As we saw, Aristotle argues that perception of the modally different sensibles together in a single *content* is achieved by means of a single subject, *plus* a perceptual mechanism by which the different modifications of the various sense organs result in the generation of a single perceptual content for the subject. Ultimately, as I will argue in the overall conclusions, the unity of the common sense is a functional type of unity: what it does can be achieved only by an integrated perceptual system constituted by the five senses, and its unity is derived from the unity of function. This is what the Relative Identity Model cannot capture; it cannot explain how the common sense functions. Thus Aristotle attempts new two ways of explaining the perceptual mechanism of multimodal perception. I call them the Substance Model and the Common Power Model, and I discuss them in this chapter.

7.1 THE RELATIVE IDENTITY MODEL

In the *De Anima* Aristotle returns for a second time[1] to the question of how a sense can at one and the same time be affected by different sensibles such as sweet and bitter, or sweet and white; and makes a fresh start. He introduces the problem thus:

> It may be objected, it is impossible that what is one and the same [i.e., a sense] should be moved at one and the same time with contrary movements in so far as it is undivided, and in an undivided moment of time. For if what is sweet be the quality

perceived, it moves the sense or thought in this determinate way, while what is bitter moves it in a contrary way, and what is white in a different way. (*DA* 426b29–427a1, translation slightly modified)

ἀλλὰ μὴν ἀδύνατον ἅμα τὰς ἐναντίας κινήσεις κινεῖσθαι τὸ αὐτὸ ᾗ ἀδιαίρετον, καὶ ἐν ἀδιαιρέτῳ χρόνῳ. εἰ γὰρ γλυκύ, ὡδὶ κινεῖ τὴν αἴσθησιν ἢ τὴν νόησιν, τὸ δὲ πικρὸν ἐναντίως, καὶ τὸ λευκὸν ἑτέρως

The solution Aristotle proposes in this section of the *De Anima* to the difficulty just raised is not unique to his theory of perception, but is one that he employs in various contexts where he is confronting a problem of unity and multiplicity in relation to the constitution of an activity or a (nonsubstantial) entity: it is being *one in number and many in being*. I call this particular application of it to the problem of perception the Relative Identity Model. It is put forward here:

Is it the case then that what discriminates, though both numerically one and indivisible, is at the same time divided in its being? In one sense, it is what is divided that perceives two separate objects at once, but in another sense it does so *qua* undivided; for it is divisible in its being but spatially and numerically undivided. (*DA* 427a2–5)

ἆρ᾽ οὖν ἅμα μὲν ἀριθμῷ ἀδιαίρετον καὶ ἀχώριστον τὸ κρῖνον, τῷ εἶναι δὲ κεχωρισμένον; ἔστι δὴ [πως] ὡς τὸ διαιρετὸν τῶν διῃρημένων αἰσθάνεται, ἔστι δ᾽ ὡς ᾗ ἀδιαίρετον· τῷ εἶναι μὲν γὰρ διαιρετόν, τόπῳ δὲ καὶ ἀριθμῷ ἀδιαίρετον

The thought Aristotle is exploring here is that the common sense is already by its very nature many beings at the same time, while being numerically one; therefore the multiple modifications of it at one and the same time should not be thought to undermine its oneness.

Before we proceed in further examining the model, let us consider a very subtle objection Aristotle himself raises against his own proposed solution:

> But is not this impossible? For while it is true that what is one and the same and undivided may be both contraries at once *potentially*, it cannot be one and the same in its being—it must lose its unity by being put into activity. It is not possible to be at once white and black, and therefore it must also be impossible for a thing to be affected at one and the same moment by the forms of both, assuming it to be the case that sensation and thinking are properly so described. (*DA* 427a5–9, with minor alterations in the translation, my emphasis)
>
> ἢ οὐχ οἷόν τε; δυνάμει μὲν γὰρ τὸ αὐτὸ καὶ ἀδιαίρετον τἀναντία, τῷ δ' εἶναι οὔ, ἀλλὰ τῷ ἐνεργεῖσθαι διαιρετόν, καὶ οὐχ οἷόν τε ἅμα λευκὸν καὶ μέλαν εἶναι, ὥστ' οὐδὲ τὰ εἴδη πάσχειν αὐτῶν, εἰ τοιοῦτον ἡ αἴσθησις καὶ ἡ νόησις

The question Aristotle examines is whether the discriminating sense (i.e. the common sense) is 'many in being' *actually, at the same time*; or is many in being only *potentially*, while being actually 'many in being' only at different times. The objection is that if the common sense was many in being only potentially but not in actuality at the same time, then the common sense would not be able to suffer different causal alterations at a time—which is what is required for complex perceptual content. Aristotle responds to the objection he has raised with an example, which aims to validate the Relative Identity Model for the common sense:

> Just as what is called a *'point'* is, as being at once one and two, properly said to be divisible, so here, that which discriminates is *qua* undivided one, and active in a single moment of

time, while *qua* divisible it twice over uses the *same dot* at one and the same time. So far then as it twice over uses the limit, it discriminates two separate objects with what in a sense is separated: while so far as it uses it as one, it does so with what is one and occupies in its activity a single moment of time. (*DA* 427a10–14, my emphasis, and translation slightly modified)

ὥσπερ ἣν καλοῦσί τινες στιγμήν, ᾗ μία καὶ δύο, ταύτῃ <καὶ ἀδιαίρετος> καὶ διαιρετή. ᾗ μὲν οὖν ἀδιαίρετον, ἓν τὸ κρῖνόν ἐστι καὶ ἅμα, ᾗ δὲ διαιρετὸν ὑπάρχει, δὶς τῷ αὐτῷ χρῆται σημείῳ ἅμα· ᾗ μὲν οὖν δὶς χρῆται τῷ πέρατι, δύο κρίνει καὶ κεχωρισμένα, ἔστιν ὡς κεχωρισμένως· ᾗ δὲ ἑνί, ἓν καὶ ἅμα.

A terminological point first: In this passage, Aristotle thinks of the point in two ways—as a substratum, entering the constitution of a further entity (for example a limit, πέρας, has a point as its substratum), and as a constituted entity in itself. He uses different expressions for each: the word στίγμα for the point taken as a limit, and the word σημεῖον for the point taken as the underlying substratum of the στιγμή (or the στιγμαί). Thus Aristotle talks of the στιγμή as being one and two at the same time, but of the σημεῖον as being used twice over at the same time. What this example establishes is that it is possible for something to have two natures *in actuality* at one and the same time.[2] The example describes the function of a point as a limit. Consider a point that divides a line in half. The point constitutes two limits, *a* and *b*, one for each half-line. The relations of the point to each of the half-lines determine its function and nature, as a limit for each of the half-lines. In this sense, the point is one and undivided as a point, while it is divided into two in its functions as a limit, since there are two different limits instantiated in it in actuality at the same time. So at one and the same time, *a* and *b* are the same point, but they are different limits. Hereby, Aristotle introduces in his metaphysics the concept of *relative identity*.

Turning now to examine the philosophical adequacy of the Relative Identity Model to provide a metaphysical account of the common sense, Aristotle reiterates that this is what the common sense needs to be capable of achieving:

> Therefore discrimination between white and sweet cannot be effected by two discriminators which remain separate; both the qualities discriminated must be present to something that is one and single. On this supposition [that both qualities are present to one discriminator], even if I perceived sweet and you perceived white, the difference between them would be evident. What says that two things are different must be one; for sweet is different from white. Therefore what asserts this difference must be one and the same, and as what asserts, so also what thinks or perceives. (*DA* 426b17–22; translation slightly modified)
>
> οὔτε δὴ κεχωρισμένοις ἐνδέχεται κρίνειν ὅτι ἕτερον τὸ γλυκὺ τοῦ λευκοῦ, ἀλλὰ δεῖ ἑνί τινι ἄμφω δῆλα εἶναι—οὕτω μὲν γὰρ κἂν εἰ τοῦ μὲν ἐγὼ τοῦ δὲ σὺ αἴσθοιο, δῆλον ἂν εἴη ὅτι ἕτερα ἀλλήλων, δεῖ δὲ τὸ ἓν λέγειν ὅτι ἕτερον· ἕτερον γὰρ τὸ γλυκὺ τοῦ λευκοῦ· λέγει ἄρα τὸ αὐτό· ὥστε ὡς λέγει, οὕτω καὶ νοεῖ καὶ αἰσθάνεται

The requirements for the discrimination between, for example, white and sweet can be summarized as follows. The common sense functions *as a sense*. It is the sense through which we perceive colors, sounds, tastes, etc. Its sense organs are the sense organs of the special senses; we have seen that the common sense does not have a sense organ that can perceive the perceptible qualities over and above the sense organs of the special senses.[3] Thus it must be that the perception of white through sight *suffices* for the awareness of white through the common sense, and similarly for the other perceptible qualities. Hence, whatever is perceptible through the special senses is thereby perceptible through the common sense. There is only one instance of perceptual awareness of the white through sight and through the common sense, not two. In other words, there is no (homuncular, or second order) sense internally perceiving the perceptual contents produced by the special senses.[4] Therefore, any account of the common sense must be able to explain its capacity to function as a sense despite not having its own sense organ but relying on the sense organs of the special senses. Secondly, any such account must be able to explain how it is that the common sense has perceptual powers that the special senses do not have (for example the common sense can discriminate white and sweet). Such perceptual powers require that the common sense be a *single* center of perceptual awareness.[5] Hence, the metaphysical challenge of complex perceptual content arises.

The common sense has to function as each of the special senses and additionally as a *sui generis* sense itself, with input through the special senses and also with perceptual powers of its own. Does the point example illustrate how a single entity can function in all these ways? The example lends itself to a variety of metaphysical interpretations. Specifically, the point can be taken to be the *substratum* that constitutes this or that limit—depending on the relations that relate the point to this or that line as their limit. Alternatively, the point can be taken to be a *limit*, essentially related to the line whose limit it is. But the common sense cannot be related to the five senses in the way the substratum point is related to the limits it constitutes, because the common sense is *constituted* by the special senses, rather than constituting them. The common sense functions, itself, as a sense, capable of perceiving sensibles that no other sense can perceive—the common sensibles—and has awareness of all the perceptual input received through the special senses. It is the *same type of entity* as each of the special senses (i.e., it is a sense); this is why it cannot be their substratum. For these reasons, I shall rather turn to explore the other possible interpretation of the example, taking the point as a limit. The example of the point taken as a limit can itself be developed in a variety of ways; the more promising one is the reading according to which the point is the center of a circle.[6] On this reading, the center point is the terminus of each radius and the terminus of all of them. One and the same point is *many* limits (i.e., many in being)—and analogously the common sense is one and many senses in actuality. But the example goes only some way toward providing the metaphysical explanation of the common sense that Aristotle is looking for: the common sense is basically a sense constituted by the special senses. The example is ultimately not apt to capture this—it is as if we were looking for a limit constituted by the convergent limits of the circle's radii, but there is no limit constituted of the overlapping limits of the radii. The interpretation of the point as the limit of the radii only differentiates between it being the limit of one and being the limit of many radii—and thus it does not provide all the metaphysical sophistication that an account of the common sense requires. (It might be thought that the point, as the limit of *all* the radii of a circle, becomes the center of a circle—i.e., something metaphysically different from being a line-limit—and thus perhaps differently empowered. Would this move offer a way of addressing the requirement that the common sense functions not merely as any one of the special senses, but as a different type of sense, with perceptual powers of its own, of a type that the special senses do not possess? It would not. Even if considered as the limit of *all* the radii, the point has no more causal powers than it has if considered as the limit of each of the radii, and certainly not powers that enable it to operate on the radii the center connects. Aristotle is seeking a model that can explain how the common sense can operate on the very same input as each of the special senses, but perform different functions with it.)

In conclusion, I submit that Aristotle proposes the example of the point and the limits in order to help us understand how different sortal beings can be co-instantiated concurrently in actuality, without any incompatibility arising. The example illustrates this successfully by showing that the limits overlap on the same point concurrently, in actuality—without any incompatibility arising. This is helpful to address the difficulty raised with the example of a surface that cannot be black and white at the same time; similarly, the common sense is supposedly unable to be altered in different ways at the same time by two or more perceptible qualities. But if so, complex perceptual content (and all the perceptual functions that depend on it) would be impossible. The solution the Relative Identity Model offers is a way of thinking of different beings or natures as co-instantiated in the same entity in the way in which different limits are co-instantiated in the same point. In this example the co-instantiated beings are different *functions* that the same point can perform. These functions are generated and defined by *external relations* that the point holds with different semi-lines; they are not real changes the point undergoes. Thus, the example of the point does show us how one thing can have multiple functional roles. Aristotle does not show how the example is to be applied to the common sense case; but the gist is clear: the common sense can be numerically one, but functionally many with respect to perceiving sensibles of different modalities. Yet, the example of the point and the limits, and the Relative Identity Model in general, do *not* help us understand how the point could become endowed with more causal powers. What we have been looking for is an understanding of how the special senses form a whole that is itself a sense, which has perceptual capacities over and above the individual senses. The example of the point is an important step in the right direction for understanding the metaphysics of the common sense, even if it does not give us the full requisite account.

7.2 THE SUBSTANCE MODEL

The Relative Identity Model has explanatory value, to which Aristotle returns in the *De Sensu* before giving yet another new account of the unity and articulation of the common sense as a perceiving subject. In the *De Anima* Aristotle had written:

> Is it the case then that what discriminates [complex contents], though both numerically one and indivisible, is at the same time divided in its being? In one sense, it is what is divided that perceives two separate objects at once, but in another sense it does so *qua* undivided; for it is divisible in its being but spatially and numerically undivided. (*DA* 427a2–5)
>
> ἆρ' οὖν ἅμα μὲν ἀριθμῷ ἀδιαίρετον καὶ ἀχώριστον τὸ κρῖνον, τῷ εἶναι δὲ κεχωρισμένον; ἔστι δὴ [πως] ὡς τὸ διαιρετὸν τῶν διῃρημένων αἰσθάνεται, ἔστι δ' ὡς ᾗ ἀδιαίρετον· τῷ εἶναι μὲν γὰρ διαιρετόν, τόπῳ δὲ καὶ ἀριθμῷ ἀδιαίρετον.

And here, in the *De Sensu* Aristotle entertains a line of thought that echoes his Relative Identity Model. He writes:

> May we not, then, conceive this faculty that perceives white and sweet to be one *qua* indivisible in its actualization [*sc. qua* combining its different simultaneous objects of perception in a content], but different, when it has become divisible in its actualization [*sc. qua* perceiving its objects separately—e.g., white, sweet, not in the same content]? (*SS* 449a10–13)

ἆρ' οὖν ᾗ μὲν ἀδιαίρετόν ἐστι κατ' ἐνέργειαν, ἕν τί ἐστι τὸ
αἰσθητικὸν γλυκέος καὶ λευκοῦ, ὅταν δὲ διαιρετὸν γένηται κατ'
ἐνέργειαν, ἕτερον;

The description in the *De Anima* passage gives us more metaphysical
detail than the description in the *De Sensu* passage. The *De Anima*
passage makes it explicit that the indivisible status and the divided
status[7] of the common sense are simultaneous—the perceiving
subject is one, although many in beings (i.e., the common sense is
one sense, which is sight, taste, etc., at once). Aristotle experiments
with explaining the indivisible and the divisible as different metaphysical levels of the perceptual faculty—'for it is divisible in its
being, but spatially and numerically undivided' (427a4–5). In other
words, Aristotle finds oneness (indivisibility) in the organization
of the common sense—it is *one* perceptual faculty, and plurality
(divisibility) in its constituents (i.e., the special senses). But what
Aristotle needs in order to explain the oneness of complex content
is unity at the level of the *actual operation of the common sense* (i.e., in
perceiving) rather than merely in its organization. Organizational
unity may deliver connectivity and communication; operational
unity, on the other hand, requires a single 'field of operation', which
in this case is the content of perceptual awareness. A faculty that is
unified only at the organizational level is one, but could be divided
in its operations, perceiving white and sweet in separate contents
at the same time). This is the very point that the *De Sensu* passage
under consideration addresses: the common sense is *divisible in its
actualization* (i.e., in perceiving each of the special sensibles—e.g.,
white and sweet— through different sense organs), but also *indivisible in its actualization* (in discerning white from sweet in a complex
perceptual content).[8] The Relative Identity Model, which to some
degree developed this line of thought, did not deliver a metaphysics
adequate to capture these two commitments.

How then can the common sense be shown to be 'one *qua* indivisible in its actualization, but different, when it has become divisible in its actualization' (SS 449a11–13)?[9] Advancing an account of the common sense as *simultaneously* divisible (when the sensibles are perceived simultaneously but in different contents) but indivisible (when the sensibles are in the same content) in its *actualization*, is no easy task. Some type of qualification needs to be made, and it is for this purpose that Aristotle starts again with a new metaphysical model. Recall that for Aristotle, for the content of perception to be one it must be present to a single subject (chapter 5, section). So Aristotle secures the oneness of the perceptual subject in the present account, and then derives the oneness of the content from it. The oneness of the subject that Aristotle is proposing in this model is the oneness of a substance. Hence, I call this the Substance Model. Aristotle writes:

> Or is what occurs in the case of the soul conceivably analogous to what holds true in that of the things themselves? For the same numerically one thing is white and sweet, and has many other qualities; for if the qualities are not separable from one another, their being is different in each case. (SS 449a13–16)
>
> ἢ ὥσπερ ἐπὶ τῶν πραγμάτων αὐτῶν ἐνδέχεται, οὕτως καὶ ἐπὶ τῆς ψυχῆς; τὸ γὰρ αὐτὸ καὶ ἓν ἀριθμῷ λευκὸν καὶ γλυκύ ἐστι, καὶ ἄλλα πολλά· εἰ γὰρ μὴ χωριστὰ τὰ πάθη ἀλλήλων, ἀλλὰ τὸ εἶναι ἕτερον ἑκάστῳ.

The proposed paradigm is that of a substance which possesses different properties, each one of which is different in being from the other properties (e.g., being sweet is different from being white), but they are not separate from one another, as it is numerically one and the same thing that is sweet and white (for example, sugar). Correspondingly, Aristotle writes,

In the same way therefore, we must assume also, in the case of the soul, that the faculty of perception in general is in itself numerically one and the same, but different in its being (*SS* 449a16–19)

ὁμοίως τοίνυν θετέον καὶ ἐπὶ τῆς ψυχῆς τὸ αὐτὸ καὶ ἓν εἶναι ἀριθμῷ τὸ αἰσθητικὸν πάντων, τὸ μέντοι εἶναι ἕτερον καὶ ἕτερον τῶν μὲν γένει τῶν δὲ εἴδει.

In a substance, each property belonging to it is a different kind of entity from the other properties (e.g., a quality, a quantity, etc.). Yet, their connection to each other in a substance is *metaphysically* '*seamless*', which is why a substance is one thing, and not many. The properties that belong to a substance are not numerically distinct (except in abstraction); they are 'fused' in the substance they qualify. They are 'fused' in it in the sense that they become dependent on it, in the way dictated by Aristotle's Homonymy Principle, which says that separating a constituent of a substance from the substance generates a new individual, only synonymously related to what it was within the substance before being severed from it, and different from what it was in definition.[10] The type of dependence of the properties on the substance is determined by the substantial form of the substance itself, which structures the substance's components according to the organization principle the substantial form stands for.[11] It follows that in the constitution of a substance there is 'difference without distinctness'. The different beings (properties) that qualify a substance are seamlessly united into a numerically one substance in virtue of its substantial form. In the case of perception, the different beings are the perceptual sensitivities the common sense has, through the sense organs of its special senses. Whatever is perceived through any of the senses is thereby perceived through the common sense. Yet, each of the special senses has a different being from the others, with respect to what it is perceptually receptive of. In the *De Sensu* Aristotle in fact differentiates the beings of the special senses with more precise descriptions than in other contexts, saying that the common sense is 'different in its being: different, that is to say, in genus as regards some of its objects, in species as regards others' (*SS* 449a18–19). That is, special senses comprising the common sense are different in *genus* from one another, in virtue of being perceptually sensitive to, for example, visual and olfactory stimuli; additionally, each special sense is different in *species* when perceiving and discerning stimuli such as, for example, hot and rough, both of which are generically tactile sensitivities, but different in species from each other.

On the Substance Model, the beings of the special senses qualify the common sense in the way that properties qualify the substance they belong to. On this model we would also expect an account of the seamlessness of (the awareness of) the perceptible qualities united into a complex perceptual content. But in the case of complex perceptual content, seamlessness ought to be achieved not in virtue of a substantial form (as it is with the properties of substances) unifying all the perceptual inputs into one (that would make discrimination impossible); but rather, in virtue of the *operation* of the common sense. It is the common sense that brings the perceptible qualities together into comparisons, discernments, etc., in a *structured* perceptual content (that is, structured in the way that, for example, white can be discerned from red). Thus, the perceptible qualities perceived through the special senses are involved in perceptual activities that result in the complex perceptual contents of the common sense. In sum, the Substance model shows that modifications of the special senses may be *physically distributed* (in the sense organs of the special senses) and yet the experiences be *metaphysically unified*, in virtue of their belonging to the same subject of awareness, the common sense. In the case of a substance, com-presence of properties does not generate incompatible results (e.g., an almond possesses the properties of being white and being sweet in every part of itself compatibly). The almond is white and sweet as the metaphysical subject to which these properties belong. The substance is, as it were, a *metaphysical catalyst* for the oneness of the properties; they come together into a oneness by fusion into the whole of the substance.[12] By analogy, the perceptual experiences resulting from the variously distributed modifications of the common sense by the sensibles it perceives through the special senses all belong to a single metaphysical subject of awareness: the common sense. This metaphysical subject of awareness acts as a 'catalyst' that brings together into one content the awareness of different perceptible qualities perceived through the special senses. Thus, the Substance Model provides a way of explaining not only how the modifications of different sense modalities are unified into one conscious content; it further explains how the perception of two different sensibles (e.g., of black and white) through the same sense modality come together in the same content.

Although Aristotle does not mention the example of discerning black from white in connection with the Substance Model, it was raised in the context of the Relative Identity Model as the most challenging difficulty for the oneness of perceptual awareness (see chapter 6). The Substance Model can best address this challenge. The challenge was that there cannot be unified perceptual awareness of white and black, because this would require the sense organ to be modified by black and white at the same time. Nothing can become black and white all over at the same time; similarly one and the same sense organ cannot be modified by them both at the same time (see *DA* 427a5–9)—hence no subject can discern them. Yet what the Substance Model allows is that, for example, a chessboard *is black and white* at the same time, even though it is not white all over and black all over; it is black and white when its surface includes black areas and white areas. The physical distribution of the modifications, even when they are in different parts of the same sense organ, does not impede their belonging to the same subject of awareness. So, even if one would have thought that something's being black and white is impossible because the two colors are mutually incompatible on the same surface, if 'being black and white' is not taken to mean that every proper part is black and white, but rather, that black and white both qualify distinct proper parts of the same subject, then the chessboard can be black and white without any proper sub-region of its surface having both colors. By analogy, in the case of the discrimination of black and white, it will not be the same proper part of the sense organ that will be modified by the perceptible qualities of black and of white at the same time. Just as *the substantial subject* can be black and white with no color overlap, so *the subject of awareness* can perceive black and white without the perceptible qualities being perceived in an overlapping way through any given proper part of the sense organ. There is a parallel between the physics of the awareness of perceptible qualities by a subject of awareness and the physics of the ownership of properties by a substantial subject.

In conclusion, the Substance model, just as a substance is unified into a single entity under its kind (e.g., being an eagle or a daisy) while also being many other kinds of thing too—say tall, small, fast, beautiful, etc.—so the common sense can be a single sense while having a variety of *functions* through its modally different sensitivities to the environment.[13] What is different about the oneness of the common sense according to the Substance Model, compared to the Relative Identity Model, is that in the Relative Identity Model Aristotle grounds the oneness of the common sense in the physical substratum of the perceptual activity (like the point underlying the limits); while in the Substance Model he attributes to the common sense oneness at the level of *functional composition*. The numerical oneness of a substance is not oneness of matter, but oneness of what is constituted of the matter, of the en-formed substance. Thus, the advantage of this account of the common sense, being modeled on Aristotle's account of substance, is that it attributes to the common sense unity at the *functional level*, the level of the senses, rather than spatiotemporal oneness at the physical level of perceptual activity. It is this level of oneness that the Relative Identity model could not provide, but was needed for Aristotle to show the common sense to be constituted of senses and itself be one *as a sense*, aware of complex contents not perceivable through the special senses; it is not sufficient to show the common sense to be simply an aggregate or a network of senses, which are physically interconnected and engaged in merely coordinated perceptual activities of their own.

The Substance Model is a breakthrough for Aristotle, and a milestone in the history of the philosophy of mind. It is a breakthrough with respect to the problem of how one and the same subject of awareness can perceive different perceptible qualities at the same time. For, the overall assumption here is that the oneness of complex perceptual content requires a single perceiving subject, and hence, *a single perceptual activity*. The Substance Model explains that the oneness of the perceptual subject is not physical, but *metaphysical*. This approach does not evoke a primitively assumed oneness of the mental subject; nor does it reduce the oneness of the mental subject to physical oneness (or oneness at some lower ground level). Rather, it endeavors to offer an explanation of the oneness of the perceptual subject from Aristotle's well-developed account of the oneness of a substance. This is oneness arising *from functional composition*. The Substance model however does not explain all that Aristotle endeavors to explain with respect to complex perceptual content. It successfully explains how white, sweet, cold, etc. can all be com-present in the same perceptual content at the same time, without mixing. But it does not explain how one can *discern* white from sweet. Discerning, contrasting, comparing, etc., are perceptual activities that involve functions *over and above* merely belonging to the same perceptual subject; additional perceptual abilities to the ones the special senses have are needed to perform the common sense's functions. We will have to look to the next model to gain a fuller understanding of how the common sense can have powers in addition to those of the special senses.

7.3 THE COMMON POWER MODEL

The Common Power model, as I call it, is the most generic model Aristotle develops, describing the common sense in terms which are compatible with some of the more specific models discussed in chapter 6 and in the preceding section of this chapter. The model is presented in the *De Somno*, and it marks a departure from the account of the senses in *De Anima* III.2.[14] In the *De Somno* Aristotle writes:

> Since every sense has something special and also something common; special, as, for example, seeing is to the sense of sight, hearing to the auditory sense, and so on with the other senses severally; while all are accompanied by a common power, in virtue whereof a person perceives that he sees or hears (for, assuredly, it is not by *sight* that one sees that he sees, and it is not by taste, or sight, or both together that one discerns that sweet things are different from white things, but by a part common to all the organs of sense; for there is one sense, and the controlling sensory organ is one, though differing with respect to what it is to be a faculty of perception in relation to each genus, for example sound or color). (*DS* 455a12–22)
>
> ἐπεὶ δ'ὑπάρχει καθ' ἑκάστην αἴσθησιν τὸ μέν τι ἴδιον, τὸ δέ τι κοινόν, ἴδιον μὲν οἷον τῇ ὄψει τὸ ὁρᾶν, τῇ δ' ἀκοῇ τὸ ἀκούειν,

καὶ ταῖς ἄλλαις ἑκάστῃ κατὰ τὸν αὐτὸν τρόπον, ἔστι δέ τις καὶ
κοινὴ δύναμις ἀκολουθοῦσα πάσαις, ᾗ καὶ ὅτι ὁρᾷ καὶ ἀκούει
αἰσθάνεται (οὐ γὰρ δὴ τῇ γε ὄψει ὁρᾷ ὅτι ὁρᾷ, καὶ κρίνει δὴ καὶ
δύναται κρίνειν ὅτι ἕτερα τὰ γλυκέα τῶν λευκῶν οὔτε γεύσει
οὔτε ὄψει οὔτε ἀμφοῖν, ἀλλά τινι κοινῷ μορίῳ τῶν αἰσθητηρίων
ἁπάντων· ἔστι μὲν γὰρ μία αἴσθησις, καὶ τὸ κύριον αἰσθητήριον
ἕν, τὸ δ᾽ εἶναι αἰσθήσει τοῦ γένους ἑκάστου ἕτερον, οἷον ψόφου
καὶ χρώματος.

Two descriptions of the common sense are given in the above passage. On the one hand, the common sense is presented as a 'common part' or 'common power' of the special senses (455a13–14: τι
κοινόν; 455a16: κοινὴ δύναμις), which each of the special senses
has, and which is involved in each special sense's specific perceptual
activities. On the other hand, the common sense is presented as the
'primary sensory organ' that is *one*, but *many* with respect to what
it is to be a sense (i.e., being sensitive to sounds or colors, etc.) (ll.
455a20–22: ἔστι μὲν γὰρ μία αἴσθησις, καὶ τὸ κύριον αἰσθητήριον
ἕν, τὸ δ᾽ εἶναι αἰσθήσει τοῦ γένους ἑκάστου ἕτερον, οἷον ψόφου καὶ
χρώματος). *Prima facie* it seems as if the former description presents
the common sense as one of several components of the perceptual
system, the latter as an all-encompassing perceptual faculty. But
the two accounts are not put forward as alternatives, but rather as a
single account, where the description of the common sense as 'primary sense organ' supposedly justifies its description as a 'common
power' or a 'common part' (see the use of γὰρ, at l. 20). The full picture is that of an overall perceptual faculty which is unified in its perceptual functions, despite the fact that different component powers
are dedicated to different perceptual tasks. It is important to appre-
ciate that on this account Aristotle considers the common sense,
and explains its role, as a unifier of the whole perceptual faculty. All
the perceptual powers are unified by the common power into the

common sense, 'in virtue whereof a person perceives that he sees or hears' (455a15–16); and the common sense can discern their special objects: 'one discerns that sweet things are different from white things' (455a19). Both of these perceptual activities require the common sense (i.e., the common power) to have access to the special sensibles perceived through all the special senses. Through them it can detect that, for example, a color is being seen—thereby becoming aware that seeing is taking place—and that the color is different from, for example, a sound concomitantly detected.

In presenting the common sense as a perceptual power that is over and above each of the special senses, and even over and above the special senses taken *collectively* (by extension of 'both together' (l. 19) to all the senses), Aristotle is pointing to the 'supervisory' and 'regulatory' perceptual *functions* (and corresponding perceptual powers) that are characteristic of the common sense. There is thus a distinction to be drawn between two types of perceptual powers that each of the special senses has: the *special* and the *common* ones. Interestingly, in this context Aristotle describes the special powers in terms of their activity, rather than their special objects (which is his usual criterion), by saying that,

> Every sense has some special [power] ... as, for example, seeing is to the sense of sight, hearing to the auditory sense, and so on with the other senses severally (*DS* 455a12–15, translation slightly modified)
>
> ἐπεὶ δ'ὑπάρχει καθ' ἑκάστην αἴσθησιν τὸ μέν τι ἴδιον, ... οἷον τῇ ὄψει τὸ ὁρᾶν, τῇ δ' ἀκοῇ τὸ ἀκούειν, καὶ ταῖς ἄλλαις ἑκάστῃ κατὰ τὸν αὐτὸν τρόπον

This account of the special powers aligns the special senses with the common sense, in so far as the power of the common sense is not identified through special objects, but is rather described in terms of its functions. (Note that defining the special powers with reference to their special functions rather than the special objects they range over is actually a more accurate definition, since the objects of the special powers are also accessible by the common power, for example when the common sense discerns red and white). Aristotle writes:

> All are accompanied by a common power, in virtue whereof a
> person perceives that he sees...and...discerns. (*DS* 455a15–17)
> ἔστι δέ τις καὶ κοινὴ δύναμις ἀκολουθοῦσα πάσαις, ᾗ καὶ ὅτι
> ὁρᾷ καὶ...αἰσθάνεται.

The common power of the perceptual system as a whole performs such operations as perceptual self-awareness (e.g., being aware that one is hearing); discerning between objects of different perceptual modalities (e.g., between the sweet and the white quality of something); and so on. Recall that, as we saw in chapter 5, in the *De Anima* the power for perceptual self-awareness was assigned to the special senses (it is by sight that we are aware of seeing) (425b12–17). By contrast, in the *De Somno* Aristotle emphatically states that it is the common power in each of the special senses that is responsible for self-awareness[15]:

> All [the special senses] are accompanied by a common power,
> in virtue whereof a person perceives that he sees or hears (for,
> assuredly, it is not by *sight* that one sees that he sees...). (*DS*
> 455a15–17)
> ἔστι δέ τις καὶ κοινὴ δύναμις ἀκολουθοῦσα πάσαις, ᾗ καὶ ὅτι
> ὁρᾷ καὶ ἀκούει αἰσθάνεται (οὐ γὰρ δὴ τῇ γε ὄψει ὁρᾷ ὅτι ὁρᾷ...).

Is it the common power that is *part* of sight that enables the perceiver to be aware that she sees, or the common power that is common to *all* the senses? This question is not relevant any more. Aristotle has shown that there is a set of perceptual functions that are common to all the special senses, which *unify* the whole perceptual system into one. He writes:

A part common to all the organs of sense; for there is one sense, and the controlling sensory organ is one, though differing with respect to what it is to be a faculty of perception. (*DS* 455a19–22)

ἀλλά τινι κοινῷ μορίῳ τῶν αἰσθητηρίων ἀπάντων· ἔστι μὲν γὰρ μία αἴσθησις, καὶ τὸ κύριον αἰσθητήριον ἕν, τὸ δ' εἶναι αἰσθήσει τοῦ γένους ἑκάστου ἕτερον

The point Aristotle is making is that *all the perceptual powers* (common and special powers) are unified in the common sense, which is one multimodal sense. The common power is not merely com-present with the special powers of each sense. There is a functional integration among powers so intimate and so fundamental that it allows the common power to be aware of the perceptible qualities perceived through each of the special senses.

What, then, is the account of the common sense emerging in *De Somno*? We saw above (section 7.2) that the Substance Model provides a way of accounting for the unity of complex perceptual content, by making use of the notion of substance as the unified metaphysical subject to which properties belong. Yet, the Substance Model could not explain how one can, for example, discern sweet and white, compare blue to red, or contrast loud and soft sounds. The reason is that the Substance Model only accounts for the unity of a single subject of awareness, but does not endow the subject with the requisite *functionality* for the performance of the perceptual tasks of the common sense. In other words, the Substance Model uses the unity of a subject of properties to explain the *unity* of complex perceptual awareness; but it cannot explain *how* the subject of awareness is also bestowed with the additional perceptual powers. That the common sense needs *its own powers* to carry out its perceptual tasks helps us understand the motivation Aristotle had for investigating further metaphysical models of the common sense. The common sense cannot be simply all the special senses working together. At least this cannot be the case if each special sense is dedicated to the perception of its special sensibles. This is because if each special sense were aware only of its special sensibles, the special senses working together would not be able to perform the additional functions the common sense performs (e.g., discerning sweet and red) since there would not be any one sense that would perceive them both, but only different senses working cooperatively. Yet, this seems to be all that Aristotle intended in his description of the perceptual system in the *De Anima*.[16] The idea motivating this position in the *De Anima* seems to be that when all the senses form a unity, the perceiver is aware of special sensibles of various types at the same time. But 'all the senses *qua* one' does not entail a single subject, or a single content. What is missing from the *De Anima* account is an explanation of how the different special senses can function as a single *subject of awareness*, given that they have incompatible perceptual sensitivities. Additionally, recall that the common sense is supposed to be endowed with powers to do more than what the special senses can do (e.g., to discern the components of complex contents); so simply clustering the special senses together cannot *ipso facto* account for what the common sense can do.

Someone might think that perhaps Aristotle's position in the *De Anima* and in the *De Somno* are to some degree in tension; for in the *De Anima*, Aristotle attributes to the special senses some of the powers that in the *De Somno* he explicitly attributes exclusively to the common sense. We already saw(pp.) that in the *De Anima* Aristotle attributes the power for self-awareness to *each* of the special senses, and also the power to discern more than one sensible of the same type at once:

> Each sense then is relative to its particular group of sensible qualities; it is found in a sense organ as such and discriminates the differences which exist within that group (e.g., sight discriminates white and black, taste sweet and bitter, and so on in all cases). (*DA* 426b8–12)
>
> ἑκάστη μὲν οὖν αἴσθησις τοῦ ὑποκειμένου αἰσθητοῦ ἐστίν, ὑπάρχουσα ἐν τῷ αἰσθητηρίῳ ᾗ αἰσθητήριον, καὶ κρίνει τὰς τοῦ ὑποκειμένου αἰσθητοῦ διαφοράς, οἷον λευκὸν μὲν καὶ μέλαν ὄψις, γλυκὺ δὲ καὶ πικρὸν γεῦσις· ὁμοίως δ᾽ ἔχει τοῦτο καὶ ἐπὶ τῶν ἄλλων.

Even so, assuming that each special sense is endowed with such discerning powers, and even if all the senses (somehow) form a unity, what sense will have the power to discriminate between perceptible qualities of modally different kinds? Unless the unity of the perceptual system involves *more* than the co-occurring functionality of the special senses, it will *not* deliver a single common subject of awareness with multimodal discriminatory powers of its own. This is just what has become explicit in the *De Somno*. Thus, on the *De Somno* account, each special sense has two types of power: a special one (i.e., sensitivity to its special objects) and a common one with other senses, in which it participates. The common power is such that it enables the sense to perform tasks that no special sense can perform on its own. If so, the common power will not be 'common' as a power that is simply replicated in each of the special senses, since this would only endow each of the special senses with an additional set of capabilities each of them can exercise. Rather, what Aristotle attributes to the special senses is a common power that is *shared* across the special senses, owned *jointly* by all of them. The common power brings together all the special senses into one perceptual system that has a singular *functionality* as one. Thus the special powers of the special senses become *aspects of this unified sense,* namely types of perceptual ability of the unified sense.

In conclusion, the special senses have a degree of independence from one another; they are embodied in their respective sense organs, and each is sensitive to its own genus of special sensibles. What this means is that the unified sense can perform specific tasks with different parts of the bodily system in which it is implemented. In this way, there is a division of labor, as different organs of the unified sense perform different functions. But the division of labor does not divide the unified sense into many; it does not undermine the unity of the perceptual system. Therefore the unified sense—the common sense—empowers the perceiver to be a *single subject* of perceptual awareness, with sensors and hence perceptual powers of different types, which give it access to different kinds of perceptible forms. It is a single sense, with various kinds of perceptual sensitivity that define its constitution and correspond to the division of labor within it. Thus the common sense can, *via* the common power of the special senses, perform operations on the input that it receives through the special senses. These operations unify the content of perception into *complex content.* Such operations include: comparisons, discriminations, and the perception of the common sensibles (movement, number, magnitude, etc.). These operations determine the type of power the common sense is, and the types of activity it can carry out with the input through the special senses.

CONCLUDING REMARKS

In this chapter we examined the three more promising models Aristotle puts forward to account for the metaphysics of the common sense and complex perceptual content. The merits and inadequacies of each model have been already discussed in detail; here I want to briefly bring out how each contributes useful insights toward the final solution. The Relative Identity Model provides a way of thinking about how different types of functionality can be co-instantiated in one and the same physical organ, by analogy with the case of a point that is the limit of many semi-lines. The Substance Model draws on Aristotle's substantial holism, and is introduced to make progress on the question of how the common sense can achieve a *seamless multimodal operation* and *seamless multimodal content* given the physical distribution of the senses in different sense organs. The Common Power Model explains how the senses have a *common* power that is *shared* across the special senses, owned *jointly* by all of them, and which controls the special senses and makes them *aspects* of common sense, namely types of perceptual ability of the unified sense. We are now in the position to understand Aristotle's final position, which I shall discuss in the overall conclusions.

Notes

1. The first is where he develops the Ratio Model, see chapter 6.
2. This point will be further discussed in chapter 7 in relation to Aristotle's general essentialist commitment.
3. See chapter 4.
4. See chapter 5.
5. With the same proviso as in the earlier chapters that the perceiver is the ultimate center of perceptual awareness, via the common sense, even if for brevity here I talk as if the common sense itself was the center of awareness.

6. Alternative readings have been discussed and criticized in the literature. For the most recent survey of additional alternative interpretations of the point example see Gregoric (2007, 149–157).

7. There may be two interpretations of Aristotle's claim that the common sense is 'different, when it has become divisible in its actualization': he may mean that the common sense is 'divided' when one perceives white by looking at the clouds and sweet by tasting milk, at the same time; or that the common sense is divided when one perceives white now and sweet later.

8. The precise connective Aristotle uses here is 'when' it becomes divisible in its actualization—but this cannot ease the conflict between divisibility and indivisibility by separating them in time, since the complex discerning content needs to be simultaneous with the perceptions of the two sensibles through the different sense organs as it discerns these two sensibles. Aristotle does not make use of time separation in his argumentation.

9. ἕν τί ἐστι τὸ αἰσθητικὸν γλυκέος καὶ λευκοῦ, ὅταν δὲ διαιρετὸν γένηται κατ' ἐνέργειαν, ἕτερον

10. See, for example *Metaphysics* 1035b24–25; and *DA* 412b10–24.

11. This principle has been argued for in the literature. I offer a contribution to the discussion in Marmodoro (2009) and (2013b). See also Scaltsas (1994).

12. What unifies all the properties that belong to a substance is *not* the semantic relation that they all share, of 'being predicated of the same subject'. Rather, it is the metaphysical relation of being in a subject that determines how all the properties relate to the substance they qualify. They are all in a subject in the same way—bereft of numerical distinctness of their own, and subsumed in the numerical oneness of the whole substance as qualifications of the whole, rather than as distinct parts of the whole; their oneness is qualitative only in being, not numerical.

13. Its modally varied sensibilities may differ between them generically or with respect to species, as we have seen before.

14. I take the *De Somno* to be a later work than the *De Anima* on the basis of the reference to the latter at 455a25.

15. Regarding this apparent tension between the *De Anima* and the *De Somno*, see pp. 259–60.

16. *DA* 425a30–b3: 'The senses perceive each other's special objects incidentally; not because the percipient sense is this or that special sense, but because all form a unity: this incidental perception takes place whenever [the common] sense is directed at one and the same moment to two disparate qualities in one and the same object (e.g., to the bitterness and the yellowness of bile); the assertion of the identity of both cannot be the act of either of the [special] senses.' See also chapter 4.

Chapter 8

Conclusions

Perception is intriguing to Aristotle. It is a fundamental phenomenon; it is challenging to account for; and it requires him to innovate metaphysically in order to understand it and explain it. Perception spans the domains of the physical and the mental, of epistemology and ontology, with complex correlations between them. Aristotle's thought develops as he examines the problem, and his method is exploratory, drafting a map of positions that he pioneers himself of both unsuccessful and fruitful approaches toward a solution. Although he does not present his final position as explicitly as we might like him to, the questions and insights that drive him are clear and upon close examination so are his views on the perceptual faculty.

Aristotle's analysis of the phenomenon of perception requires him to develop his theory of *causal powers* further,[1] exploiting the notion of potentiality at different stages of activation. His theory of powers is uniquely suited to the problems that arise in perception because crucially Aristotelian powers retain their identity through different levels of activation and transmission of their causal influence. On the other hand, when applied to the analysis of perception, his powers ontology acquires a sophistication that makes it a viable theory of causal powers for today's metaphysics.

But it is not just metaphysics and ontology that are advanced by Aristotle's treatment of perception. His account of how we can perceive *objects* from perceiving properties through our sense organs is groundbreaking, both in being the first to identify the problem of cross-modal binding and in offering an innovative solution to it. He recognizes that perceiving properties (e.g. color, smell, taste) through the senses is not sufficient for perceiving objects—first, because the senses do not provide a 'setting' wherein the perceived properties can come together into representations of objects; secondly, because even if there was such a setting, nothing would bring the perceived properties together into representations of objects.

The resolution Aristotle gave is the topic of this book. Aristotle reckons that in addition to the properties of objects that are perceived through the senses, there are further aspects of the objects that are perceived, which are themselves the epistemological foundation for our perception of objects. Their perception is far more complex than that of the properties of objects, requiring additional ontology and great metaphysical complexity at the levels of physical and mental explanation. These *further perceivable aspects* of objects are the so-called common sensibles (movement, rest, number, shape, size), which are perceived through the special senses, but not by any one of them on its own. The additional ontology that is thus required is the *common sense*, which is a *sui generis* sense in that it has no sense organ of its own for the detection of sensibles, but relies on the special senses for its perceptual input. The required *metaphysical complexity* is found, on the one hand, in the constitutional relation between the special senses and the common sense; on the other, in the correlation between the physical and the mental for the generation of perceptual contents that contain multimodal sensibles. In addressing these challenges, Aristotle ultimately offers an account of the *unity of the subject* of perception and the *unity of perceptual awareness*.

The perceptual faculty is physically confined within the remit of the sense organs. The sense organs are dedicated to specific domains of sensibles, each of which are different types of perceptible quality—color, sound, taste, etc. Given this perceptual input, Aristotle wants to explain how the world is 'revealed' to us through our perceptual faculty. The problems that Aristotle has to address in developing his account of perception range from the physical contact between the perceptual faculty and the world to the content of the resulting perceptual experiences. In offering an analysis of the physical process, Aristotle follows his general approach of explaining the causal interaction between the perceptible qualities in objects and the sense organs in us in terms of their respective causal powers. His account shows how such interaction comprises the fullest activation of the sensibles in the objects and of the sense organs of the perceptual faculty. This account is the foundation of Aristotle's conception of a world bustling with colors, sounds, tastes, etc., which we are able to perceptually enjoy by fully activating them in perception.

The account Aristotle offers of the way the senses enable us to discover the world by 'registering' the presence of its perceptible qualities generates a challenge for Aristotle's explanation of the perceptual faculty. There is a physical partition of the perceptual faculty according to the genera of detected sensibles, due to the dependence of perception on unimodal sense organs. We perceive colors through sight, sounds through hearing, smells through smelling, etc., but there are multifarious ways in which these sensibles are combined in our perceptual awareness. How does this come about?

The problem generated by a perceptual awareness of sensibles of different modalities is that none of the sense organs can bring about such a multimodal awareness. Each sense organ detects sensibles of one modality, and so none can detect multimodal content. If so, as

a way out of the problem, Aristotle could ascribe perceptual awareness to some other activity than the interaction of the sense organs
with the sensibles. For example, it could be an activity that received
input from the sense organs of different modalities and was specifically generating perceptual awareness of multimodal content. But
the price for this move would be divorcing the special design of
each sense organ, which enables it to be sensitive to sensibles of its
own modality, from the awareness of these sensibles. Another way
of thinking about the problem would be to start with the assumption that there could be a central 'universal detector' of sensibles of
any modality. But this would be the very denial of the significance
of the dedicated design of each sense organ. If there could be universal detectors that could give rise to the awareness of sensibles of
any modality, then the unimodal sense organs would not be needed
in the first place.

Aristotle had good reason to think nature did not go this way—
rather, unimodal sense organs detect sensibles, bringing about
awareness thereof. But then, the problem remains: how does multimodal perceptual awareness arise from modally dedicated sense
organs? Aristotle's answer is simple: the awareness of sensibles
perceived by the special senses is thereby also available to the perceptual faculty centrally, as a constituent of complex perceptual
contents. The complex contents arise either as a result of how the
world is, or as a result of how we perceive it. And this is possible on
account of, broadly speaking, two perceptual mechanisms for complex multimodal perceptual content: the first is the mechanism of
perceiving common sensibles (e.g., shape, size, number, movement
etc.) and the second is the mechanism of perceiving differences
between various sensibles (e.g., discerning white from sweet). The
awareness of differences between sensibles is the most fundamental
perceptual ability, whereas the perception of the common sensibles
is the ground for our awareness of objects in the world.

How is the awareness of the sensibles that are perceived by the special senses made available to the perceptual faculty centrally, as a constituent of complex perceptual contents? It is here that we reach the heart of Aristotle's contribution with his account of complex perceptual content. He answers this question through original, ingenious, and highly sophisticated metaphysical accounts of how the special senses combine with the common sense to make up a perceptual faculty that delivers multimodal complex perceptual contents. Additionally, he carefully examines a number of alternative accounts, which he believes would not give the answer, not only so that he can bring out their metaphysical shortcomings as possible solutions to the problem, but also so as to engage in greater detail and sophistication with the conditions on the unity of the perceptual faculty.

An intuitively straightforward model Aristotle proposes to start with is to apply his own original metaphysical account of mixing to perception. His idea in the Mixed Contents Model is attractive: if the content of perception is one, but complex, then it may be in a state of mixture. Aristotle has elsewhere offered a successful metaphysical account of mixtures by employing his conception of being in potentiality. In general terms, mixtures pose a difficult philosophical problem only because they are constitutionally uniform but also complex. They are uniform as a mixture, but complex in that they literally consist of the mixed items, which survive in it, rather than of what the mixed items have transformed into. Aristotle undertakes to explain uniformity and complexity of mixtures, and does so by showing that the there is a way in which the mixed items can be both present and absent (transformed) in a mixture. In the mixture, the ingredients have 'deviated' from their nature due to the impact of each on the others; but at the same time this 'deviation' is not permanent. In some cases, when the influence on each other subsides (e.g., the sea water evaporates), the two original items (salt and water) emerge again. What is significant about this is the pos-sibility that the original items are recovered, which shows that they had survived all along in the mixture.[2] This is the principle Aristotle tries to use to give an analysis of complex perceptual content. If the sensibles that impact upon a sense organ simultaneously mix, then the generated perceptual content is one, because of the uniformity of the mixed sensibles; and yet the two sensibles survive in it, in potentiality.

Aristotle is clear about the shortcomings of the Mixed Contents Model for perceptual content. Whereas in the case of mixtures the content is uniform, in the case of complex perceptual content, the content cannot be uniform. It is not sufficient that the sensibles be potentially present in the complex content—they need to be dis-cernible in it. Furthermore, the Mixed Contents Model could not serve to explain multimodal complex perceptual content. Sensibles of different modality do not mix, and even if some could mix (e.g. cold and sound) there would be no sense organ that could be sensi-tive to the resulting multimodally mixed sensible.

Along a similar line of investigation Aristotle explores the pos-sibility of accounting for the oneness of complex perceptual con-tent through the physiology of the sense organs. He envisions each sense organ as divided into parts that are sensitive to specific types of sensibles of that sense modality. (The assumption here is that there are types of sensible at the level of genera and also within a given genus.) With this model Aristotle tries to exploit the oneness of a sense organ for accounting for the oneness of the content, while introducing specialization of the organ's parts to explain multiplic-ity. The idea is that the unity of a genus and the multiplicity of its species would account for the unity and multiplicity of complex perceptual content. So a visual perceptual content could contain different colors whose awareness derives from different parts of the sense organ of sight. This is what I call the Multiple Sensors Model.

Aristotle does realize that this model cannot deliver an account of complex content. He is not explicit about the various ways in which the model fails, but one can see that the model would give to perceptual content either too much unity or too little. Either, as with the eyes, there will be a single content from the contributions of both eyes; or each part of a sense organ would function as a different sense organ, which brings one back to the original problem of the unity of their content.

Taking a much more abstract approach, Aristotle next attempts the Ratio Model for the unity of the common sense and its multimodal complex contents. The simplest way to think about the contribution the Ratio Model makes is this: it offers an explanation of unity and multiplicity in the way that these can be thought to exist in patterns (or structures). A sufficiently abstract pattern can have multiple realizations. For example the pattern of a cross can be found in the shape of jewelry, or in the shape of buildings. Aristotle seems to think there is a pattern in the comparison between the types of the senses and the types of their perceived sensibles. His intuition is not simply that there is a similarity between the relation of the types of sense (as sight to hearing) and the relation of the types of their perceived sensibles (so color to sound). He thinks also that each relation (ratio) exemplifies a *oneness* which is *one and the same* with the *oneness* exemplified by the other relation (ratio). Just as 1/3 is a relational structure that is one, and exemplifies the same oneness as 4/12, so the multimodal common sense is a relational structure that is one (sight to hearing to smelling, etc.), and its unity is the same as the unity of its multimodal perceptual awarenesses (color to sound to odor). Ultimately, the oneness of the relational structure of the senses and the relational structure of their complex contents points to the oneness of the operational unity of the senses and of their unified complex contents. Profoundly insightful as this metaphysical suggestion is, it does not provide an account of how these unities are brought about. It does not tell us *how* the senses are operationally unified, or how this results in the unification of their complex contents. For this we need to look further to the subsequent models of the common sense and its perceptual contents.

Aristotle explores, more promisingly, the following ways in which complexity and oneness can combine. With the Relative Identity Model he pursues the idea that something that is physically one, whether an entity or a process, could in special circumstances make up two objects or activities. Aristotle illustrates this model using the example of a point, which is numerically one, but makes up two or more different limits, on account of its functional roles in relation to the lines it is the limit of. This model goes some way in illustrating how the modifications of the one sense organ could be thought to make up different experiential contents (e.g., of white and sweet). There are however important dissimilarities between the two cases. The different (contrary or at any rate incompatible) *physical* modifications that a sense would have to undergo to allow perception of complex perceptual content cannot be likened to different functional roles (such as being the limit of); and they are not relational properties. The reason why this model cannot explain the unity of complex content is that it presupposes that one and the same perceptual faculty would be functionally related to modally disjoint sensibles (i.e., unities of modally different senses). Thus the model cannot be used to unify modally different sensibles into complex contents, since such contents lack modal uniformity. Furthermore, the model cannot explain attribution of functional powers of its own to the perceptual faculty, such as discerning modally different sensibles. The reason it cannot attribute such powers to it is that, according to the model, there is nothing that unifies the faculty at the functional level; rather the opposite, it is functionally divided but physically one. Even if ultimately it cannot account for the unity of complex perceptual content and the additiona:

perceptual capacities the faculty of perception as a whole has, the Relative Identity Model does offer a way of thinking of the unity of the perceptual faculty and the multiplicity of its sense organs and respective sensitivities. One of the descriptions Aristotle gives of the common sense (i.e., the faculty of perception) is in terms of the special senses *operating as one*. So in this description one can think of the common sense as a single sense organ that has special functional relations to different types of sensibles; this organ instantiates different senses just as the point instantiates different limits on account of its relations to the different lines of which it is a part. So the Relative Identity Model can account for a type of oneness that the faculty of perception can lay claim to, and a kind of functional multiplicity derived from the way the faculty interacts with its environment.

In conclusion, the Relative Identity Model cannot explain either the oneness of complex perceptual content, or the additional perceptual powers that the faculty of perception has as one sense, over and above the powers that the special senses have. Nevertheless, the Relative Identity Model captures aspects of the physical unity and functional multiplicity of the common sense that characterize its constitution and role in perception.

In his effort to show how unity is compatible with multiplicity of being and even physical separateness, Aristotle introduces the Substance Model. Here is the problem that it addresses: The common sense is composed of the special senses, which are physically distributed in the sense organs responsible for the awareness of the special sensibles. But the common sense is also able to have awareness of perceptual contents that contain multimodal sensibles, perceived wholly or partially (in the case of common sensibles) through the special senses. This ability results from the metaphysical structure of the common sense and the additional powers it possesses. So the common sense is a faculty that is composed of sub-faculties of different types, which operate collectively under the common sense to give rise to perceptual contents that are composed of sensibles of different types. The operation of the common sense is *seamless*, as its perceptual contents *are seamlessly complex*, despite the multiplicity of functionalities involved and the physical distribution of the sense organs. In brief, this is the common sense *seamless operation and seamless content* challenge that Aristotle needs to address. We have seen so far that although the first three models we examined cannot adequately address this challenge, the Relative Identity Model does offer an insight into how different types of functionality can be co-instantiated in one and the same physical organ. The Substance Model is introduced specifically to make progress on the *seamless operation and seamless content* challenge.

As we know from the *Metaphysics*, Aristotle's account of substances is holistic, and delivers metaphysical and functional seamlessness. Substances for Aristotle are unified wholes, rather than aggregates of parts. The key for their unification is their functionality. The substantial form is the type of the functional unity a substance has. There is a pattern to it, first a developmental and then an operational pattern for each substance, within which the functional parts of each substance have their place. Hence, a substance is constituted of activities, and their respective parts, which comprise the functional unity of the whole. It is the role of each activity within the whole that makes it a component of the substance, and gives it its identity in the whole. Substantial unity is not only compatible with complexity; it presupposes it. Multiplicity of being in a substance, therefore, results from the functional complexity that grounds its unity. The unity of the components is seamless because their identity is derived from their place in the functionally unified whole. This is what Aristotle brings to the problem of the unity of the common sense and its contents. The connection with his theory of substance is that the common sense is a functional unity, as substances are, and that such unity is compatible with multiplicity of function, which requires multiplicity of being. In so doing he is exploiting the significance of activity for the unity of both the perceptual faculty, and the contents of its awareness. The perceptual faculty is unified in its activity, which produces multimodal perceptual awareness. Both are complex, but they are seamlessly unified in the way that substances are seamlessly unified through their functional holism.

The final model Aristotle develops is the Common Power Model. With this model, Aristotle attributes to the special senses a common power that is *shared* across the special senses, owned *jointly* by all of them. The common power brings together all the special senses into one perceptual system that has a single *functionality* as one. Thus the special powers of the special senses become *aspects of this unified sense*, namely types of perceptual ability of the unified sense. The Common Power Model does not provide a full account of the common sense and its content, but rather focuses on an important aspect of the structure of the common sense. I consider it complementary to the Substance Model, in the sense that the Common Power Model clarifies a metaphysical consequence implicit in the functional organization of the common sense— namely the need for a common power 'controlling' all the powers of the special senses. Thus, the two models are complementary also in the sense that the Common Power Model adds to the ontology of the common sense something that the Substance Model itself did not require (i.e., the common power and its controlling function with respect to the special powers of the five senses).

Recall now the Substance Model: there is an aspect of the model that might mislead us in our understanding of the Common Power Model. The Substance Model introduces the substantial form as a possible way of accounting for the unity of the common sense. One might think that Common Power Model is not quite a different model—it is rather a redescription of the Substance model.

Thereby one might assume that when Aristotle talks of the common sense as a controlling sensory organ in the *De Somno*, he is still thinking of the common sense as a substantial whole, with its own substantial form. But the roles of a substantial form and a controlling power are not the same. It is important here to focus on where the difference lies. The substantial form unifies, it does not control. The substantial form can be thought of as a structural universal that confers roles on the constituent activities and parts of the substance, thereby contributing to their individuation within the whole and to their unity as a whole. A controlling power need not do this; it in other words can control without individuating or unifying what it controls. Aristotle offers two distinct metaphysical accounts of the common sense—one focusing on its unity, with the Substance Model, and one focusing on its controlling function over the five senses and their perceptual powers, with the Common Power Model.

My overall conclusion is that the Substance Model and the Common Power Model *combined* provide a fuller account of the perceptual faculty than either of them does on its own. The first accounts for the unity of the common sense and the second for the status of the common sense as a perceptual power itself, over and above its unifying role in relation to the five senses. Thus the common sense gives more than mere unity and structure to the senses that constitute it. It empowers and enriches its constituents with functionalities their union alone could not secure. Its operation results in the generation of new content (e.g., awareness of the common sensibles), over and above unifying the existing content from the special senses (e.g., discerning white from sweet). The generation of new perceptual content, and the unification of existing perceptual content into further contents, is the nature and role of the common sense: 'for there is one sense, and the controlling sensory organ is one, though differing with respect to what it is to be a

faculty of perception in relation to each genus (e.g., sound or color)'
(*DS* 455a20–22).

Notes

1. That is, beyond what he has already achieved in his physics and metaphysics.
2. For Aristotle there is no creation *ex nihilo*.

BIBLIOGRAPHY

In addition to the primary texts and the ancient, medieval, and modern commentaries:

ACKRILL, J. (1987), *A New Aristotle Reader*, Princeton: Princeton University Press.
ARMSTRONG, D. M. (1997), *A World of States of Affairs*, Oxford: Oxford University Press.
Armstrong, D.M. (2000), 'The Causal Theory of Properties: Properties According to Shoemaker, Ellis and Others', *Metaphysica* 1(1): 5–20.
Armstrong, D.M. (2004), *Truth and Truthmakers*, Cambridge: Cambridge University Press.
Averroes (1562), *Aristotelis Omnia Quae Extant Opera*, Venice: Apud Iunctas.
BARNES J., M. Schofield, and R. Sorabji (1979) (eds.), *Articles on Aristotle: Vol. 4: Psychology and Aesthetics*, London: Duckworth.
BARNES J. (1984) (ed.), *The Complete Works of Aristotle: The Revised Oxford Translation*, Princeton: Princeton University Press.
BEERE, J. (2010), *Doing & Being: An Interpretation of Aristotle's Metaphysics IX*, Oxford: Oxford University Press.
BIRD, A. (2005), 'The Ultimate Argument against Armstrong's Contingent Necessitation View of Laws', *Analysis* 65: 147–55.
BIRD, A. (2007), *Nature's Metaphysics*, Oxford: Oxford University Press.
BLOCK, I. (1961), 'The Order of Aristotle's Psychological Writings', *The American Journal of Philology* 82 (1): 50–77.
BLUMENTHAL, H., H. Robinson, and A. C. Lloyd (1991) (eds.), *Aristotle and the Later Tradition*, Oxford: Clarendon Press.
BOSTOCK, D. (1991), *Plato's Theaetetus*, Oxford: Oxford University Press.

BRADSHAW, D. (1997), 'Aristotle on Perception: The Dual-Logos Theory', *Apeiron* 30(2): 143–61.

BRENTANO, F. (1867), *Die Psychologie des Aristoteles, insbesondere seine Lehre vom nous poiêtikos*, Mainz: F. Kirchheim.

BROACKES, J. (1999), 'Aristotle, Objectivity, and Perception', *Oxford Studies in Ancient Philosophy*, 27: 57–113.

BROADIE, S. (1993), 'Aristotle's Perceptual Realism', *Southern Journal of Philosophy* 31(Supplement): 137–59.

BURNYEAT, M. (1990), *The Theaetetus of Plato*, Indianapolis: Hackett.

BURNYEAT, M. (1992), 'Is an Aristotelian Philosophy of Mind Still Credible? (A Draft)', in Martha C. Nussbaum and Amélie Oksenberg Rorty (eds.), *Essays on Aristotle's* De Anima, Oxford: Oxford University Press, 15–26.

BURNYEAT, M. (1995), 'How Much Happens when Aristotle Sees Red and Hears Middle C? Remarks on *De anima* 2.7–8', in Martha C. Nussbaum and Amélie Oksenberg Rorty (eds.), *Essays on Aristotle's* De Anima, Oxford: Oxford University Press, 421–34.

BURNYEAT, M. (2001), 'Aquinas on "Spiritual Change" in Perception', in D. Perler (ed.), *Ancient and Medieval Theories of Intentionality*. Studien und Texte zur Geistesgeschichte des Miltelalters, Leiden: Brill, 129–53.

BURNYEAT, M. (2002), '*De anima II 5*', *Phronesis* 47(1): 28–90.

BYNUM, T. W. (1987), 'A New Look at Aristotle's Theory of Perception', *History of Philosophy Quarterly* 4(April): 163–78.

CASTON, V. (1996), 'Why Aristotle Needs Imagination', *Phronesis* 41(1): 20–55.

CASTON, V. (1997), 'Epiphenomenalisms, Ancient and Modern,' *The Philosophical Review* 106(3): 309–63.

CASTON, V. (1998), 'Aristotle and the Problem of Intentionality', *Philosophy and Phenomenological Research* 63(2): 249–98.

CASTON, V. (2000), 'Aristotle's Argument for Why the Understanding Is Not Compounded with the Body', *Proceedings of the Boston Area Colloquium in Ancient Philosophy* 16: 135–75.

CASTON, V. (2002), 'Aristotle on Consciousness', *Mind* 111: 751–815.

CASTON, V. (2004), 'The Spirit and the Letter: Aristotle on Perception', in Salles (ed.), *Metaphysics, Soul, and Ethics in Ancient Thought*, Oxford: Clarendon Press, 245–320.

CATAN, J. R. (1981) (ed.), *Aristotle: The Collected Papers of Joseph Owens*, Albany: State University of New York Press.

CHARLES, D. (1984), *Aristotle's Philosophy of Action*, Ithaca: Cornell University Press.

CHARLES, D. (2000), *Aristotle on Meaning and Essence*, Oxford: Oxford University Press.

CHARLES, D. (2009), 'Aristotle's Psychological Theory', in J. J. Cleary and G.M. Gurtler (eds.), *Proceedings of the Boston Area Colloquium in Ancient Philosophy* 24, Leiden: The Netherlands: Brill, 1–29.

CHARLES, D. (2009), 'Aristotle on Desire and Action', in D. Frede and B. Reis (eds.), *Body and Soul in Ancient Philosophy*, Berlin: De Gruyter, 291–307.

CHARLTON, W. (1981), 'Telling the Difference Between Sweet and Pale', *Apeiron* 15: 103–14.

Choi, S. (2012), 'Intrinsic Finks and Dispositional/Categorical Distinction', *Nous* 46(2): 289–325.

COHEN, S. MARC (1992), 'Hylomorphism and Functionalism', in Martha C. Nussbaum and Amélie Oksenberg Rorty (eds.), *Essays on Aristotle's* De Anima, Oxford: Oxford University Press, 57–73.

COHEN, SHELDON M. (1982), 'St. Thomas Aquinas on the Immaterial Reception of Sensible Forms', *The Philosophical Review* 91: 193–209.

CORCILIUS, K. and P. GREGORIC (2010), 'Separability vs. Difference: Parts and Capacities of the Soul in Aristotle', *Oxford Studies in Ancient Philosophy* 39: 81–120.

Crane, T. (1996) (ed.), *Dispositions: A Debate*, London: Routledge.

DAY, J. (1997), 'The Theory of Perception in Plato's *Theaetetus* 152–183', *Oxford Studies in Ancient Philosophy* 15: 152–83.

DENNISTON, J. D. (1950), *The Greek Particles*, 2d ed. (orig. publ. 1934) Oxford: Clarendon Press.

Ellis, B. and C. Lierse (1994), 'Dispositional Essentialism', *Australasian Journal of Philosophy* 72(1): 27–45.

ELLIS, J. (1992) (ed.), 'Ancient Minds', *The Southern Journal of Philosophy*, Suppl. Vol. 31: 81–119.

Ellis (2010)

ESFELD, M. (2000), 'Aristotle's Direct Realism in De anima', *The Review of Metaphysics* 54(2): 321–36.

EVERSON, S. (1997), *Aristotle on Perception*, Oxford: Oxford University Press.

FREDE, D. (1992), 'The Cognitive Role of *Phantasia* in Aristotle', in Martha C. Nussbaum and Amélie Oksenberg Rorty (eds.), *Essays on Aristotle's* De Anima, Oxford: Oxford University Press, 279–95.

FREELAND, C. (1992), 'Aristotle on the Sense of Touch', in Martha C. Nussbaum and Amélie Oksenberg Rorty (eds.), *Essays on Aristotle's* De Anima, Oxford: Oxford University Press, 227–48.

GAUKROGER, S. (1981), 'Aristotle on the Function of Sense Perception', *Studies in History and Philosophy of Science* 12: 75–89.

GILL, M. L. (1980), 'Aristotle's Theory of Causal Action in *Physics* III 3', *Phronesis* 25: 129–47.

GOTTLIEB, P. (1993), 'Aristotle Versus Protagoras on Relatives and the Objects of Perception', *Oxford Studies in Ancient Philosophy* 11: 101–19.

GRANGER, H. (1990), 'Aristotle and the Functionalist Debate', *Apeiron* 23: 27–49.

GRANGER, H. (1992), 'Aristotle and Perceptual Realism', *Southern Journal of Philosophy* 31(Supplement): 161–71.

GREGORIC, P. (2007), *Aristotle on the Common Sense*, Oxford: Oxford University Press.

GUTHRIE, W. K. C. (1957), *In the Beginning: Some Greek Views on the Origins of Life and the Early State of Man*, Ithaca: Cornell University Press.

HALDANE, J. (1983), 'Aquinas on Sense-Perception', *Philosophical Review* 92: 233–39.

HAMLYN, D. (1977), *Aristotle's De Anima*, Books 2 and 3, Oxford: Clarendon Press.

HAYDUCK, M. (1897), (ed.), Ioannis Philoponi *in Aristotelis de anima Iibros commentaria*. CAG XV, Berlin.

HEIL, J. (2003), *From an Ontological Point of View*, Oxford: Clarendon Press.

HEINAMAN, R. (1990), 'Aristotle and the Mind-Body Problem', *Phronesis* 35(1): 83–102.

HETT, W. S. (1957), *On the Soul, Parva Naturalia, On Breath*, London: Heinemann.

HICKS, R. D. (1907), *Aristotle, De Anima*, Cambridge: Cambridge University Press.

HOFFMAN, P. (1990), 'St. Thomas Aquinas on the Halfway State of Sensible Being', *The Philosophical Review* 99: 73–92.

HOLTON, R. (1999), 'Dispositions All the Way Round', *Analysis* 59(1): 9–14.

HUSSEY, E. (1983), *Aristotle's Physics. Books III and IV*, Oxford: Clarendon Press.

JOHANSEN, T. K. (1996), 'Aristotle on the Sense of Smell', *Phronesis* 41(1): 1–19.

JOHANSEN, T. K. (1998), *Aristotle on the Sense Organs*, Cambridge: Cambridge University Press.

JOHANSEN, T. K. (2005), 'In Defense of Inner Sense: Aristotle on Perceiving That One Sees', *Proceedings of the Boston Area Colloquium in Ancient Philosophy* 21: 235–76.

JOHANSEN, T. K. (2006), 'What's New in the *De Sensu*? The Place of the *De Sensu* in Aristotle's Psychology', in R. King (ed.),. *Common to Body and Soul. Philosophical approaches to explaining living behaviour in antiquity*, Berlin: De Gruyter, 140–64.

JOHANSEN, T. K. (2012), *The Powers of Aristotle's Soul*, Oxford University Press.

JOHNSTONE, M. (2012), 'Aristotle on Odour and Smell', *Oxford Studies in Ancient Philosophy* 43: 143–83.

KAHN, C. H. (1966), 'Sensation and Consciousness in Aristotle's Psychology', *Archiv für Geschichte der Philosophie* 48: 43–81. Reprinted in Barnes, Schofield, and Sorabji, *Articles on Aristotle 4: Psychology and Aesthetics*, London: Duckworth (1979), 1–31.

KING, R. A. H. (2006) (ed.), *Common to Body and Soul*, Berlin: De Gruyter.

KOSMAN, L. A. (1975), 'Perceiving that We Perceive: On the Soul III, 2', *The Philosophical Review* 84(4): 499–519.

KOSMAN, L. A. (2005), 'Commentary on Johansen', *Proceedings of the Boston Area Colloquium in Ancient Philosophy* 21: 277–83.

HEIL, J. (forthcoming), 'Causings' in J. Jacobs (ed.), *Causal Powers*, Oxford: Oxford University Press.

LEAR, J. (1988), *Aristotle: The Desire to Understand*, Cambridge: Cambridge University Press.

LORENZ, H. (2007), 'The Assimilation of Sense to Sense-Object in Aristotle', *Oxford Studies in Ancient Philosophy* 33: 179–220.

MAGEE, J. M. (2000), 'Sense Organs and the Activity of Sensation in Aristotle', *Phronesis* 45(4): 306–30.

MAKIN, S. (2006), *Aristotle: Metaphysics Theta*, Oxford: Oxford University Press.

MARMODORO, A. (2006), 'It's a Colorful World', *American Philosophical Quarterly* 43 (1): 71–80.

MARMODORO, A. (2007), 'The Union of Cause and Effect in Aristotle: Physics III 3', *Oxford Studies in Ancient Philosophy* 32: 205–32.

MARMODORO, A. (2009), 'Do Powers Need Powers to Make Them Powerful? From Pandispositionalism to Aristotle', *History of Philosophy Quarterly* 26(4): 337–352.

MARMODORO, A. (2011), Review of Gregoric P. (2007), *Aristotle on the Common Sense*, in *Philosophy and Phenomenological Research* 83 (1): 234–37.

MARMODORO, A. (2012), 'Aristotle. Psychology', in R. S. Bagnall et al. (eds.), *The Encyclopaedia of Ancient History*, Malden, MA: Wiley-Blackwell, 221–46.

MARMODORO, A. (2014a), 'Causation Without Glue: Aristotle on Causal Powers', in C. Viano, C. Natali, and M. Zingano (eds.), *Aitia I. Les quatre causes d'Aristote. Origines et interpretations*, Louvain: Peeters, 221–246.

MARMODORO, A. (2013), 'Aristotle's Hylomorphism Without Reconditioning', *Philosophical Inquiry* 36(1–2): 5–22.

MARMODORO, A. (forthcoming), 'Potentiality in Aristotle's Metaphysics', in K. Engelhard and M. Quante (eds.), *The Handbook of Potentiality*, Springer.

MARMODORO, A. (2014b), Review of Johansen's *The Powers of Aristotle's Soul* in the *British Journal for the History of Philosophy* 22 (1): 174–91

MARMODORO, A. (forthcoming), 'Aristotelian Powers At Work; Reciprocity without Symmetry in Causation' in J. Jacobs (ed.), *Causal Powers*, Oxford: Oxford University Press.

MARTIN, C.B. (1992), 'Power for Realists', in J. Bacon, K. Campbell, and L. Reinhardt (eds.), *Ontology, Causality, and Mind*. Cambridge: Cambridge University Press, 175–86.

MARTIN. C. B. (2008), *The Mind in Nature*, Oxford: Oxford University Press.

MATTHEN, M. (forthcoming), 'The Individuation of the Senses', in *The Oxford Handbook of the Philosophy of Perception*, Mohan Matthen (ed.), Oxford: Oxford University Press.

MCDOWELL, J. (1973), *Theaetetus (Clarendon Plato Series)*, Oxford.

MCDOWELL, J. (1998), *Mind Value and Reality*, Cambridge, MA: Harvard University Press.

MELLOR, D.H. (1974), 'In Defense of Dispositions', *Philosophical Review* 83: 157–81.

MILLER, F. (1999), 'Aristotle's Philosophy of Perception', *Proceedings of the Boston Area Colloquium in Ancient Philosophy* 15: 177–213.

MODRAK, D. (1987), *Aristotle: The Power of Perception*, Chicago: University of Chicago Press.

MOLNAR, G. (2003), *Powers: A Study in Metaphysics*. Oxford: Oxford University Press.

MOREL, P-M. (2010), 'Âme, action, movement. Responsabilite' psychique et causalite' motrice chez Aristote', in F. Fronterotta (ed.), *La Scienza e le Cause a Partire dalla* Metafisica *di Aristotele*, Naples: Bibliopolis, 383–412.

MUMFORD, S. (2009), 'Passing Powers Around', *The Monist* 92(1): 94–111.

MUMFORD, S. AND R.L. ANJUM (2011), *Getting Causes from Powers*, Oxford: Oxford University Press.

NUSSBAUM, M. C. and H. PUTNAM (1992), 'Changing Aristotle's Mind', in Martha C. Nussbaum and Amélie Oksenberg Rorty (eds.) *Essays on Aristotle's De Anima*, Oxford: Oxford University Press, 27–56.

NUSSBAUM, M. C. and A.O. RORTY (1992) (eds.), *Essays on Aristotle's De Anima*, Oxford: Oxford University Press.

O'CALLAGHAN, C. (2012), 'Perception and Multimodality', in *Oxford Handbook of Philosophy and Cognitive Science*, Margolis, Samuels, and Stich (eds.). Oxford: Oxford University Press.

OSBORNE, C. (1983), 'Aristotle, De anima 3.2, How Do We Perceive that We See and Hear?', *Classical Quarterly* 33(2): 401–11.

OSBORNE, C. (1988), 'Perceiving White and Sweet (Again): Aristotle: De anima 3.7, 431a20–b1', *Classical Quarterly* 48(2): 433–46.

OWENS, J. ([1976] 1981), 'Aristotle: Cognition a Way of Being', *Canadian Journal of Philosophy* 6: 1–11; reprinted in J. R. Catan (1981): 74–80.

OWENS, J. (1980), 'Form and Cognition in Aristotle', *Ancient Philosophy* 1: 17–27.

OWENS, J. (1981), 'Aristotelian Soul as Cognitive of Sensibles, Intelligibles, and Self', in J. R. Catan (1981): 81–98.

PASNAU, R. (1997), *Theories of Cognition in the Later Middle Ages*, Cambridge: Cambridge University Press.

PASNAU, R. (2002), *Thomas Aquinas on Human Nature: A Philosophical Study of Summa Theologiae: 75–89*, Cambridge: Cambridge University Press.

PASNAU, R. (2002), 'What is Cognition? A Reply to Some Critics', *American Catholic Philosophical Quarterly* 76: 483–90.

PERLER, D. (2001) (ed.), *Ancient and Medieval Theories of Intentionality*. Studien und Texte zur Geistesgeschichte des Miltelalters, Band 76, Leiden: Brill.

PHILOPONUS. (1897), Ioannis Philoponi in Aristotelis De anima libros commentaria, Hayduck (ed.), Berlin: Reimer.

POLANSKY, R. (2007), *Aristotle's De Anima*, Cambridge: Cambridge University Press.

PREUS, A. (1968), 'On "Dreams" 2, 459b24–460a33, and Aristotle's Ὄψις', *Phronesis* 13(2): 175–82.

PRICE, A. W. (1996), 'Aristotelian Perceptions', *Proceedings of the Boston Area Colloquium in Ancient Philosophy* 12: 285–309.

ROSS, W. D. (1955), *Aristotle, Parva Naturalia, A Revised Text with Introduction and Commentary*, Oxford: Clarendon Press.

ROSS, W. D. (1961), *Aristotle, De Anima*, Oxford: Clarendon Press.

ROSS, W. D. (1979), *Aristotle's Physics: Revised Text with Introduction and Commentary*, Oxford (orig. published 1936): Clarendon Press.

RYLE, G. (1963), *The Concept of Mind*, Penguin Modern Classics.

SALLES, R. (2005) (ed.), *Metaphysics, Soul, and Ethics: Themes from the work of Richard Sorabji*, Oxford: Oxford University Press.

SCALTSAS, T. (1994), *Substances and Universals in Aristotle's Metaphysics*, Ithaca: Cornell University Press.

SCALTSAS, T. (1996), 'Biological Matter and Perceptual Powers in Aristotle's *De anima*', *Topoi* 15(1): 25–37.

SCALTSAS, T. (2009), 'Mixing the Elements', in *Blackwell Companion to Aristotle*, George Anagnostopoulos (ed.), Oxford: Blackwell.

SCHOFIELD, M. (2011). 'Phantasia in *De Motu Animalium*', in M. Pakaluk and G. Pearson (eds.), *Moral Psychology and Human Action in Aristotle*. Oxford: Oxford University Press, 119–34.

SHIELDS, C. (1997), 'Intentionality and Isomorphism in Aristotle', *Proceedings of the Boston Area Colloquium in Ancient Philosophy* 2: 307–30.

SHIELDS, C. (2007), *Aristotle*, London and New York: Routledge.

SHOEMAKER, S. (1984), *Personal Identity*, Oxford: Blackwell.

Shoemaker, S. (1998), 'Causal and Metaphysical Necessity', *Pacific Philosophical Quarterly* 79(1): 59–77.

SILVERMAN, A. (1989), 'Color and Color-Perception in Aristotle's *De anima*', *Ancient Philosophy* 9(2): 271–92.

SIMMONS, A. (1994), 'Explaining Sense-Perception: A Scholastic Challenge', *Philosophical Studies* 73(2–3): 257–75.

SISKO, J. (1996), 'Material Alteration and Cognitive Activity in Aristotle's *De anima*', *Phronesis* 41(2): 138–57.

SISKO, J. (1997), 'Space, Time and Phantasms in Aristotle, De memoria 2, 452b7–25', *Classical Quarterly* 47: 167–75.

SISKO, J. (1998) 'Alteration and Quasi-Alteration: a Critical Notice of Stephen Everson, Aristotle on Perception', *Oxford Studies in Ancient Philosophy* 16: 331–52.

SLAKEY, T. J. (1961), 'Aristotle on Sense Perception', *The Philosophical Review* 70, 470–84.

SMYTH, H. W. (1980 [1920]), *Greek Grammar*, Cambridge, MA: Harvard University Press.

SORABJI, R. (1971), 'Aristotle on Demarcating the Five Senses', *Philosophical Review*, reprinted in J. Barnes, M. Schofield, R. Sorabji, *Articles on Aristotle: Vol. 4: Psychology and Aesthetics*, London: Duckworth (1979), 76–92.

SORABJI, R. (1972), 'Aristotle, Mathematics, and Colour', *Classical Quarterly,* New Series 22(2): 293–308.

SORABJI, R. (1974), 'Body and Soul in Aristotle', *Philosophy* 49(187): 63–89. Reprinted in J. Barnes, M. Schofield, and R. Sorabji, *Articles on Aristotle: Vol. 4: Psychology and Aesthetics,* London: Duckworth (1979), 42–64.

SORABJI, R. (1991), 'From Aristotle to Brentano: The Development of the Concept of Intentionality', in H. Blumenthal, H. Robinson, and A.C. Lloyd (eds.) *Aristotle and the Later Tradition,* Oxford: Clarendon Press (1991), 227–59.

SORABJI, R. (1992), 'Intentionality and Physiological Processes: Aristotle 's Theory of Sense-Perception', in Martha C. Nussbaum and Amélie Oksenberg Rorty (eds.) *Essays on Aristotle's De Anima,* Oxford University Press (1992), 195–225.

SORABJI, R. (2001), 'Aristotle on Sensory Processes and Intentionality: A Reply to Myles Burnyeat', in D. Perler (ed.), *Ancient and Medieval Theories of Intentionality,* Leiden: Brill, 49–61.

THEMISTIUS (1900), *In Aristotelis Physica Paraphrasis* (CAG V.2), H. Schenkl (ed.), Berlin.

THORP, J. (1980), 'Le mecanisme de la perception chez Aristote–etude de quelques problemes', *Dialogue* 19: 575–89.

TOWEY, A., (2000) (ed.), *Alexander of Aphrodisias on Aristotle on Sense Perception,* Ithaca: Cornell University Press.

TWEEDALE, M. (1992), 'Origins of the Medieval Theory that Sensation is an Immaterial Reception of a Form', *Philosophical Topics* 20(2): 215–31.

TYE, M. (1995), *Ten Problems of Consciousness: Representational Theory of the Phenomenal Mind,* Cambridge, MA: MIT Press.

TYE, M. (2009), *Consciousness Revisited,* Cambridge, MA.: MIT Press.

WARD, J. K. (1998), 'Perception and *logos* in *De anima* II 12', *Ancient Philosophy* 8, 217–33.

WATERLOW, S. (1982), *Nature, Change and Agency in Aristotle's Physics,* Oxford: Oxford University Press.

Waterlow, S. (1983), 'Instants of Motion in Aristotle's Physics VI', *Archiv für Geschichte der Philosophie* 65(2): 128–46.

WITT, C. (2003), *Ways of Being: Potentiality and Actuality in Aristotle's Metaphysics,* Ithaca: Cornell: University Press.

WOOLF, R. (1999), 'The Coloration of Aristotelian Eye-Jelly: A Note on On Dreams 459b–460a', *Journal of the History of Philosophy* 37(3): 385–91.

GENERAL INDEX

INDEX LOCORUM